D0272253

Natural

Natural

The **Jimmy Greaves** Story

DAVID TOSSELL

Foreword by Sir Geoff Hurst

First published by Pitch Publishing, 2019

Pitch Publishing
A2 Yeoman Gate
Yeoman Way
Worthing
Sussex
BN13 3QZ
www.pitchpublishing.co.uk
info@pitchpublishing.co.uk

© 2019, David Tossell

Every effort has been made to trace the copyright.
Any oversight will be rectified in future editions at the
earliest opportunity by the publisher.

All rights reserved. No part of this book may be reproduced,
sold or utilised in any form or transmitted in any form or by
any means, electronic or mechanical, including photocopying,
recording or by any information storage and retrieval system,
without prior permission in writing from the Publisher.

A CIP catalogue record is available for this book
from the British Library.

ISBN 978-1-78531-490-2

Typesetting and origination by Pitch Publishing

Printed and bound in India by Replika Press Pvt. Ltd.

CONTENTS

FOREWORD
By Sir Geoff Hurst

JIMMY Greaves was a genius in the art of scoring goals. There are people in different walks of life to whom you can give that label and Jimmy was exactly that in what he did.

If there were 20 players in a crowded penalty area, he had the ability to find a yard or two on his own. And the other beauty of his game – something that he was very good at compared to other players who found themselves in those positions in front of goal – was that he always expected the ball to come to him, no matter what. It could hit a defender; it could hit a post it; it could come off a team-mate; but he would always expect the ball to finish up at his feet. Lesser goalscorers don't have that anticipation and it is almost a shock when the ball comes to them. They lose their composure. But Jim knew what to do, how to control it and put it away.

He was such a great player that he probably didn't have to work as hard and dedicate himself as much as people with lesser talents. Many of us – and I include myself – had to work a lot harder to get somewhere close to the ability he had. His record at Chelsea and Tottenham was phenomenal and, heading into the World Cup in 1966, he was one of England's five world-class players, along with Bobby Moore, Bobby Charlton, Gordon Banks and Ray Wilson. Jimmy had been ill with hepatitis so was probably not quite at his best during that period, but had he not been injured in the group games I don't think there would have been any question of Alf Ramsey leaving him out of the team.

I obviously regard it as a huge piece of luck that I was able to play in the latter stages of the tournament and in the final. It wasn't something that I expected. I was just happy to be in the squad. But that is sport, and I was ready to play and able to take the chance when it came along. As disappointed as he was, it never stopped me getting along with Jim in later years.

He was always such a laid-back guy and an unbelievably funny character, which came through in the things he got involved in after football; his television career, the writing and his theatre shows. He was just a natural in everything he did. I did a show with Jimmy and Gordon Banks at Wembley, just before the 2014 World Cup in Brazil, and we had pictures taken backstage with the trophy. The guy from FIFA who was looking after it explained that only players who have won the World Cup are allowed to actually hold it in their bare hands. Everyone else, including the handler himself, had to wear white gloves. Jimmy piped up, 'Hang on. That means if it gets nicked there are only our bloody fingerprints on it!' I was in tears even before we went on stage.

Another thing that comes to mind is being parked outside my front door listening to the radio when Jimmy described Wayne Rooney as looking like SpongeBob SquarePants. I was laughing, even though I had no idea at that stage who the hell SpongeBob SquarePants was. When I looked it up and saw pictures, I laughed a hundred times more. It was a typical Jim comment. When he once described me as one of his best guests on his theatre show I was very flattered, considering how funny he was.

Like most people, I had absolutely no idea at all – none whatsoever – about the extent of his problems with drink after he retired from playing. I was astonished when it came out in the papers. There had never been any rumours in the football fraternity. It was a huge shock. It is a great credit to him as a person to be able to stop drinking as he did and get on with a fantastic career in other areas. He never talked about it with me and I doubt with many other people outside of his family. He just carried on working.

You never know how others find people, but I would be very surprised if anybody would have had any reason to be unhappy with Jimmy on or off the field. There are some people you can get on with, but you recognise that others might not find it so easy. But I can't imagine anyone would think anything other than Jimmy was a terrific, funny guy and great company. And what a player – one of the greats. His goalscoring record is astonishing and I don't think we will ever see anyone like him again.

INTRODUCTION

*'I found it so natural to score goals. I had
absolutely no idea how good I was. It was easy for
me, to be honest'*

IT all happened too fast for the White Hart Lane crowd and
television viewers to fully appreciate. They just knew that they
had seen something very special.

As usual, *Match of the Day* had chosen to show Tottenham
Hotspur's game against Manchester United, their first meeting
of the 1965-66 season. The opportunity to drop some of English
football's biggest stars – Bobby Charlton, Denis Law and George
Best for the League champions; Jimmy Greaves and Dave Mackay
for Spurs – into people's living rooms on a Saturday evening
was not one the BBC was going to pass up, as they proved by
featuring the fixture six times in the show's first three seasons.
When Greaves scored a dazzling third goal in the middle of a 5-1
triumph, the show's producers congratulated themselves on their
selection, while those watching from their sofas, had they been
able to foresee technical advances, might have cursed that slow-
motion replays were still a few years away.

In the modern age we can use the Internet to find, pause,
analyse and marvel at the genius of the greatest goalscorer in the
history of English football. With Spurs two up and the October

clouds erasing the shadows over the pitch that have framed the early exchanges, Mackay pushes the ball forward to Greaves, his back to goal, 30 yards out. This being the 1960s, when defenders frequently mistake the number on a forward's jersey as a target to aim at, Greaves finds the United centre-half, Bill Foulkes, clambering all over him.

Greaves doesn't go down. He retains his balance, leaving Foulkes the one on the ground as he pivots towards goal. Perhaps it is the somewhat tentative nature of the turn that has the United defenders back on their heels, unprepared for the burst of acceleration that he unleashes. In a flash, he has sliced through and away from four of them. Pause the picture now – he looks like a sprinter breaking the tape a yard ahead of a string of pursuers. Meanwhile, substitute John Fitzpatrick's clumsy attempt at a sliding tackle has scarcely registered in Greaves's peripheral vision, let alone disturbed his single-minded path into the penalty area.

As United goalkeeper Pat Dunne advances, there is a barely perceptible hitch in Greaves's stride, just enough to convince the keeper he is about to shoot, sufficient to commit him to a dive. Instead, without any loss of speed, Greaves continues on his diagonal course in the direction of the right-hand goalpost, slipping beyond Dunne's groping left hand before side-footing the ball into an empty net from six yards.

'Oh, beautiful football,' exclaims commentator Kenneth Wolstenholme. 'What a great goal; a fabulous goal,' he declares. Toilet rolls are thrown joyously to the field and white-coated snack vendors hop around excitedly in front of the bouncing terraces. The *Tottenham Herald* will predict that, 'the memory of his lone-goal dash will stay with the 58,000 crowd for many seasons to come', while the *Sunday People* describes Greaves as having, 'snatched the third after beating four men inside the space of his own hall carpet'.

There are various versions of this footage on YouTube. Collectively they have achieved around half a million views.

Dunne and Foulkes could have been responsible for every one of those clicks without fully comprehending how Greaves had made them look so foolish. He himself was no more able to explain his genius. Comments such as, 'I have a weak shot, but I lay tremendous stress on accuracy' from his 1966 book *My World of Soccer* were about as close as he got to self-analysis.

It was goals like that – the moments that made him an automatic presence in the England team for the 1966 World Cup until fate, injury and Alf Ramsey intervened – that were brought to mind when the unhappy news emerged in May 2015 that Greaves had suffered a stroke, robbing him of his ability to walk and making speech painfully difficult. Equally shocking, and heartbreaking, were the images released a month later that emphasised the severity of his condition. Behind the optimistic thumbs-up Greaves offered to photographers, the eyes no longer flashed, the extended moustache that had become a trademark of his later years, and which always seemed to frame a mischievous smile, now just seemed to droop in a gesture of melancholy.

In the subsequent three years, various pictures were released of Greaves: paying a final visit to White Hart Lane before the bulldozers went to work; being greeted by Harry Kane, the modern-day wearer of his mantle as leader of the Spurs and England attack, during a trip to the club's training ground. Yet when one put down the newspaper or turned off the computer, those brutal images quickly lost their power to haunt, replaced – for those of us old enough or sufficiently aware of his history – by a flash of ball into goal, another ghosted finish past a flat-footed defence. Such is the strength and purity of his legacy.

Importantly, the outpouring of affection that greeted each new photograph and update on his health was not driven by any sense of regret for what his life might have been; rather a simple sadness that someone who had given so much pleasure on and off the field was suffering. That absence of conflicted emotion is remarkable when one considers how his later years could have turned out; when one recalls what happened following his premature retirement from the game at 31 after 366 league goals for Chelsea, AC Milan, Tottenham and West Ham, plus 50-odd more in cup competitions and 44 for England.

For five years, alcoholism tore apart everything in his life; his business interests, his friends, his marriage and, finally and inevitably, his self-esteem and health. Until, one day in early 1978, when he decided that he had lost enough and vowed never to drink again. With the same single-mindedness that characterised his work around the penalty area, he brought himself back from self-destruction. For good.

Where others in his position, including some high-profile figures in his own profession, are condemned to the dark cycle of relapse and rehabilitation, a sober and sound Greaves found himself back in the bright lights of public life, unafraid of judgement and undaunted by any cruel onlookers waiting for him to melt down before their eyes. Offered the opportunity to become a television pundit, a role he had neither coveted nor prepared for, he became one of the most recognisable faces on British television throughout the 1980s, complete with a catchphrase and a *Spitting Image* puppet. Just as his instincts had carried him past uncompromising defenders, so his personality and empathy with the ordinary viewer had been the basis of his television performance, an intangible quality he would be no more able to define than his knack for finding the net.

Journalist Martin Samuel, who became a friend when ghost-writing Greaves's column in *The Sun*, said this about him in the *Daily Mail* after he fell ill, 'Many players are described as great footballers, but Jim was the genuine article. Yet more than that, he is a great man, too, one who has never received the credit he is due for making the second act of his life as magnificent a triumph as the explosive first.'

He adds, 'Jim said to me he was prouder of that second phase of his career than he was of being a footballer, because of what he had come through to get there. The football was natural, a gift. His second career took work. In 1996, he kindly let us have his place in La Manga for a week after we had just had our first son. The first thing I noticed was that there were a couple of bottles of white wine in the fridge. They were for Irene or whoever. I asked him about it and he said that of course he had alcohol in the house. He never let that aspect of his life define him.'

In the later years of his own life, Brian Clough was one of those who acknowledged the great triumph of Greaves's rehabilitation. 'The greatest goalscorer of his time is among those who have made the greatest comebacks from the drink,' he wrote in his autobiography in 2002. 'Nobody admires what Jimmy has achieved more than I do – setting about a completely fresh start to his life, leaving the bottle alone completely and achieving it in spectacular fashion. Fantastic!' Facing up to his own addiction, he concluded, 'I have to draw my inspiration from Jimmy.'

Mostly, however, Greaves is recalled either as a sporting superstar of the 1960s or a broadcasting pillar of the 1980s. The alcoholic haze of the in-between years never tarnished the achievements of his first career, but nor, as Samuel suggests, did they amplify his second coming as much as was perhaps his due. In the end, that is a compliment. He made it easy for everyone else to forget those dark times, even if he had to carry their burden for the rest of his life.

Being an alcoholic never became the aspect of his life that characterised Jimmy Greaves. He never succumbed so deeply to his addiction that he became a George Best-type figure, someone who had to die for communal memory to return unambiguously to the glory of his achievements on the field rather than the shambling caricature of his later years. Nor did he take the path chosen by Tony Adams, acknowledged as much in his years of rehabilitation for his devotion to helping others escape his own pitfalls as he is for his caps, cups and championships. Greaves went in a different direction. He spoke about his alcoholism at the time in interviews and a book and then left it behind, preferring to fight his battles in private. Within a few years he had become 'Greavsie', the joking sidekick to Ian St John's 'Saint'. Rarely was he the reformed alcoholic.

Adams suggested in his 2017 book, *Sober*, that Greaves could have done more to publicise the work of Alcoholics Anonymous. That he didn't, he said, 'was a bit of a shame as I am sure he would have had so much to pass on to people who had newly stopped drinking'.

Greaves's son, Danny, suggests, 'He decided he didn't want to drink anymore, but he didn't want to preach to others about how they should live their life. That is Dad in a nutshell. He will quite happily tell you how he feels and tell you what he will do, but that doesn't mean that you have got to do that. That is why it came across that giving up drink was easy for him and why he was still the footballer or the TV pundit rather than the ex-alcoholic.'

Away from the spotlight, however, Greaves was not without empathy for those in whom he recognised the same demons that he had stared down. Cliff Jones, a Tottenham team-mate, readily admits that it was the example of Greaves that may have saved everything he held dear. By the mid-1980s, Jones was working as a coach at a north London school and denying to himself that his dependence on alcohol had reached threatening levels. After one particularly volatile Christmas, his wife, Joan, seized upon what she saw as her last hope.

'She got in touch with Jimmy,' Jones relates. 'My drinking had become a great concern to my family and she knew that he had been through the same thing. She asked him to come and see me.'

Greaves, who had remained in touch since their playing days but was not among his immediate circle of friends, wasted no time in coming to the point of his unexpected New Year visit. 'Look, Cliff,' he began, 'you have got a wonderful family, a nice home, you have got a job. Do you want to lose those things?'

16

'Of course not,' Jones replied. 'What are you talking about?'

'It will happen if you continue drinking. It happened to me.'

'So, what do I do then, Jim?'

'Go to Alcoholics Anonymous.'

'You are fucking joking. I don't need to do that. I am not an alcoholic.'

Jones reflects, 'Of course, he was right. He understood me and could see I was going through what he had been through. I began going and 29 June 1985 was the last time I had a drink. It was all down to Jim coming to see me and giving me a push in the right direction. It is always there. For people like Jim and me it is a day at a time. Every day that you don't pick up a drink you are happy. It doesn't always work for everyone, but that is the philosophy. Jimmy brought that to me and it changed my life; not just my life but my family's. He has always been there for support when I have needed it.'

Nick Owen, who worked alongside Greaves in various television roles, recalls Greaves's generous spirit by relating an event while they were working together on *Star Soccer*, the Midlands regional football show, in the early 1980s. 'A very close friend of mine at the time had become an alcoholic. He was in despair and didn't know how to get himself out of it, so he asked me if there was a chance he could spend some time talking to Jimmy. Of course, Jimmy said yes, so one Saturday evening before our programme my friend came in and Jimmy spent an hour talking to him in his dressing room.

'It did my friend the power of good. It was such a lift because he was football mad and to talk to Jimmy, who had been through it and knew what it was like and could talk sympathetically about it, was excellent for him.

'That was Jimmy. He was a lovely bloke and became a great friend. We would always be off to the bar in mid-evening after we had written our scripts. I would have a pint of lager and he would have a Coke. I would say, "Jimmy, are you all right with this? Do you mind?" And he wouldn't mind at all. With hindsight, it must have been bloody difficult for him.'

It is impossible to relate the life of Jimmy Greaves without going into his battle with alcoholism. Quite what drove him towards his dependency is uncertain, as it is for so many who have been similarly afflicted. The death of an infant child, the isolation and anguish he felt in his brief time in Italy, the devastation of missing the 1966 World Cup final, a drinking culture around football that could potentially push anyone beyond the threshold of mere indulgence, the loss of purpose and routine caused by premature retirement; all could conceivably have been triggers.

Yet alcohol won't dominate this book; reflecting the way in which Greaves himself refused, just in time, to allow it to take over his existence. The goals of his earlier years, the highs and lows of his playing career, the on-screen laughs of later life; they are the essence of this story.

And if the Manchester United defenders of 1965 should read this, they will probably still be wondering by the final page how Jimmy Greaves made such fools of them.

1

A BOY AND HIS BALL

*'I honestly don't know if I ever wanted to be a
footballer or not. It was something that was born
in me and I was told that from the age of one
upwards I kicked a ball. It was the most natural
thing that came to me.'*

T HE likeness was so striking, the smile such an exact
replica, that it looked as though Patrick Kluivert's head
had been superimposed on to the body of a young boy. In
fact, the cheerful face belonged to the former Dutch international
striker's nine-year-old son, Shane. His happiness, captured on
camera in the summer of 2017, came in the form of a five-year
endorsement deal with the footwear giants Nike. The news was
delivered by Shane to his 120,000 followers on Instagram.

Let's just pause there. Nike. A five-year deal. For a nine-year-old
with a fan base of 120,000.

By the time he reached that same age, Jimmy Greaves, who
would go on to become one of the sport's greatest goalscorers, had
yet to play a single organised game of football. His social network
consisted of those within shouting distance of his front door in
Dagenham and the only pair of boots he'd ever owned had long

since come apart at the toes. Not that it mattered as the one leather football he'd ever played with was now in shreds and he and his friends were back to playing with a tennis ball.

These days, the fields in Parsloes Park, across the road from the former Greaves family home in Ivyhouse Road, host very few of the games of twenty-a-side or three-and-in that were a feature of the recreation grounds of post-war Britain. You are more likely to be greeted by the ducks that wander in curiosity from the ponds to the footpaths than by kids laying down jumpers for goalposts. Instead of the seven-days-a-week ad hoc contests that were the cornerstone of the childhood of Greaves and his contemporaries, football activity consists mostly of the organised Sunday morning matches in competitions such as the Echo Junior Football League.

The games are staged on the marked fields by a clubhouse that sits at the intersection of three thoroughfares through the park. Few of those in attendance will have any idea that one of the sport's icons grew up only yards away, and was denied the use of these fields during his earliest years because they were commandeered to grow the potatoes that would be picked by Italian prisoners of war from a nearby camp.

Kit is freshly laundered, boots match the modern-day trend of reflecting the full range of the spectrum and coaches carry holdalls containing more footballs than Greaves and his pals would have laid eyes on in their entire childhoods. For every watching parent who merely wants their child to enjoy football in a spirit of fun and friendship, there are those who support – and sometimes goad – with passion fired by the hope of professional contracts or the fear of unfulfilled dreams; perhaps even echoes of their own.

Michael Calvin, author of *No Hunger in Paradise*, a study of modern player development, notes that Premier League clubs are now prioritising children between the ages of six and nine for identification and recruitment. Which means that any nine-year-old playing in front of Greaves's former home who has not yet been identified as a prospect by a professional team may have missed the boat already. A year before Kluivert junior signed his Nike contract, John McDermott, the head of development at Tottenham, had told an audience in South Carolina that he knew of one Premier League team that was paying a nine-year-old £24,000 per year. In September 2017 came the story of the six-year-old who was training with Manchester United, Manchester City, Liverpool and Everton before he could even tie his own shoelaces.

Modern football, as Greaves was credited as saying, is indeed 'a funny old game', and not one that young Jimmy – despite the obsession with the sport that fuelled his childhood – would ever have imagined.

James Peter Greaves was born on 20 February 1940 in Manor Park, now a part of the London Borough of Newham but then within the old county borough of East Ham, a mile or so from West Ham's Upton Park ground. Within months, however, the German bombs that had begun falling dangerously close to home forced the Greaves family to move about five miles east to Dagenham. 'My first memory is sleeping in the Anderson [air raid] shelter in Dagenham,' he told *The Times* in an article about his childhood. 'I can still sniff its unforgettable smell – a mixture of cats' pee and hot cocoa. We slept in the shelter most nights and the adults were always going on about Hitler and bloody Germans.'

With dad Jim, mum Mary and older siblings Marion and Paul, the boyhood lived by young Jimmy was unremarkable; no discussion of a child prodigy and certainly no agents lurking on street corners with boot contracts.

He did what other children of the 1940s did: he spent hours out of doors making up all kinds of games; some born out of the Luftwaffe's raids on London. 'We all collected shrapnel and one of our street games was nipping out with buckets of water to put out incendiary bombs.' He collected cigarette cards showing his favourite footballers and cricketers; he enjoyed trips to the 'pictures' on Saturday to see the latest American movie stars and adventure serials; and he accepted powdered eggs and milk and corned beef as staples of his diet because he knew no different. 'We were all painfully thin, and short, with pipe-cleaner legs. Rationing was supposed to have improved the diet of the working class, but it didn't do much for us.'

And, of course, he played plenty of football. The Greaves house had a garden that stretched away from the house like a pitch. Until the potatoes were dug up from the fields across the way, it was here, or on the streets outside if lighting was needed or the garden was being used to grow vegetables, where Jimmy and his mates would spend hours playing until all the skin came off their tennis ball and, finally, it split. 'I belong to the very last generation in Britain which played in the street. On our estate, no one had cars, so there was no fear of being run over.'

Greaves would recall that he 'arrived as a footballer out of the blue', with no great family tradition in the sport. His dad had played as a modestly-talented amateur wing-half or centre-half and had been a useful hockey player in the army in India. Yet Greaves remembered that 'nobody gave me any real coaching'. But what his father was able to offer him, at the age of five years old, was more valuable than any technical guidance; it was his own leather football. With that, Jimmy became the most sought-after playing companion in the neighbourhood.

Greaves senior served as chairman of a small local club, Fanshaw Old Boys, whose players became Jimmy's first sporting heroes and happily allowed him to have a kickabout with them when he tagged along to games. And when the club was about to discard one of its old footballs, it was Jimmy who ended up with the prized possession.

Not by talent or skill – of which he already had more than most of his peers – Jimmy had become 'the centre of our football world'. The ball was his entry ticket to endless games with boys up to the age of 15, who were happy to allow a slip of a kid to play with them in return for the chance to kick around something better than an ageing tennis ball. No game could take place without him being picked for one of the teams. Even though the older boys displayed a reluctance to scare off such an important figure, Greaves still needed to develop keen instincts for self-preservation to survive physically. 'That was the best thing that happened to me as a youngster,' he said, 'playing with those lads three times my own age.' After that, even the brutal defences of Italian football would hold few fears.

A veteran of hundreds of street games, Jimmy played his first organised match at the age of nine at Southampton Lane School, scoring twice from his inside-right position with his family watching the action from their kitchen window. Greaves's school team then won the local league in his second year in the team.[1]

It was at Southampton Lane that Greaves had encountered, in a Mr Bakeman, someone who possessed 'the best knowledge of the game I had met in a teacher'. More typical throughout his school years was a sports master of whom Greaves said, 'I doubt if he knew as much about the game technically as my mother.'

Again, it was fate and circumstance that proved to be his most effective coaches. When the toes of the cheap boots he was wearing fell apart after only a couple of weeks, he had been forced to learn to kick properly with his instep to avoid pain and discomfort. And his father's promotion from a guard on the London Underground's District Line to driver on the new Central Line as it expanded out into Essex led to the family moving to Hainault, where the concrete and rubble that formed the back garden meant that Greaves found himself back out in the street kicking a tennis ball. 'When shooting I had to hit it just right, otherwise I would not make contact at all,' he recalled. The proper ball used in official matches was easy to master by comparison.

Away from football, Jimmy enjoyed listening to nature programmes on the radio, but family holidays spent hop picking in Kent – 'it took us five hours' drive in a cranky old lorry to get there'

---

1   Greaves's recollection varies from autobiography to autobiography as to whether they won the local cup in the same year or were beaten in the final.

– were the closest he came to the idyllic countryside rambles he heard being portrayed on the radio. 'I was convinced life happened somewhere else for other kids,' he admitted, content to allow his favourite sport to fill the void that everyday existence appeared to have left.

The 11-plus exam that would determine his secondary school destination threw up exactly the result he hoped for. 'I spent so long trying to understand the questions that I had no time to fill in the answers,' he told *The Times*. Failure in the exam hall allowed him to attend Kingswood Secondary Modern in Hainault rather than being stuck at a rugby-playing grammar school. Not that success on the football field was easy to come by. It took Kingswood three miserable years of failure before things suddenly clicked in Greaves's fourth year at the school and a cup and league double was achieved – 'the strangest thing I have ever known happen in the game at any level', he would note.

As Greaves's goals from his inside-forward position fired his school team towards success in that 1954-55 school year, so he came to the attention of a broader audience. 'I idolised Jimmy when I was a kid,' recalled future England team-mate Martin Peters. 'He was three years older than me and I remember him playing for his school side against ours and scoring 11 goals in a 13-0 victory.'

In the Dagenham district team he found himself playing alongside opponents who would eventually become professional peers; Terry Venables, Ken Shellito, Mike Harrison and John Smith. And against someone who would line up alongside him in one England youth team game and eventually be his coach at West Ham during the final months of his League career. John Lyall recalled, 'When I first played against him in the Corinthian Shield Under-15s final, he wasn't a goalscorer at all. He was playing for Dagenham Schools and he ran my Ilford team ragged. He had a dribbling talent and a passing talent that was way above anything else on the field … Jimmy dribbled rings around us that day and, although he didn't score, someone obviously spotted a talent that could be exploited.'

Venables remembered Greaves as 'an awesome player even then', explaining that he would 'come alive' when the ball reached him, 'dancing around four or five players and scoring fantastic goals'. Venables was so in thrall to Greaves, three years older than he was, that he followed him home on the bus one day, hoping to absorb some insight that might help him emulate his hero. The only result of his spying mission, though, was a long walk home.

When his father was approached by Tottenham scouts after an appearance for London Boys, it was the first time that Greaves seriously considered that he might be able to earn a living from football. Despite being from West Ham territory, it was always Spurs with whom he felt the closest affinity – although he would watch his football at local non-League teams competing in the Athenian, Corinthian, Isthmian and Spartan Leagues. His father, Jim, set his sights firmly on a Tottenham apprenticeship for his son after being impressed by a meeting with manager Arthur Rowe, who had developed the 'push and run' style of football that won the League Championship in 1950-51. Young Jimmy was suitably happy with such a plan, despite the temptation of remaining at Kingswood long enough to earn the chance to win a schoolboy cap at cricket for Essex.

It was selection for the Essex Schoolboys football team, however, that brought him into contact with a mysterious bowler-hatted character who was to change his life; a man who, for reasons of paranoia resulting from previous accusations of poaching young players, often went by the name of Mr Pope, even though those in professional football knew his true identity as Jimmy Thompson, Chelsea Football Club's starmaker.

'Jimmy Thompson was the best scout there was,' says Les Allen, another Dagenham boy who had been spotted by Thompson while playing local amateur football. 'He was a special man. He knew what he wanted and Ted Drake, the manager at Chelsea, gave him carte blanche to get any players he wanted. He lived in Romford, which was quite a good area for picking up players. He was well known for persuading a lot of boys that West Ham were after to go to Chelsea instead. He told me about the good players that were at Chelsea: a lad my age called Colin Court, who played for Wales schoolboys, and Roy Cunningham, who played for the Scottish schoolboys. Jimmy Thompson went all round the country getting the best players, so it was a good club to join.'

With Greaves's leaving date from school only a month away and Tottenham his apparent destination, Thompson, excited by what he had seen on the field, knocked on the door of the Greaves home. 'He was a genius,' was Thompson's description of his target. 'He would never touch it with his head, but downstairs – cor!' In those days, the sight of a bowler-hatted man on the doorstep usually meant that an insurance payment was due, but for Greaves that headgear was to have an entirely different significance. 'Every time for years to come that I was to make a major decision in my football career, the bowler hat would be around,' he said.

A young member of Chelsea's playing squad, defender John Sillett, had been as impressed as Thompson by his first sight of Greaves. 'I saw him in a game at White Hart Lane,' he remembers. 'I think it was for London Schoolboys. Him and a lad called David Cliss. I thought, "These two can play." Next day, Jimmy Thompson came into the club and asked if anybody had seen the game and what did we think of the players? I said, "Cliss impressed me a lot and the feller up front, Greaves, he scored a couple of good goals." Jimmy said, "They are both coming to Chelsea." That was the first time I really took notice of him.'

Thompson had called Drake after watching Greaves score five goals in a game to tell him he had seen 'a player of a lifetime'. A man on a mission, he introduced himself at the family's front door and walked confidently into the kitchen to announce, 'Put the kettle on, ma, and we'll have a cup of tea.' Mary, far from being affronted, was charmed, even if this smooth talker did always seem to be speaking out of the side of his mouth as if suspicious of spies behind the sofa. To Greaves senior, Thompson issued the instruction that Jimmy should sign for Chelsea, while laying out all the supposed faults of the set-up at Tottenham.

As part of his period of contemplation, Greaves's dad went to see Ernest Allen, father of Les, who had grown up in the same neighbourhood and was in the early days of a professional career at Stamford Bridge. 'I was from just close by to Jimmy,' Allen explains. 'I was in Bonham Road, where a few of us turned out to be professional players: for instance, Ken Brown and Dickie Walker, who were centre-halves for West Ham; my brother, Dennis, who played for Charlton; and Terry Venables, who lived opposite us. I don't know if Jim's dad went to the same working men's club my father went to on a Sunday for a pint at lunchtime, but he did talk to him. My dad told him what a good club Chelsea was for the young players.'

Another factor in the Greaves family's decision was the ill health that had struck down Arthur Rowe, the man so admired by Jim senior. Forced to take six months away from the manager's role at Spurs before he would finally step down in the summer of 1955, it meant Thompson could not have timed better the visits that became more frequent as he further recognised the talent before him. 'As the glibness rushed on in a torrent so I moved farther and farther away from White Hart Lane,' recalled Greaves, who was being swayed by the presence of other East Enders at Stamford Bridge and the club's push towards that season's League Championship, their first major trophy.

Intriguingly, Bill Nicholson, the man who – as an eventual successor to Rowe at Tottenham – felt most closely the Greaves family's change of heart, cast a shadow of impropriety over the decision in his autobiography three decades later. 'Arthur Rowe anticipated that Greaves would sign as one of his apprentices,' he noted. 'Why Greaves chose Chelsea can only be answered by him. Tottenham failed to sign many good young players through the years because they never paid inducements to the parents of schoolboys.'

Meanwhile, West Ham manager Ted Fenton had also made a couple of visits, but his powers of persuasion were limited by his club's struggle to get themselves out of the Second Division. Future England colleague George Cohen, born four months before Greaves, recalls the buzz around the London football scene over his impending decision. 'He was the one people were watching,' he says. 'He was a sensation and people were asking, "Where is Jimmy Greaves going?" I first met him at Arsenal. We were sitting next to each other on the bench watching London Boys play Scotland Boys, I think it was. He had a big name and when I asked him where he was going he said he was going to stick with Chelsea. He was very, very self-assured as far as his football was concerned.'

A further career option, a job as a compositor at *The Times*, where his dad had set him up with an interview, was never likely to be considered seriously once Thompson had taken his wide-eyed target to tea at the Strand Palace Hotel, offering him a glimpse of grandeur he had only seen in magazines and movies. Nor was remaining at school, where he had battled through exams in spite of being 'a tortoise when it came to reading', requiring twice as long to get through a textbook as his classmates. In later years, it was discovered that he suffered from dyslexia.

In the end, despite his father's loyalty towards White Hart Lane, the decision was in Jimmy's own hands. Chelsea it was. Tottenham and West Ham would both have to wait.

'I should like to take you to the ground personally to meet Mr Drake,' a triumphant Thompson told him on hearing of his choice. Thinking that he was to be given a private audience befitting an apparently prized prospect, Greaves was surprised, and a little crestfallen, to discover a whole group of young players waiting to be given train tickets by Thompson when he reported to Liverpool Street Station. Among them were Shellito and Cliss, two boys he'd been particularly impressed by during a game for London Schools.

The boys were offered a Polo mint and handed a Tube ticket to Fulham Broadway, from where they made the short walk to sit outside Drake's office inside Chelsea's stadium.

One by one, they were summoned by Thompson, the numbers in the waiting area steadily reducing as they were ushered out of another door into a billiards room, unseen by their fellow hopefuls. 'It was all pretty nerve-wracking,' Greaves remembered, eventually getting his turn in front of Drake. There were few personal comments, merely a reminder of the duties of boys assigned to the ground staff and an assurance that, 'I expect you to be a distinguished player in the years ahead'.

Waiting in the billiard room he found Chelsea's youth manager, Dickie Foss, whom he would later describe as 'one of the few people who really helped me develop as a player'. Greaves was to sign amateur forms and be paid £5 a week for his duties around the club, with £2 of that being an accommodation allowance that his mother had to sign for to prove she had received it. There was the promise of an extra £2 when he turned 16 several months later.

For now, it was hardly a life-changing milestone for the Greaves family. They had not even managed to finagle any of the white goods, sofas or new overcoats for mum that many clubs were offering in exchange for junior's signature – despite Nicholson's later innuendo. They didn't go entirely empty-handed, though. Just back from a trip across the water to watch some racing, Thompson, who loved to gamble on the horses as well as schoolboy footballers, handed Greaves's dad £50 worth of Irish five-pound notes.

2

TEENAGE KICKS

*'I am an entertainer. If I have a certain something
that the public want to read and talk about, then
let them do all the reading and talking they want.
I'm doing my job.'*

LONG before he became a professional footballer at Chelsea, Jimmy Greaves became a professional businessman. His entrepreneurial partner, John Sillett, chuckles at the memory. 'He turned up at Stamford Bridge and we got on great together. Nobody frightened him and whatever discipline there was at Chelsea at that time didn't worry Jimmy one iota.'

Greaves might never have been at the top of his class academically, but his school record was good enough to save him the menial chores of boot cleaning and shower scrubbing to which most of his new colleagues were assigned in their roles on the Chelsea ground staff. The brighter recruits were given tasks that took advantage of their brains, which meant that Greaves was given a relatively cushy job in the comfortable confines of the administration office. There, he found himself handing out luncheon vouchers to the players and making tea – endless cups of tea – for club secretary John Battersby and his staff.

His duties gave him the opportunity to eavesdrop on some interesting meetings, such as the club's negotiations to sell striker Bobby Smith to Tottenham in December 1955. He lingered a little longer over the milk and sugar that day as he experienced the thrill of being privy to such a big story. It was the luncheon vouchers that provided his entry into the world of business. 'That is how we first got together,' Sillett recalls. 'We used to go to a restaurant called Annabel's down the road. You took these five-shilling luncheon vouchers and you got a meal. Jimmy gave me about 20 of them and I sold them and we split the money. That is how our friendship started. Another thing we did together was sell men's shirts. I had a contact at West Ham who could get these shirts. I used to buy them for 10 shillings and sell them for a pound. I told Greavsie about it and he came in with me. This was all before he got in the first team.

'Things were very relaxed at Chelsea then. There wasn't any sense that you had to watch out. It was pretty open that you could do those sorts of things. We used to be able to sell our match tickets – our complimentaries. The players would get them together and we'd go and sell them to the spivs waiting outside Stamford Bridge.'

For all his wheeler dealing, Greaves didn't entirely escape manual labour: he was drafted in to assist the workmen putting up the stadium's first floodlights, which were eventually unveiled early in 1957. Football had to wait until the afternoons, when the large group of junior players attached to the club were split into separate groups; one training at Stamford Bridge and the other using the club's Welsh Harp training ground in Hendon. There was even a third unit, as midfielder Terry Bradbury recalls. 'I went out as an apprentice electrician for a couple of years. Those of us who did that used to train in the evenings and never saw the others except for matches.'

It meant that competition for places in Chelsea's various elevens was ferocious. Greaves played his first official game in Chelsea colours for the junior team, effectively the club's fourth XI, against Watford on 20 August 1955, when it took him only one minute to score the first of his two goals in a 5-1 win. Shortly after, he broke his nose in a midweek trial match, although his fear of hospital and desire not to miss any games prevented him seeking any treatment. A further break a few months later straightened it for him anyway.

Greaves's form won him elevation to the youth team, where he scored 17 goals in 20 games in the South East Counties League. He also made the Middlesex team that won the final of the FA County Youth Cup against Staffordshire. 'He was the best goalscorer I ever saw,' says Bradbury – and that's not the final time you will read that comment in this book. 'He could score from nothing. His pace over the first five yards gave him just enough time and space. He wasn't the best trainer and he didn't do much tracking back, but he didn't have to. He had people like me to get the ball and give him the ammunition he needed up front. It all came so naturally to him.'

Yet before his first season was up, Greaves, fed up with making tea and frustrated by what he perceived as his slow progress, decided he'd had enough. Selection for Chelsea's FA Youth Cup games, the highlight of the team's calendar, had eluded Greaves. Instead, his place for those matches went to Peter Brabrook, a couple of years his senior, who was a regular in the reserves and in the process of breaking into the first team.

'There were plenty of youngsters on the club's books better than me,' was the way he viewed his situation. He went to see Dickie Foss and told him he would play on as an amateur but that he wanted to take a job as a messenger in a publishing house, hardly a step up from tea boy. 'Fossy tried to talk me out of it. He was one of the few people in those days who thought I had a future in the game.' Yet his new life proved even more humdrum than the Stamford Bridge office and, after only a week, he returned to Chelsea. Foss simply nodded and sent him out to join training. To the best of Greaves's knowledge, club manager Ted Drake was unaware of the whole episode.

There was no doubting the progress he made during the following season, 1956-57, scoring a staggering 114 goals for a variety of teams. Chelsea's South East Counties League records show him hitting 53 goals in 18 games, and a total of 77 in 30 competitive games for the club's youth team. And he found a way to make himself known to Chelsea's senior players in the club.

'We didn't train with the youth team,' explains winger Frank Blunstone, a member of Chelsea's title-winning side of 1954-55. 'The only time we saw them was Monday mornings, when they were brushing the terraces while we trained at Stamford Bridge. Every Tuesday we used to have a first team versus reserves match and this particular week we were short of players. We'd had a few injuries on the Saturday so they sent for a couple of kids. These two 16-year-olds turned up and were in the reserves. Albert Tennant, the coach, was on the touchline shouting out instructions with a megaphone. We had been playing about 20 minutes and this little kid picks up the ball and sets off on a run. He goes past one man, then past another and, all of a sudden, out comes the megaphone: "Get rid of the ball!" He carries on, goes past another one. "For Christ's sake, get rid of the ball!"

'He carries on, draws out Reg Matthews – who plays for England – dips his shoulder, sends him the wrong way and rolls it in the corner. He jogs back to the halfway line, turns to the coach and says, "You didn't tell me when, Albert." Of course, that was Jimmy Greaves. It was the first time I ever noticed him. I thought then, "Blimey, what a confident kid and what a sense of humour." After that we used to look to see how the youth team had got on and it was always, "Oh, Jimmy got another three."'

If Greaves's output was remarkable, then equally so was the dominance of the Chelsea youngsters, winning 23 of their 24 league games and scoring a phenomenal 159 goals. A side that included Barry Bridges, scorer of 28 league goals, and David Cliss, who totalled 19, regularly achieved double figures. Meanwhile, letting them in at the other end, Greaves recalled, 'never bothered us because we were confident we would score four or five in reply'.

Having won the South East Counties League in 1954-55 and relinquished the title in Greaves's first season at the club, Chelsea's youth-team title in 1957 was the first of seven consecutive triumphs under the leadership of Foss, someone whom Greaves described as a stern character who was 'never satisfied'.

'He always told you if you played badly and rarely mentioned the game if you played well,' Greaves explained. Forward Les Allen adds, 'Dickie was straightforward and knew his football. If you didn't do your bit he told you in no uncertain terms.' Greaves would come to acknowledge that Foss's honest and direct approach – he would never criticise anyone behind their back – turned him from a schoolboy into someone who, if not quite yet a man, was getting ready to take his place in a man's world.

Greaves had made his debut for Chelsea's reserve team against Bristol City in September 1956, and his first appearance for the England youth team came the following February. After seeing his team go behind early on against the modest opposition of Luxembourg at Upton Park, Greaves helped himself to four goals in a 7-1 victory. A week later, he scored three and set up two more in another 7-1 win, against Wales at Ninian Park, Cardiff. The *Daily Mirror* wrote that he was 'the shining light of the England forward line'. By the time the team's busy schedule for the season had ended, he had won seven youth caps.

The moment was approaching when, he assumed, Chelsea would ask him to sign as a professional. He was taking nothing for granted, however. He had already seen young hopefuls discarded ruthlessly by Drake; boys such as future England centre-forward Joe Baker – brother of another youth-teamer, Gerry Baker – who was given only a month's trial before being released. Yet Jimmy Thompson promised, after meeting with the manager, that no such fate awaited him.

The assurance meant a lot coming from Thompson, whom Greaves would describe as 'the finest professional I ever met' after Thompson fell out with Chelsea and left the club a couple of seasons later. Thompson's tip-off gave Greaves the confidence to decide to make Chelsea sweat before committing himself to a future at Stamford Bridge. Surely, if anyone would acknowledge the value of someone with such ability to score goals it would be Drake, who had netted 171 times in 238 League games during a career that brought him two League titles with Arsenal and five England caps. Greaves felt that what he could potentially bring to the club deserved to be recognised financially. 'The more I delayed signing, the more frantic Chelsea became,' he explained.

It was while he was walking along Fulham Road with his girlfriend and future wife Irene Barden, that Thompson pulled up alongside him in a car and told him to go and see Drake to sort things out once and for all. Greaves chose to tell the manager that he needed more money and was thinking of signing elsewhere. Drake's response melted his resolve. Far from kicking Greaves out of his office, the manager threatened to resign if his boy wonder didn't commit to Chelsea. Disarmed and overcome by a sense of responsibility towards Drake, he signed without holding out for any kind of bonus.

Greaves's final act of the 1956-57 season had been to lead Chelsea's youth team to victory in an international tournament in Amsterdam, scoring three goals in wins against PSV Eindhoven and FC Schalke before adding another in a 2-1 victory against Anderlecht in the final. He returned to the city as the last part of the build-up to the new campaign, preparing to march decisively to the forefront of English football.

It was a week before Chelsea began their League season against Tottenham Hotspur. Greaves, newly turned professional, scored twice in the first team's 4-2 win against Ajax, leaving *Daily Express* reporter Bob Pennington in no doubt about what he had witnessed. 'The biggest, brightest boost Chelsea have had for more than a decade,' he wrote, 'was the sensational – yes, sensational – form of 17-year-old inside-left Jimmy Greaves.'

His own memory of that game was somewhat less emphatic. 'I played fairly well in Holland,' he said, admitting that 'I still wasn't prepared for what came next' – which was Drake approaching him after training later that week to tell him he would be playing in the first game of the Division One season.

A London derby to open a new campaign brought a crowd of almost 53,000 to White Hart Lane, enough to wobble the knees of most teenaged debutants. Greaves always insisted in his early years, however, that pre-match nerves were 'not in my make-up'. His view was, 'I either play badly or I play well. It's as simple as that and any fretting I do before the game is not going to help.'

Sillett adds, 'You would never see him that nervous in the dressing room. I never did anyway. You would look across and he would be having a puff on a cigarette. He never looked that worried about anybody.'

As years progressed – and especially when he was trying to understand his dependence on alcohol – he would observe that the stresses of the game made him a different, more edgy, character in the dressing room. And it is hard to believe that even the carefree 17-year-old had no butterflies at all as he took his No.10 shirt down from its dressing-room peg for the first time and slipped on a pair of oversized, but comfortable, white shorts. At least he was not as worried as some rookies might have been when looking at the opposition team-sheet. With English football still largely following the protocols of the WM formation, where the right-half took prime responsibility for marking the inside-left, the man in direct opposition would be Danny Blanchflower. The Tottenham and Northern Ireland captain was a player with a reputation for thoughtful, creative football; not for kicking lumps out of greenhorn forwards.

Greaves had what was, for the most part, a promising more than spectacular debut. He caught the eye with one particular run that took him past Blanchflower, centre-half Maurice Norman and Scotland defender John Ryden before forcing a save from goalkeeper Ron Reynolds. But five minutes from the end came the moment that would ensure him headlines and rave reviews as he earned Chelsea a point with a right-foot finish. 'I simply ran a loose ball into the net when the game was growing old,' he recalled. 'It was enough for the newspaper reporters.'

In that night's *Evening Standard*, Bernard Joy noted that Greaves had 'the cheek of an East London cockney', while the write-up from Desmond Hackett, chief sports writer of the *Daily Express*, was one for the Greaves scrapbook. 'Jimmy Greaves gave the greatest show I have ever seen from any young player,' he recorded. 'I do not want to rave, although I find it hard not to stand up and shout: This boy will be box-office magic.' Admitting he might be accused of being hysterical – which would by no means have been the first time in the excitable Hackett's career – he turned to Blanchflower for support, quoting him as concluding, 'This boy is a natural. He seemed to know just what to do.' Even the more reserved *Times* suggested that 'Greaves may have a rich future'.

Greaves was a little more restrained in his own analysis. 'Honestly, I felt lost,' he told reporters in a quiet voice outside White Hart Lane. 'The pace frightened me. It was killing. I did not think I had a good game. I felt out of it because things seemed to happen so fast.'

The press pictures of his goal caught the youngster's baggy shorts billowing in the style of those worn by English players in bygone years. Hackett's report noted Greaves opting for 'shorts in the baggy style of old soccer immortality Alex James'.

Greaves would explain that his choice of styling was down to fate and functionality rather than any kind of gimmicky look-at-me fashion statement. 'I remember having a pair of shorts thrown at me that came down past my knees.' Too preoccupied with the game to protest, his debut goal persuaded him that the shorts had been a lucky charm and he stuck with them, adding that 'they were so darned comfortable'.

Not everyone was quite so bowled over, of course. One reader's letter in the *Daily Express*, appearing in print several days later, stated, 'I don't know how a lad with only one effective foot can be said to be greater than Duncan Edwards and Johnny Haynes.'

Greaves scored again in his next game and added two more in a 5-1 win against Birmingham City. But he also came in for some fierce criticism from opposition players for neglecting to visit City goalkeeper Gil Merrick after the game, having been involved in the third-minute collision that saw the England international leave the field concussed.

Word of Greaves's ability was spreading quickly, reaching the ears of the England selectors, who named him ahead of West Bromwich Albion striker Derek Kevan for the Under-23 team to face Bulgaria late in September – a 'startling development', according to *The Times*. After scoring Chelsea's goal against Kevan's West Brom team a week before that international date, he elicited more praise. 'I came here just to see this kid Greaves,' said Aston Villa trainer Bill Moore. 'He is all they say he is, and more.'

With only eight League games – and six goals – behind him, Greaves made his first appearance in England Under-23 colours in front of 56,000 fans at Stamford Bridge. As usual, it was a goal-scoring debut. Denied with a diving header earlier in the game, he converted after an Alan A'Court effort had been parried and added his second in a 6-2 win 13 minutes from time following a combination between Haynes and Brabrook. He also missed a late penalty, but such was his performance that he was easily forgiven. *The Times* somehow turned his error into a positive, noting it affectionately as a sign that he was 'taking life very nonchalantly for one so young'.

Greaves's instant rapport with Fulham's Haynes, which would be long-lasting, earned him further compassion. 'Johnny Haynes and Jimmy Greaves are natural performers,' wrote Jim Gaughan in *The Star*. 'There has been nothing like this from an England pair since the great days of Raich Carter and Wilf Mannion.' In

The Times, Geoffrey Green predicted, 'Unless one makes a horrible mistake, a great new inside-forward partnership for the future was born last night. By the end they were thinking and looking alike as a pair of identical twins.'

The following month, playing in a 3-2 win against Romania at Wembley, Greaves scored with a first-time shot after only 35 seconds and threatened twice more before netting again from a Stan Crowther delivery on 24 minutes. On this occasion, *The Times* declared, 'Once in possession he has an electric quality – the craft of a Carter perhaps, spiced with a dash of Mortensen. With it all he has the quickest of reflexes and a cool brain.'

Some observers had already seen enough to demand his elevation to the full England team. Three days after his goals against Romania, a 4-0 victory by England's seniors against Wales was considered disappointing enough for Greaves's absence to be noted by most; and his immediate inclusion demanded by some. Two weeks later, his backers felt the national selectors had not gone far enough in merely naming Greaves as a standby player for England's Wembley game against Northern Ireland. His father, Jim, however, attempted to dilute the media clamour with a dash of realism by reminding reporters, 'Jimmy is young. There is plenty of time. It is very wise to let him get the feel of a top match like this before sending him out to play in one. Jimmy is happy even to be considered.'

One man not sorry to see Greaves overlooked for a full call-up was his club manager, who said his selection as non-playing 12th man was 'just the blooding he needs'. Drake had warned from the outset that he would stand his young star down as soon as he felt he was being asked to play too much football. In mid-November, after a run of seven games in which he had scored only once, Greaves was called into the manager's office. 'I am resting you for 10 days,' Drake informed him.

'I was being dropped,' Greaves acknowledged, 'but so gently that it wouldn't have cracked an eggshell.'

Drake had already taken steps to alleviate some of the pressure on his precocious starlet by limiting his exposure in the press, as Norman Giller recalls. 'We were both 17 and I was assistant sports editor on the West Ham local paper, the *Stratford Express*, where we had a sports staff of two,' he explains. 'As Jimmy had been born in our circulation area I arranged an interview with him at Stamford Bridge. When I got there, he said, "Sorry, mate. Can't talk to you. The boss has told me not to give any more interviews." Ted was worried that he was getting too much attention. So we went for a cuppa at the Bridge Café and our 60-year friendship started there.'

The proposed 10-day absence from the Chelsea first team turned into several weeks. Greaves found it took longer than he had expected to rekindle the energy and adrenalin that had propelled him through the opening matches of the season and it was not until Christmas Day that he was reinstated to the side for the home game against Portsmouth. He scored four goals as Chelsea won 7-4. Back in form, a report of his two-goal performance in Chelsea's 3-1 mid-January win against Everton described him as the '17-year-old post-dated gift to England power to come' and, the writer noted, he 'performed the hip wiggle-waggle I thought the exclusive property of Marilyn Monroe'. He followed up by scoring again for England Under-23s in their 3-1 win against Scotland at Goodison Park.

Inconsistent in the League, Chelsea expected to mount a run in the FA Cup when, after beating Doncaster Rovers, they were drawn at home to Darlington of the Third Division North. Yet, having found themselves 2-0 down at half-time, Chelsea could only draw 3-3, at which point Greaves was one of the players left out of the replay as Drake opted for greater experience. The plan backfired horribly as Darlington scored three unanswered goals in the second half to win 4-1, their giant-killing feat captured by Pathé News and played to cinema audiences around the country. Frank Blunstone recalls, 'I didn't play either because I was injured, but we all went up on the coach. After the game Ted Drake is doing his top. Jimmy is sat there and he said something and was smiling. Ted said to him, "What have you got to smile about? You can't even get in this bloody team." Jimmy said to me, "Great. I got a bollocking and I didn't even play."' Greaves did, however, reclaim the No.10 jersey from Les Stubbs for the next game.

Despite going without a goal in his final eight games, he finished his debut season in the first team as top scorer with 22 goals in 35 matches. The potential in their midst was apparent to all. 'It was obvious at once that here was a real talent,' says defender John Mortimore, who joined the club from non-League Woking in 1956. 'He had amazing balance, ball control and vision. Jimmy would often give me the run-around in training.'

Yet some parts of his game remained a mystery. 'I played with him for a couple of years and I still couldn't tell if he was left- or right-footed,' says Blunstone. 'He was so brilliant either side. He wasn't one of those where you had to send him on the left or send him on the right. He wasn't bothered; he could go either way.'

Sillett continues, 'I always thought his favourite foot was his left. But I would often room with Frank and he would say he was right-footed. I used to ask Greavsie which was his favourite and he used to say, "I don't mind – any of them."[2] He was even better than I thought. I couldn't believe the pace he had over 10 yards. He was lightning. As schoolboy I had qualified to do the 100 yards sprint for the county, but Jim would leave me standing. He was so sharp off the mark. At that time there was a sprinter called McDonald Bailey[3] and Greavsie took him on over 50 yards at Stamford Bridge and beat him. That's how he got away from defenders. He didn't have the kind of running action that looked quick. He looked casual, but his balance was unbelievable. It was like the grass was burning under his feet.'

---

2   Greaves was naturally left-footed, but worked hard to improve his right. 'Sooner or later both feet will be the way I want them,' he said in 1966.

3   Trinidad-born athlete who won a 100 metres bronze medal for Great Britain in the 1956 Olympics and jointly held the world record at the distance between 1951 and 1956.

Greaves credited Chelsea coach Albert Tennant, who loved to make his players run, for increasing his speed even further. Noticing that Greaves was somewhat flat-footed, he taught him to run on the balls of his feet. 'While I was improving the actual positioning of my feet, I also learned to balance my body properly,' he said. Search online and watch Greaves in full flow and you can see the effect of Tennant's guidance. At top pace, his upper body and arms barely seem to move. They hold steady, perfectly balanced, as his legs glide forward, almost appearing to hover an inch or two above the turf. There is never any suggestion that he might topple forward with the strain or risk flailing arms throwing him off balance.

Yet there was more to Greaves than mere quickness across the grass. 'His control was good,' says Sillett. 'You would not bet on him getting more than three a season with his head, but on the ground he was unbelievable. You would see him dribble past people and then he would pass it into the net. That is a well-known saying. He wouldn't crash them in.'

Blunstone also pays tribute to Greaves's instincts in the penalty area. 'We used to joke with him that he was a lucky little bugger because he used to just stand in the box and the ball would come to him and he would tap it in. He said, "It is nothing to do with luck. When the ball comes in the box and the defender is there, I always say to myself that he is going to miss it. And if he does, I am there." Many players would think it is the defender's ball and ignore it. But if the defender missed, Jimmy was on it.

'He played mostly on the left with me at the start and he was brilliant. You did have to be careful putting crosses in for him because he was only about 5ft 7in. People commented that he wasn't very good in the air, but he used to tell us, "If you put the ball on my head I will show you whether I am any good in the air." And he was right, he would put it away. He wasn't going to be able to jump with Jack Charlton and challenge people who were 6ft 4in for headers, but if you picked him out he would put it away for you.'

Even though it eventually came to nothing, Greaves had already done enough to create ripples of speculation about a possible call-up for England's World Cup squad in Sweden. The talk grew louder after the tragic loss of Manchester United centre-forward Tommy Taylor, one of the victims of the air crash in Munich in February 1958 in which eight members of the young team that had captivated the nation died.

Meanwhile, alongside his successful senior duties, Greaves had returned to the Chelsea youth team to bolster their bid for the FA Youth Cup, a tournament in which they totalled 44 goals in five games to reach the quarter-finals, Bridges accounting for 21 of them. Greaves scored two in a 4-1 victory over Southampton in the last eight before Chelsea beat Arsenal 3-1 in each leg of their semi-final. Greaves scored once in the home game before grabbing a hat-trick in the return.

He scored again at Stamford Bridge in a 5-1 win against Wolverhampton Wanderers and the two-legged final was as good as won. Or so Chelsea's precocious youngsters believed. Two days later, they took the field at Molineux with the strut of overconfidence and without the determination required to win a cup final, even one in which they already held a four-goal advantage. With Wolves forward Ted Farmer single-handedly wiping out the deficit, Chelsea were beaten 6-1 to lose the trophy 7-6 on aggregate.

'We felt we had let the club and its supporters down, and in particular Dickie Foss,' Greaves recalled. Foss saw the shell-shocked looks on his players' faces in the dressing room and knew that a lesson had been learned by all. 'Never go out on to a football field with your big heads on,' he told them by way of emphasis.

It was actually Greaves's second cup final of the season. The inaugural European Inter-Cities Fairs Cup had been rumbling along since 1955, set up by UEFA as a tournament between cities that staged trade fairs. The one team per city rule – which existed into the 1970s – saw London initially represented by an all-star team, bringing together players from all the major clubs. When the competition began, Greaves had still been brewing tea in the Stamford Bridge office; by the time London hosted Barcelona at Stamford Bridge in the first leg of the final in March 1958, he was leading the attack, having scored in the semi-final to help them overhaul a first-leg deficit against Lausanne. He opened the scoring after 10 minutes of the final, but a 2-2 draw made Barcelona the favourites to lift the trophy. They did so emphatically with a 6-0 win on the very day that Greaves and his Chelsea youth colleagues were being thrashed by Wolves, making him, in effect, the answer to a pub quiz question about players losing two major finals via six-goal hammerings on the same day.

A part-time youth team player he might still have been – and only 18 years old – but Greaves was now a married man. In March, he and Irene, an Essex girl from Harold Hill whom he'd met at a school youth club, had staged their wedding at Romford Register Office. With Irene having already fallen pregnant, it was a quick and small ceremony, which the couple had agreed would attract 'no fans, no fuss'. And no hint of the kind of celebrity magazine deal that, a few decades later, would have earned the couple enough to get them on the property ladder. Instead, their first home together was a one-bedroom rented flat inside Southern League Wimbledon's old ground at Plough Lane. There, one of the brightest talents in the English game could be found supplementing his income by weeding the terraces for £8 per week. At least it enabled him to buy his first car, a 1937 Opel convertible for which he paid £30 to Irene's brother, Tom.

'I can't say my marriage was rapturously received by the football world,' Greaves recalled. 'There were plenty of people around to tell me I was too young and that my football would suffer through having to think in terms of a home life as well as a career.' He would come to believe that the reverse had been true, steering him away from the kind of bachelor life that could give a manager fits. 'We knuckled down to proving everybody wrong. I played as hard and as well as I have ever played, simply so that nobody could point a finger at me and say, "I told you so."'

Yet marriage was not going to dilute his enjoyment of the social scene that flourished around the Chelsea team, as it did at most clubs at that time. 'One of my jobs,' laughs Sillett, 'was to get the players out of the pub over the road before kick-off. We used to have a drink in the Queen's Arms in Chelsea and we got to know all of the actors. We got on great. We used to go to film premieres and got complimentary tickets to the Chelsea Palace to go and see all the shows.'

Greaves's choice of attire was reflective of the way he approached the task of scoring goals; neat and business-like. 'He always looked smart,' Chelsea board member Brian Mears remembered. 'He favoured the City look in an era when most players wore blazers, club ties and flannels. He used to wear knotted, sober ties. His shoes looked like they had just come out of the box and his hair was always short and razor cut.'

It was Sillett who had become Greaves's most frequent running mate. 'He would say, "Come on, Snoz. Let's go out." That was where my nickname came from; it was Jimmy. The Londoners at that time were all a bit on the confident side. I had come from the New Forest, and it was amazing to be among the Cockneys and hear how sharp they were. And all the young Cockney kids had cars. It took me years to get one. But Greavsie had a car more or less straight away and he used to drive me around everywhere.

'We used to go around together a lot. I married a girl from Upminster and we used to live close by before they moved. I went to the hospital when Irene had her first baby.[4] Greavsie said, "Come on, mate, let's go and celebrate." Blimey, did we celebrate? We went to The Bell in Upminster and I got in terrible trouble with my mother-in-law. She came looking for me and we were in the cellar in the pub.'

---

4   Daughter Lynn, born in October 1958.

One of the early Greaves performances to enter football folklore occurred on the second Saturday of the 1958-59 campaign, when League champions Wolves arrived at Stamford Bridge. Greaves, who had already bagged three goals in the first two games of the season, tore the visiting defence apart to score five times in a 6-2 win. At 35 years old, Billy Wright was still captain of England, approaching his 100th cap, and destined to lead Wolves to another title that season. 'Jimmy turned him inside out,' notes Blunstone.

'It was cruel and sad to see Wright bowing to the attacking genius of Greaves,' wrote the *Daily Mirror*. It was the sight of Greaves in full flight that persuaded Wright that his distinguished career was nearing the end. 'That was the day I decided to give it just one more season,' he admitted. 'I realised I couldn't keep up with the pace of the First Division for much longer. Mind you, Jimmy gave every defender he came up against that season the runaround. I always felt that his very best years were at Chelsea because he had no fear and just did what came naturally.' In later years, Wright revised his view of history by claiming that he had not even been responsible for marking Greaves that day. One thing beyond dispute is that it was one hell of a performance.

Peter Bonetti, who would begin his long tenure as Chelsea's goalkeeper the following season, is another who believes that Greaves was at his most brilliant in those formative years at Stamford Bridge. 'I always maintain that was when he was at his best. His early performances for Chelsea were mind-blowing. It's part of his legend how he convinced Billy Wright he should hang up his boots. He was like greased lightning and used to unbalance defenders with his speed and dribbling skill. After many of his goals you would find at least three defenders on their bums wondering what had happened. He was a nightmare for goalkeepers to face because he was never predictable with his finishing.'

Except with the regularity of it, of course. After 10 games of the campaign he had scored 16 times and, when Chelsea visited

Leicester City in March, his 26th goal equalled Tommy Lawton's single-season record for the club. By the time defeat at Birmingham City in the final game saw Chelsea finish in a disappointing 14th place in Division One, Greaves had increased that total to 32 goals. He had also scored in each of his team's two FA Cup matches.

And he had made a mark, even in defeat, on a young future England defender. 'When I was 15 years old I had a trial with Blackpool,' Bob McNab recalls. 'On the Saturday they played Chelsea at Bloomfield Road and I was given a ticket just behind the goal, just outside the left post. Actually, I sat on the iron pipe on the small wall between the running track and the standing fans. I will never forget that Chelsea had a free-kick about 25 yards from the goal line, approximately in line with the left side of the D. This young boy, Jimmy Greaves, struck the free-kick with the outside of his left foot, almost bending the ball into the far post. I had to duck down to avoid it. I can still picture it to this day as I'd never seen anyone bend a ball with the outside of their left foot.'

Meanwhile, Greaves's return of goals for England's Under-23s had slowed somewhat. When he failed to score in an impressive 3-0 win against Italy in Milan at the end of the season, his tally for the team had dipped to seven in eight games. Yet England manager Walter Winterbottom, who had travelled to watch the youngsters after his senior side had squandered a two-goal lead in a 2-2 draw against the same opposition at Wembley a day earlier, had seen enough to convince him that the time was right to put Greaves on to a bigger stage.

Back at the team hotel, Winterbottom sought out Greaves and team captain Jimmy Armfield, the Blackpool right-back, and told them they would not be going on to Germany with their colleagues. Instead, they would take the night train to Zurich, hop on a private jet supplied by Swissair, and fly from Heathrow to Rio de Janeiro with the senior England team for the start of their summer schedule.

England's 1958 World Cup campaign in Sweden, their third under the leadership of Winterbottom, had ended when the USSR beat them 1-0 in a play-off following their preliminary group, denying them a place in the quarter-finals. Having some years earlier won agreement that the former nine-man England selection panel should be reduced to himself and two others, Winterbottom had begun to put in place his plans to rebuild the team for the 1962 tournament in Chile. Household names such as Tom Finney and Stanley Matthews were no longer being selected; Billy Wright was embarking on his farewell tour.

In five games since the World Cup, they had remained unbeaten, including a 5-0 Wembley win against the USSR and a home win against Scotland. But draws against Northern Ireland and Wales and the lost lead against Italy proved that Winterbottom's project was still in its embryonic stage. Five players had made their debut in that period and Manchester United's Bobby Charlton had established himself as a pivotal member of the team with five goals, but the manager was ready for further experiment. Greaves watched as Armfield, along with Wolves' Norman Deeley, won their first caps in a 2-0 defeat in Brazil. Greaves recalled 'shaking like a leaf and constantly looking over my shoulder while 200,000 Brazilians broke the sound barrier' and remained convinced that the seven non-playing members of the squad had a tougher time than those on the field.

Greaves reckoned that an unfancied England team had played quite well against the world champions and was surprised, a few days later, to be told he was replacing Peter Broadbent for the game in Lima against Peru. He was also caught off guard in the dressing room before the game when Winterbottom began issuing specific instructions and reminders to his players, directing him to operate in tandem with Bobby Charlton at the centre England's attack and for the pair to remain in close proximity. He had never heard Ted Drake say anything more than 'all the best' to his Chelsea colleagues.

The trembles he'd felt sitting on the sidelines in Rio were absent as he took the field in Lima. Winterbottom's assurance that his England future did not depend on one match had put him in a relaxed frame of mind and eager to begin his full international career. Yet it was to be a miserable experience. 'I don't know how the score wasn't 24-1,' Greaves recorded of the home team's 4-1 victory in their first-ever game against England. 'We were thrashed,' he admitted. 'Made to look inept.'

The consolation for Greaves was his 58th-minute goal, drawing goalkeeper Rafael Asca from his line before scoring with his left foot. It promoted Charlton to recall, 'Not for one moment of an experience which might have been so discouraging did his performance suggest he was out of place.'

Greaves retained his place against Mexico a week later, an engagement that found the England team booked by the host football federation into a seedy hotel in the suburbs of Mexico City. Squeezed three or four to a room, the England players at least knew it was not a ploy by their hosts to gain an advantage. The Mexican FA had stuck its own players there, too. The English party checked out and joined the travelling journalists in more salubrious digs in the centre of town.

Blistered by sunbathing in the heat and breathless because of the high altitude, England suffered a 2-1 defeat that sent them north to Los Angeles with three losses behind them. 'To my knowledge, no one died on the tour, so that disaster was perhaps an exaggeration,' said Haynes, recalling the press criticism piling up on top of them. Haynes believed it was no coincidence that England struggled at the end of a long, arduous domestic season, an opinion that would echo for decades into the future.

Arriving in California, Greaves and his team-mates went to see Sammy Davis Jr in concert, watched horse racing at Hollywood Park and appeared on morning television in an attempt to drum up interest in their game. Winterbottom had been scarred by the United States before – the infamous 1-0 upset in Brazil during the 1950 World Cup – and an unwanted game in Wrigley Field[5] offered the prospect of traumatic flashbacks more than any potential upside. Sure enough, England went behind in the ninth minute, before rescuing their reputation with eight goals of their own. Greaves, who failed to find the net, admitted, 'We didn't exactly cover ourselves in glory.'

He came home with the view that a period of rebuilding was no time during which to be undertaking the toughest tour in world football. In the end, only six of the touring party would return to South America for the World Cup three years later. But there was never any doubt that Greaves, already one of the game's biggest stars after only two seasons of top-flight football, would be among them.

---

5   A minor league baseball ground, not to be confused with the similarly-named, more famous stadium in Chicago.

3

THE ROAD TO MILAN

*'My responsibility is to my family, and that means
doing my job as well as I can and earning as much
as I can to build them the best life possible'*

JIMMY Greaves began the 1959-60 season with a hat-trick in
a 4-4 draw against Preston North End at Stamford Bridge.
His biggest champion in the media, Desmond Hackett, was
on hand to throw the full force of his admiration at readers of the
Daily Express. Not only did Hackett determine that Greaves was
'undoubtedly destined to become the Player of the Year and of
many years to come',[6] he also described him as 'a rarity, fitted to
be named in the noble football lineage of Matthews, Finney, Carter
and Doherty'. He continued in full hyperbolic overdrive:

> Jimmy's third was unforgettable, a masterpiece to go into the
> gallery of unforgettables like the Lofthouse goal that beat
> the Austrians; the one that Matthews carved out to win the

---

6   Greaves never did win the Footballer of the Year award, voted for by the Football
    Writers' Association. Future team-mate Trevor Brooking voices an opinion held by
    many when he says such an oversight 'remains a mystery to me'.

Cup. Greaves went straight down the centre of the pitch. Without any discernible effort by Greaves, husky, lunging Preston players were left in an untidy trail as Greaves moved on to the glory of his goal. There was nothing of the feinting, mazy runs of Matthews. Greaves moved to his destruction of the defence with the ball so close it seemed to be part of his genius-gifted feet. When Greaves finally nicked the ball into goal a hushed, awed silence broke into an ovation. None of your hysterical noise from gloating fans. This was a dignified rising of 43,000 applauding, deeply impressed fans.

Greaves scored the only goal at Manchester United four days later, but more typical of Chelsea's inconsistency was the 6-3 defeat against the same opposition at Stamford Bridge the following week, a game in which Greaves was noted by one journalist to have 'looked like a forlorn small boy'. Frank Blunstone remembers, 'Jimmy came in and said that if we had scored six they would have scored seven.'

The 'we'll score more than you' attitude that ran through the successful youth team in which Greaves had grown up was working in reverse when it came to the more competitive, cut-throat world of First Division football. Chelsea's attack could be relied upon to score regularly, but such was their lack of organisation and playing pattern that no amount of goals could ever guarantee victory. Even when they scored four to beat Burnley three days after the United defeat, one report identified that Chelsea's problem was 'how they stop their opponents scoring five'.

Full-back John Sillett admits, 'We were a bit thin at the back; we weren't the best defence in the world. Me and my brother Peter were full-backs and Reg Matthews in goal was a nervous wreck, bless him. He would throw one in now and again and the times I have seen a great mix-up between him and Pete. There was one time they both wanted to clear it and Reg kicked it and it hit Pete straight in the stomach and went in the goal. Everybody was in stitches.'

Less amusing were trips to the division's tougher outposts, such as Bolton Wanderers, where an inexperienced and fragile team's lack of preparation was evidenced by the 6-0 thrashing that awaited them later in the season. 'The best days,' Sillett recalls with sarcasm, 'were trips to Bolton in February when the ground was frozen and you would get in the dressing room and hear them banging on the door. Crash, bang, wallop: "Bloody pansies up from London." They had a back four of Hartle, Hennin, Higgins and Banks and they were the hardest back four in the country. They never took prisoners. You would hear them shouting, "Little Greavsie is here, and I suppose he thinks he is going to score. The only kicks he will get are from Hartle, Higgins and Banksie." He would look across the dressing room at me and say, "Good game this, innit, Snoz." We were all trembling when we went out there. I remember him eventually scoring there once and saying sorry to them. He said, "They will kick the stuffing out of me now."'

Greaves recalled one game where his Chelsea team-mate, Micky Block, had been floored by a Tommy Banks tackle. 'You're losing your touch, Tommy,' Roy Hartle called over, 'He's still wriggling.' And, remembering the cinder track around the Bolton pitch, future Tottenham team-mate Cliff Jones adds, 'Wingers always used to come back from Burnden Park with gravel rash.'

Manager Ted Drake appeared powerless to do anything about Chelsea's inconsistency. His pre-game instructions amounted to nothing more than circling the dressing room and delivering his usual good luck message. John Mortimore says, 'I had a lot of respect for Ted and he gave the players responsibility on the field, but I cannot remember any long tactical talks.'

By the time Greaves was at the club, Drake, who had led Chelsea to the 1954-55 League title in his third season in charge, seemed to some of his players to be more concerned about looking after a bad back than anything else. He had swept into Stamford Bridge on a wave of innovation, changing the club crest and nickname to rid them of their 'Pensioners' image and introducing more training with the ball, but as time went on he appeared content to hide in his office and leave preparation of the team to trainer Jack Oxberry or coach Albert Tennant. 'Ted only came on the pitch every now and again to show you something,' Blunstone recalls. 'But even then, it was in his suit. He wasn't a coach.

'When we won the League it was just one of those seasons. We had a good balance, we got confident and things went our way. Perhaps other teams weren't as strong. It was similar to Leicester winning the Premier League. It wasn't going to happen again. The team we won the Championship with was a good side, but it was getting on. We had older players and we started to struggle.'

To replace those ageing characters, Drake – the first man to be a champion of England as both player and manager – became obsessed with following the trail blazed by Matt Busby and his 'Babes' at Manchester United. 'I scoured London,' he said years later. 'I went out to prove that if Matt Busby could go out and find youth boys then I could do exactly the same.' He enjoyed the 'Drake's Ducklings' name that became attached to his own group of prodigies, but Blunstone argues, 'Too many of them came in, five or six at one time. It is hard work when you get that.'

Despite being one of the beneficiaries of such an approach, Greaves recognised that Chelsea weren't blessed with the same resources of talent that had taken United to the title in the two seasons following Drake's success. They needed more experienced players to help guide the youngsters. 'You could play badly at Chelsea and still get in the side. It was a bit of a joke really,' he said. A lack of ambition, he believed, had pervaded the club. 'We played as hard and as well as we knew how, yet we never expected to win anything,' he argued. 'We didn't even particularly expect to win our matches.' The surprising emotion of victory was experienced only 14 times in 42 League games in 1959-60 as Chelsea finished 18th, Greaves scoring 29 goals in 40 matches.

Sillett recalls Drake 'throwing the book at us' at half-time in some games and becoming 'very frustrated', but there was little the manager could offer technically or tactically to address Chelsea's decline. 'He was just a long-ball man. And he wanted you to tackle. And Albert Tennant just wanted you to be really fit. The only time you got on the pitch was when the first team played the reserves on a Tuesday. Most of the time in those days I was in the reserves, and you used to hate to see Greavsie coming near you. He would drop his shoulder and go one way and you would go the wrong way. He would go, "Unlucky, Snoz."

'Jimmy thought he didn't need that much training. He was a bit anti-establishment in that way. In those days you would be doing laps of the pitch and he and my brother were the worst two trainers I have ever met. They used to go around together and Peter was captain at that time. I would go running past. I never had ability, so I had to have fitness on my side. You would hear them say, "John, what are you doing that for? You won't be playing." They knew the side way before everyone else. Jimmy never loved the cross-country or running around the streets. He didn't think that was a lot of good. He said, "When it comes to football it is between you, the ball and your opponent." He had great belief in his ability to score goals. And there was no pattern of play to work on in training. You just played the ball into Jimmy.'

What particularly galled Greaves was the lack of empathy displayed by Drake, one of the great front men, towards his own strike force. 'He was not a forward's man,' said Greaves, who remembered the manager spending much of his time 'climbing on the forwards' backs' and finding fault with them, no matter how many goals had been allowed at the other end. Blaming winger Peter Brabrook for a goal conceded after he gave away the ball at the other end of the field stuck in Greaves's mind as a typical example of Drake's apparent prejudice.

Not that the defenders were entirely free of Drake's quirks of mood. After a heavy defeat at Wolves during the following season, Drake would make a point of praising John Sillett for his performance. 'Next match we had Crewe at home in the FA

Cup,' Sillett explains. 'We had a pre-match team meeting in the billiard room upstairs. Ted said, "John Sillett gave one of the best performances at Wolverhampton that I have had from any defender since I have been manager here. And I am dropping him." And then we lost against Crewe at home.'

Greaves would come to think of Chelsea as 'a huge, shambling, good-natured outfit that bumbled along like an overgrown amateur club'. It gave off an aura that would be described, in the delightful language of sports writing of the era, by Peter Morris. 'You could call Chelsea the Gaiety Girl of football,' he wrote in *Charles Buchan's Football Monthly.* 'Precocious, pretty to watch ... capricious, often captivating ... always unpredictable. Yet loved by peers and painters, stage-folk and errand boys, city gents and country squires.'

Greaves wanted more than to be a loveable loser and to pick up individual honours like that bestowed on him at the end of the 1959-60 season, when he was named Young Footballer of the Year.[7] He could not help but wonder whether a better future lay away from Chelsea. Such thoughts occupied his summer break before he determined that he would 'give it another go at Stamford Bridge' in the hope that the team could turn things around.

There was to be no such transformation. Greaves began 1960-61 with two goalless games before grabbing a hat-trick against Wolves to start a run of nine goals in five games, including another treble against Blackburn. On that occasion, the *Daily Mirror's* Bill Holden described Greaves as 'one of the few personality players whose presence on the field is as startling as a supercharger on a family car'. His first goal, created by a typical burst of acceleration and finished with inevitable disdain, was 'an individual masterpiece'.

Yet as Chelsea approached the final weekend of October, they had won only four games out of 16. Although his team were about

---

7 Sponsored by the *Sunday Chronicle,* the award was inaugurated one year earlier as a way of commemorating Billy Wright's 100th England cap and was won by Jimmy Armfield. It was discontinued after Greaves won it in its second year.

to win four matches in succession, Greaves decided that he could wait no longer to make his move. 'I found that I'd had enough,' he said. 'What made me laugh earlier was just frustrating.'

He confided in his friend, Sillett. 'I am putting in a transfer request, Snoz. I will be leaving the club soon.'

'No you won't,' came the reply. 'You can't leave Chelsea.'

But Greaves was determined. On 4 November, he met the board. 'I had ambition and I wanted to play in top-class football, so I had to get away,' he recalled. His view was that he was 'carrying the team on my shoulders'. Sitting before chairman Joe Mears, secretary John Battersby, Drake and a collection of directors – with Irene at his side – Greaves outlined his belief that his career was going nowhere and that he could not see any advancement if he remained at Chelsea. Director Brian Mears, the chairman's son, recalled, 'My father summoned me to his home to attend a meeting Greaves had convened. He had requested a move and preliminary talks were going on. I was surprised to see his wife Irene there. Despite lengthy talks, [they] could not be dissuaded from thinking that their future lay beyond Stamford Bridge.'

Greaves fielded the anticipated questions about loyalty to the club, although he noted that there was no great attempt to state a footballing case for why he should stay at Chelsea. Instead, he sensed that the thought of the transfer fee appealed to the directors.

The meeting adjourned after 15 minutes. 'They gave me a good hearing and I think they saw my point of view, but they made it clear they thought my decision was bordering on the diabolical.' Greaves sensed that increasingly over the coming weeks. 'There were those who made me as welcome as a python that's wandered into an old ladies' tea party,' he recorded. While Joe Mears remained polite and friendly, Battersby, he believed, became petty and difficult, taking offence at Greaves walking into the club office, as he had done hundreds of times before, in contravention of the 'office staff only' sign. 'Jimmy's last few months at Chelsea were a strain on us all,' Brian Mears would admit, 'and difficult for everybody concerned.'

In his first autobiography, written only two years later, Greaves claimed that his transfer request remained secret for weeks until journalists got wind of the story.

He had a short memory. News hit the papers almost immediately. He was even putting his name to a column about it in the *Daily Express* within a couple of weeks. 'Yes, I still want to leave Chelsea,' he wrote on 25 November, a few days after he had demonstrated his value once again with a hat-trick against Manchester City. 'I've been two years making up my mind so I won't change it now.'

Reiterating that his desire to 'play for a club which will go places' remained his motivation, he signed off, 'Don't think me a big head because I still want to leave Chelsea. They are a fine club, but I feel the time has come for me to go.'

The manner in which *The Times* had reported that 6-3 victory over City merely emphasised the lack of gravitas surrounding Chelsea that made Greaves so anxious to leave:

> 'Cor!' said the taxi driver as we bowled down the Fulham Road on Saturday evening away from Stamford Bridge and its tail lights stabbing the early mist of night. 'That was a real three bob's worth.'

At first, there were few who believed he was going anywhere. Which English club, for a start, would be able to afford the fee that Chelsea would demand? And the rich teams in Spain and Italy appeared likely to be blocked by their federations from signing any more foreign players. Proving that they had a sense of humour over the whole business, Chelsea responded when they received an official bid of £5 from Oaklands FC, who played on Mitcham Common but assured Chelsea that their target 'will be excused carrying goalposts to our pitch'. Joe Mears wrote back to assure

Oaklands, 'If we decide to secede to his request to join a better club I will ask my directors to consider this offer.'

It was not long, however, before Greaves was given an inkling of his possible destination. 'My father was desperate that Greaves did not go to Tottenham,' said Brian Mears. 'It would have caused an outrage among the Chelsea fans.' Instead, the chairman called to tell Greaves there was a chance that he could end up in Italy; that it was looking increasingly likely that clubs there would be allowed to include more than one overseas player from the end of the current season. Greaves 'was ready to walk there playing a barrel organ if they wanted me to'. It was, in his mind, 'the jackpot. I was being asked if I wanted to become a rich man.'

Even though Mears had told him that 'if I agree to selling you to Spurs the supporters will want to lynch me', Greaves did retain some initial wariness over the talk about Italy, wondering whether the notion of an end-of-season move was something the chairman was using in the hope that he might have changed his mind by then. He did not believe Chelsea had yet received a concrete offer from anyone. The intrigue of the situation was soon to increase when he was called upon by an Italian visitor, Roberto Favilla, who claimed to be representing an Italian club. Favilla returned a few weeks later saying he was sure that the restrictions on foreign players would be lifted by the Italian authorities and that AC Milan were very interested. Greaves remained sceptical about how much Chelsea knew about what was going on.

Yet wheels were now in motion. The next move was made by the renowned Italian agent Gigi Peronace, who had negotiated the transfer of John Charles from Leeds United to Juventus for £65,000 in 1957. Peronace – of whom Greaves said, 'If a crocodile could talk it would sound like [him]' – was charged with speaking to Chelsea on behalf of AC Milan and, in early April 1961, the second-placed club in the Italian league announced that they had secured an option to sign Greaves for £73,000. 'It means no other Italian club can attempt to sign Greaves if our ban on importing foreign players is lifted,' Luigi Scarambone of the Italian Football Federation announced.

Writing in the *Daily Express* once more on 11 April, Greaves admitted, 'I hope to be playing inside-right for Milan. As I say that I heave a mighty sigh.' He described the relief of having to keep such a big secret from everyone except family and his closest football friends, such as team-mates John and Peter Sillett and Ken Shellito. 'He confided in Jimmy Hill as well,' John Sillett recalls. 'He was a big friend of his because Fulham were our neighbours. Those of us in the know all had to keep it quiet. The worst thing about the move was that he hated flying. He and Peter would always sit in the back. When I asked them why, they said, "Because there's never been a plane that backed into a mountain." But money was Jimmy's king in those days. He was always thinking, "I can buy this now and I can do that now," and was always going to invest money in business. He was going to look after his future, which in those days was not heard of. And the difference in money was unbelievable – he would be the equivalent of a millionaire. He didn't want to go, but he was a young married man with a family and he couldn't say no.'

His initial excitement at his impending move was obvious to those around him. A somewhat morose Malcolm Allison, pondering a future outside of football after his playing career had been ended by the loss of a lung to tuberculosis, was running a bar in London at the time and ended up serving the player who now had a world of opportunity at his feet. 'His hope and optimism had taken me out of myself,' said Allison, explaining how their meeting inspired him to return to the sport he loved in a coaching role.

The deal that had Greaves so fired up was a £15,000 signing bonus, payable over the three years of his contract, with £1,000 up front; £130 per week in wages, plus win bonuses; and a lavish apartment in the Milan suburbs. Not bad for someone currently earning £20 a week, and only £16 during the summer. 'I didn't hesitate to grab at the bonanza. I wanted my money and here it was in truck loads.'

No one should have been surprised to see wages becoming a central factor in the year's biggest transfer. It had, after all, been at the heart of the storyline of the season.

The Professional Footballers' Association, the players' union, had endured the sport's Victorian shackles for long enough. As the new season had begun they were prepared to go to war to achieve four objectives that were formalised at their annual general meeting: abolition of the maximum wage; the right of players to receive a percentage of transfer fees; a new retain-and-transfer system; and a new form of contract. What particularly angered the union was the ability of a club to retain without pay any player who refused to accept renewal of his contract on whatever terms had been offered.

Yet it was the first of those contentious issues, the £20 per week maximum wage, that was driving Greaves towards the Continent. It was also the element of the debate that attracted most headlines, being the simplest of the issues to present to a public that seemed, by and large, sympathetic to the players. In November 1960, as Greaves was approaching his Chelsea bosses to request his move, one Member of Parliament, Philip Goodhart, described the Football League as 'inefficiently organised, semi-bankrupt and all too often a thoroughly bad employer'.

Newspapers explaining the dispute pointed out that only the best players at the highest level earned the maximum wage of £20, and that the average across the industry was £14.10s. 'Even a great footballer like Jimmy Greaves, for instance – a regular for his country, top of the tree – often finds a mere £16.17s.1d on his pay chit in a week where there are no extras,' one report pointed out.[8]

---

8 In one of his autobiographies, Greaves claimed that Newcastle had offered him a signing fee of £1,000 around this time, plus an extra £50 per week for working as a car salesman.

The realities of life for even the most elevated of footballers was illustrated by the case of the man who had been Greaves's England captain over the previous two seasons, Blackburn's Ronnie Clayton. The holder of the most prestigious on-field role in the game was forced to get up at dawn to mark up the papers in the newsagents and tobacconist shop that offered a financial lifeline.

'The money wasn't that great in those days,' Clayton told me in 2007. 'You had to look after your own future, which was why I had the shop. You can't imagine John Terry having to do that. You could never be sure when a club might decide they'd had enough of you and the players didn't have much of a leg to stand on.' And Clayton was one of the lucky ones, having found a way of investing enough of his earnings in a small business that would provide for his family beyond his playing days.

Burnley inside-forward Jimmy McIlroy, a Northern Ireland World Cup midfielder and another of football's biggest stars, had just admitted in his autobiography, published in 1960, that 'fear of retirement is constantly troubling us'. His bleak assessment of his future prospects was, 'I'll just scrub along and hope things turn out for me.'

As the dispute continued throughout the 1960-61 season, the Football League made various counter-offers, including a rise in the minimum wage of £2 to £12, and a wage of £10 per week for those on the transfer list. The PFA's two biggest concerns – maximum wage and the retaining system – had not been addressed, causing Greaves to comment after one round of negotiations, 'It is certainly not what I had hoped for – and I had not hoped for the moon.' A series of player meetings were held in which the PFA was given approval to issue notice of a strike to take effect on 21 January, 1961. Asked about the reality of such a threat, Greaves confirmed, 'It is on the cards. All the footballers I have spoken to are very determined to see this thing through – even the reserves. And they are the ones in most danger should clubs have to make cuts.'

As the players' deadline approached, the League offered the abolition of the maximum wage; longer contracts and a minimum retaining wage per division. The retain-and-transfer system remained untouched. The PFA dug in their heels. Three days before the strike date, League officials met the union delegation again, including PFA secretary Cliff Lloyd and chairman Jimmy Hill. After two and a half hours of talks, Minister of Labour John Hare, who had sat in on the meeting, announced that agreement had been reached on the issue of the retain-and-transfer system. If a player refused the terms offered by his club he would be placed on the transfer list on 31 May. If he was still on the list on 30 June he would receive a minimum wage based on his team's division. If there was no transfer by 31 July he would be on a monthly contract while the League Management Committee resolved the issue.

'Players win' was the popular headline the following day. It was premature. While the PFA officials had the power to agree a deal there and then, it transpired that the League Management Committee had no such authorisation. The League clubs, unconcerned about how such an obvious U-turn would be perceived, rejected the deal at their next meeting at the Café Royal.

Greaves, who in the course of the season had become the youngest player to reach 100 Football League goals, looked on as events played out. At least he had his own way out of the deadlock; a plane ticket to Italy.

There was more than mere money playing on Greaves's mind, however. For a start, Chelsea were getting no better, even though he was on his way to scoring 41 goals in 40 First Division games. By the time news broke of his likely move to AC Milan, his haul included three hat-tricks, plus five in a game against West Bromwich Albion and four against Newcastle United. His efforts could not lift his team higher than 12th come the end of the season, while their FA Cup hopes lasted no longer than a third-round defeat at home to Crewe Alexandra. Match reports frequently referred to the lack of support he received from his team-mates.

Before the season was up, Chelsea would bring in former Scotland wing-half Tommy Docherty from Arsenal to work as coach under Drake. Asked what he thought of Chelsea's defence during his job interview, Docherty, with the comedic banter that would make him a media darling during two decades in management – and frequently land him in trouble – responded, 'A jellyfish has more shape.' When he turned up for work, he was informed by Drake that he'd not wanted him. And he was shocked at the lack of pattern and purpose he observed in the club's training sessions. Docherty, who would succeed Drake as manager the following season, could see why Greaves wanted no more part of it. 'One of the biggest disappointments of my career was when they sold Greavsie,' he says. 'I think if we had kept him we could have won the League four or five times. He is the best goalscorer I have seen.'

Meanwhile, Greaves was beginning to view a new country as a safe haven from the tragedy that had struck his family. In October, Jimmy and Irene's second child, Jimmy Jr, had contracted pneumonia when four months old and was found dead in his cot at the family home in Hornchurch. 'His condition worsened and there was nothing anyone could do,' Greaves would write many years later. The family was at least spared the ordeal of an inquest, but Greaves recalled, 'Jimmy's death devastated us. It nearly drove us out of our minds. We were inconsolable. If ever there was a time in my life when I had wanted to call back yesterday, it was the day young Jimmy died. Though we had Lynn our grief lay before us, our joy seemingly behind us. You grieve for the death of any loved one but when it is for your own child, no words can describe that grief.' It was shortly after their son's death that Irene discovered she was expecting another child. Italy seemed like 'a fresh start'.

In the days when men were expected to choke down their emotions and not encouraged nor expected to open up to each other, John Sillett was among the few with whom Greaves shared his pain. 'He just said how much it hurt him,' Sillett recalls, his usual joviality receding at the memory. 'He had this car and when he gave you a lift you had to take hold of this bit of string. You would get in and then he would tie the passenger door to the driver's door so one of them wouldn't fly open. He would talk a lot sat in the car because he didn't like other people listening too much. It really broke him up. It was a tragedy and he was so young to have to experience and deal with something like that.'

Darkly, Sillett adds a comment that will be returned to later. 'I think that was really the start of the drinking.'

The next stage of Greaves's transfer to AC Milan was a medical, undertaken over two days at a private Italian hospital in London. It revealed that two of his vertebrae had broken and fused together. Such news came with the warning that his back could seize up by the time he was 30. Greaves was shattered, yet Milan mistrusted the diagnosis enough to fly their own doctor to London and set up an appointment the next day with a specialist in Harley Street. Relief greater than that offered by any drug arrived with the specialist's assurance that 70 per cent of adults lived quite comfortably with the condition, which was probably caused by energetic childhood activity. There was, Greaves and his prospective employers were assured, no threat to his livelihood.

He was clear to pursue his new career, but not before he had been the subject of discussion in the House of Commons. Labour MP Denis Howell, a future Minister of Sport, called the impending transfer of Greaves and other British players to Italian teams 'serious to the morale of the country'. Describing a 'major crisis' facing football, Howell urged that a foreign-style system should be examined whereby teams played in municipally-owned stadia, with the low rents allowing them to afford higher salaries. He praised Fulham's Johnny Haynes for reportedly rejecting a move to Italy and said of talented English players, 'It is up to us to stand by them, allow them the opportunity to develop their talent and not to fail them.'

Greaves ended his Chelsea career in spectacular fashion. On the final weekend of April, one day after Italian football had voted to allow its clubs to sign more overseas players, he was made captain for the final match of the season at home to Nottingham Forest. 'I had never seen him nervous before,' Sillett reveals.

'I would love to go and score one goal, Snoz,' Greaves whispered. 'Just one goal to finish off. I had this dream I would not score at all.'

Greaves went out and scored all the goals in a 4-3 victory, including a decisive last-minute penalty, and was carried around the pitch on the shoulders of adoring fans who harboured no bitterness towards their departing star. 'He was a hero,' says Sillett. 'They clapped him all around the pitch. He was idolised. They had never seen anything like him; nothing like this goalscoring machine. He would score, put his hand up – no kissing or cuddling – turn around and go back to the centre circle to start the game again. They loved that.'

Greaves called it 'a very emotional moment' and admitted, 'I did feel sadness at the fact that I was leaving Chelsea.' Yet such feelings turned to anger when Chelsea informed him that, as he was still their player, he had to take part in an end-of-season trip to Israel. When he refused, he was suspended by the club for 14 days, which resulted in him missing England's game against Mexico at Wembley. 'I was choked. This was the club that had preached loyalty to me, the club to which I had given everything for four seasons.'

And then another funny thing happened. After one final, abortive attempt to create a whole new retain-and-transfer system, the PFA made its peace with the Football League. The new agreement, including the end of the maximum wage, could now take effect. Johnny Haynes would soon be earning £100 per week at Fulham, having turned down his own offer of £10,000 per year from Milan. 'It was more a question of feeling than of logic,' Haynes explained.

Greaves was left wondering about the logic of his own move. What on earth had he done? As proud as he felt over the victory he and his fellow professionals had achieved, 'their success made my contract with Milan look a bit sick'. As the most lethal goalscorer in English football, his earning potential would leave him not so far short of the disposable income he would have in Italy, where he anticipated that his cost of living would be much higher.

Even before the latest turn of events his 'initial euphoria' about playing and living in Italy had been waning, to be replaced by doubts. As the father of a young family, he was hardly a regular on the nightclub circuit, but, even so, enjoyed the life London offered; a night at the dogs, for example, especially if it was watching his own greyhound, Burren Bridge, who had given Greaves his first win as an owner at Romford in December.

And now the Italian governing bodies were warning that foreign players would only be released to play in internationals if it was a World Cup game and if there was no clash with domestic fixtures, casting doubts over Greaves's role in the England team at the 1962 World Cup finals.

He spoke again to his club chairman. 'I want to remain at Chelsea,' he told him. Joe Mears reminded him that Chelsea had already accepted £10,000 and it was inevitable that Milan would take up the option of completing the transfer. Mears and Battersby attempted to remind Greaves how much he would love football in Italy and how much it would add to his game. 'I had no agent or adviser and I was 21,' he recalled. 'What do you know at that age?'

Battersby felt confident that the club could wriggle free from their part of a transfer that had not yet been concluded, but feared that the player's own commitment had passed the point of no return. 'You have to go, Jimmy,' he told him. Mears was at least open to offering a salary similar to that of Haynes for a year, moving him to a bigger house and then granting him a transfer to an English club if Greaves could find a way to convince Milan to let him stay at home.

Greaves knew that a simple refusal to go to Italy could lead to Milan invoking a FIFA ban that would exclude him from all levels of football. He would need to win a legal battle. To fight his corner, Chelsea appointed R. I. Lewis, a renowned legal brain whose stuffed-shirt, old-school British attire and attitude – all wing collars and bowler hats – was guaranteed to clash with the slick and streamlined styling of Italians such as Peronace.

Greaves and Chelsea had little more to fall back on than a promise that the club would pay back the £10,000 deposit on the transfer and that Greaves would return his £1,000 signing bonus. 'We will rely on their sense of fair play,' the chubby-faced Lewis insisted. It didn't seem like much to be pinning hopes on as Greaves set off for Rome with the England team. Lewis and Mears joined him and went in search of the AC Milan officials, tracking them down in their hotel. An initial discussion, staged without Greaves, left Lewis in a pessimistic mood. Another meeting was set for the following day, at England's headquarters at the Quirinale Hotel, on the Via Nazionale. Haynes recalled the hotel being 'a madhouse of agents, official and directors … of scouts and journalists'.

Milan vice-president Dr Mino Spadacini asked Greaves outright, 'Do you want to come to Italy?'

'No,' he replied truthfully. 'I feel I have made a mistake and I want to play for Chelsea.' Spadacini left the hotel muttering darkly.

If his hope had been to dissuade Milan from insisting that the transfer went ahead, then Greaves could hardly have made life more difficult for himself by his intervention in the final 12 minutes of England's game at the Stadio Olimpico. With Italy leading 2-1, he advanced on the Italian penalty area and slipped the ball to his left for Gerry Hitchens to fire an equaliser. In a near identical move five minutes from time it was Greaves taking a Haynes pass in his stride and shooting across the keeper from the left side of the box to seal England's victory. 'I pushed the ball square to Greaves, coming up in support, and there was a sudden blur of white and the little man had it snuggled in the back of the net,' said Haynes.

Milan president Andrea Rizzoli purred, 'I think he was magnificent. It was his split-second thinking and lightning shot that gained England's winning goal in just the manner that Milan want.'

Having returned home, via another goal in England's defeat in Austria, Greaves reassessed his situation. He reckoned he could earn £7,000 a year in England if he included possible commercial opportunities. He still wanted out of the Milan deal. He and Lewis set off for Italy once more, this time landing in Milan and then driving five hours to Alassio, a coastal town where they would meet again with club officials in the 'icing cake walled villa' belonging to Spadacini. Greaves was left waiting on a veranda overlooking a plush lawn while Lewis made his final bid for his client's emancipation. But Milan came back with a new offer. There would be more money up front than originally offered; £4,000 of his signing bonus when he put pen to paper and the rest when he reported for training. The transfer would go ahead.

Greaves signed and Milan announced he would be playing for them in a friendly two weeks later. Now it was Chelsea's turn to sweat, fearing that he would be injured in an appearance they had not sanctioned. After all, they had not yet received their money. The FA even intervened on their behalf in an attempt to prevent him facing Brazilian team Botafogo. 'We sent a telegram to Milan,' the FA said, 'telling them we could not clear the Greaves transfer until the money was paid.' Greaves played anyway, making it unscathed through a 2-2 draw and scoring the equalising goal. He returned to London to prepare for his new life and to count what little was left of his £4,000 after he had paid £1,000 on legal fees, a similar amount on a new Jaguar and thrown a farewell party.

'Do something for me,' he'd said to John Sillett. 'Organise a place where we can have a late drink, where they don't chuck people out, because I am going to have a going-away party and invite all the players. We will have a good old booze-up on me.'

Sillett used to drink at the Parsons Green Bowling Club and explains, 'The landlord there would stay open until three in the morning if you were spending. I said, "You must have jellied eels and as much lager as you can get in." Jimmy got every player a Ronson table lighter because they all smoked in those days. It was a great going-away gift. We had a great night.'

Yet Greaves would soon be wondering whether the good times were gone forever.

4

THE ITALIAN JOB

*'I just know that we are going to be miserable in
Milan. I just know, that's all.'*

WHEN Jimmy Greaves read the first sentence on page
6 of the *Daily Express* on 24 August, 1961, it became
clear that the interview he'd agreed to had produced no
ordinary football tale. Nor would it be the anti-Milan manifesto
that he had probably planned: 'Jimmy Greaves, who might be
described as the Maria Callas of British football, sat last night in
the front room of a semi-detached house in Essex rocking with
fatigue and blanketing himself with gloom as thick as mud.'

Used to having his views projected without question by
football writers happy to hang on his every word, it must have
seemed like a good idea to speak out and tell the world that Italy
was not for him. Yet instead of Desmond Hackett, the bowler-
hatted foghorn of English football journalism who'd been at
Greaves's shoulder throughout each step of his career, the man
preparing to describe his every tick and twitch to his readers
was a stranger, the journalist and lyricist Herbert Kretzmer. A
man accustomed to sparring across the table with literary giants
such as John Steinbeck, Truman Capote and Tennessee Williams

and cultural icons like Duke Ellington and Sugar Ray Robinson, Kretzmer was never going to give a young footballer an easy ride or blandly relay his 'get me out' message. What emerged from an interview conducted hours after Greaves returned home just days into his Italian employment was a painfully honest portrait of a contradicted 21-year-old; someone clearly in turmoil over a life-changing decision made without meaningful advice or any real insight about what he was getting into.

That a man who would later compose the English lyrics for the musical *Les Miserables* would start his piece with a reference to a talented, troubled opera singer, might not have been a great surprise, but what was a revelation in terms of sportswriting of the era were passages that accused Greaves of 'confusing his family, antagonising his advertisers, and putting the patience and tolerance of his myriad British supporters through an agonising, testing time'.

The piece had been headlined, somewhat sardonically, 'The agony of being Mr Greaves', and, ironically, sat above an advert related to travel sickness. Within it, Greaves insisted, 'I don't want to go back to Milan. I must be a mug. I can't explain it.' Yet, sitting in the living room of Irene's brother's house, Kretzmer appeared to view him as a spoilt brat, referring to his bonus payment of 'a guaranteed £15,000 spread like rich, creamy butter over three years'. It was, he said, 'hardly the blackest of prospects for a footballer who, at his English peak, could point only to a careful £500 in the bank and the ownership of a second-hand Standard Vanguard'.

Kretzmer continued, 'I engaged Mr Greaves's attention for an hour in an endeavour to get the record straight. I report this morning that it is one record that defies any such effort. Mr Greaves is the most confused young man I have clapped eyes and ears on this year.' Greaves, he continued, evaded every question:

He stammered and stumbled and said 'I just dunno' so many times that I lost count. He clicked his fingers and slapped his thigh in the most abject unhappiness. He appeared to be incoherent and irrational. I am not over-dramatising his effect when I say that at times he seemed almost shell-shocked.

Showing a vulnerability never detected in the penalty box, Greaves told Kretzmer, 'I've developed an awful sense of insecurity in the last week and there is nothing I can do about it.'

He had hardly set off for Italy with the wind beneath his wings. After his efforts to wriggle out of his commitment to Milan, it was no surprise that Greaves should drag his feet when it came to getting himself to the airport to begin what had become an obligation rather than an adventure. He had been told to report on 17 July, but with he and Irene expecting another child shortly after that date he was going nowhere until he was satisfied about his family's well-being. When he sent his new employers a telegram telling them not to expect him, Milan responded with a threat to fine him £50 for every day he was absent. Greaves cabled them again – the instant messaging of its time – and re-stated his position. This time the club backed down. Greaves eventually flew to Italy on 12 August, less than a week after the birth of his second daughter, Mitzi.

Having already shown up late at the wrong airport on one previous visit, Greaves now made the mistake of deciding to fly out via Venice, where he held a meeting about a boot deal with Italian footwear company Valsport. This time he was a full day late arriving at the club's pre-season base in Gallarate, 25 miles north-west of Milan. The Milan manager, the intimidating Nereo Rocco, was not impressed. 'I was in his bad books from the start,' Greaves recalled.

Rocco was not a man best viewed from his wrong side. Newly appointed as manager after Giuseppe Viani suffered a heart attack and was moved to the role of technical director, he had wanted no part of a transfer forced upon him by Viani and club president Andrea Rizzoli. He bore a resemblance to the kind of character who provided the muscle in Hollywood gangster movies and Greaves quickly discovered that the look did not do him a disservice.

Holder of one Italian cap as a winger, Rocco had made his name by turning little Padova into a force in Serie A. His approach to achieving success in Milan was to stick rigidly to the defensive-minded *catenaccio* system on the field and a strict and stifling disciplinary regime off it. Greaves felt he had entered a prison camp, where every minute of the day was accounted for and players were forced to spend each moment in close proximity to each other, with no space or time to themselves. Already isolated by being unable to speak the language, he felt further intimidated by the close attention of the manager, who insisted on sitting opposite him at mealtimes and ordering food for his new signing. 'If he could have had me glued to the end of his nose he would have,' he said.

Not usually his favourite pastime, training assumed greater importance, but even that offered Greaves little release. He found it to be low impact and lacking in purpose. He might have taken to smoking more than his usual five per day if it had not been for the fact that players were rationed to two, one each at lunch and dinner. It was little wonder that defender Cesare Maldini, a future Italy manager, remembered 'Yimmy' – as his team-mates called him – spending an inordinate amount of time polishing his Jaguar in an attempt to keep himself occupied.

Ordered to tuck his shirt into his shorts during training, Greaves enjoyed a small victory by refusing, but he was particularly infuriated by Rocco's habit of standing in the middle of the training pitch and tapping players with a stick if he felt they needed geeing up. 'He never touched me with it,' Greaves noted, 'which was just as well because, as big as he was, I swear I'd have let him have it back across his nut.'

Meanwhile, although understanding that not everyone was going to speak English, Greaves became mystified why nobody bothered to find ways to communicate with him. He sat through tactical discussions with no effort made to explain to him the gist of the team's approach. The odd piece of translation passed on by a club masseur, who had been a prisoner of war in England, was his only insight into the conversation.

Even if he had been able to communicate his despair to his colleagues, he doubted he would have had much of an audience. The Italian players, he sensed, were used to their working conditions and went about their days without complaint. They appeared more intent on expending their energy in endless arguments over games of head tennis.

And when he tried to ingratiate himself with the locals – aware of the accusations that he was aloof – it seemed to go wrong. Greaves had noticed a group of young females who would regularly wait outside the training ground waving to the players. One day, seeking to generate some good public relations, he drove them in with the intention of getting these clearly committed fans some signed items from his team-mates. Horrified at the arrivals in their midst and the likely response of their manager, his colleagues quickly informed him that he was hosting a renowned group of prostitutes.

'I felt like doing a bunk,' Greaves concluded. So when his solicitor, R. I. Lewis, turned up to visit while on holiday, he took the opportunity to unload his problems. After Greaves had scored one and set up two goals in a 3-1 win against Parma in a friendly and played in a further warm-up game against Hungarian team Honved, Lewis managed to negotiate a 48-hour period of compassionate leave for him to return to England. He was sent on his way with the words of Milan secretary Bruno Passalacqua, who remarked, 'Greaves is a good boy. I am sure that once his family is in Milan he will give no trouble of any kind.'

So it was that Greaves found Kretzmer before him, analysing him in the manner of a psychotherapist rather than a sports hack. According to the writer, Irene looked at her husband with 'large, doe-like eyes' and assured him, 'It'll be all right, Jimmy. I'll be all right.'

To which Greaves replied, 'No it won't be. You'll hate it.'

He appeared to be thinking out loud, wondering why he had signed for Milan and blaming his decision on 'an illusion'. Oblivious to the observer in their midst, Irene reminded Greaves that he had no choice but to return to Italy. 'We've got nothing here,' she said. 'We've sold our house.'

Kretzmer noted that 'Greaves possesses a markedly withdrawn and solitary personality', which would have surprised those who had known him well at Chelsea, but was indicative of the mind-altering predicament in which he found himself. Kretzmer also declared that he had 'always been quixotic, casual and ruinously unpunctual in his personal discipline', although where he had drawn that information from went unmentioned.

Contrary to the jovial figure that the British public would come to know and love a couple of decades later, Greaves told Kretzmer, 'I'm not temperamentally suited to being, like, a public figure. I hate it. Many's the time in the last three years when I've wished I'd never seen a pair of football boots in my life.' Of course, this was the stresses of Italian life talking. If he had stayed in London such words would never have dropped from his lips.

'It'll be all right, Jimmy,' Irene reassured him once more. Yet Greaves was in no way comforted. 'I am all alone in this,' he said. 'It's nobody's fault. It's mine.'

Greaves was less forthcoming to other reporters. Photographed packing up pieces of furniture, he issued quotes stating that he would see how his first year in Italy unfolded before making any long-term decisions. 'I will quit only if I can't square up my problems with Milan,' he added cryptically.

His furlough expired, he returned to Milan, as he was bound to, with *The Times* noting that 'Greaves has lost public sympathy'. He was accompanied by PFA chairman Jimmy Hill, who had been asked by the *Sunday People* to help Greaves deliver the column he was contracted to write, and who also saw his role as helping 'improve his relationship with the Milan club so that he would find it easier to settle down and produce his best football'. Hill also travelled with a 'hidden agenda' of persuading Milan that it would be better for all concerned if they put Greaves up for sale and allowed him to return to England.

Greaves arrived back in Italy promising to honour his three-year contract. Publicly, his employers made the right noises about being sympathetic to his concerns, committing to finding a female companion to help Irene settle in, although vice-president Mino Spadacini sounded a slightly sinister note when he stated, 'I am sure Greaves's nostalgia will soon pass.'

At last it was time for his Serie A debut at Vicenza, a 3-0 victory. Hill recorded that 'he juggled, dallied and feinted, threw in some clever stuff and those fans just adored him'. Greaves's debut goal was a little more prosaic, a 55th-minute penalty. A week later came his first competitive appearance in front of the fans at the San Siro Stadium. Even though he didn't score, another three-goal victory against Catania sent everyone home happy. He netted his first two home goals in a 4-3 win over Udinese – a brave header and a left-footed penalty – but by the time he had added a close-range finish and another spot-kick in a 3-2 defeat by Sampdoria at the San Siro, Milan had won only three of their six matches and had the derby game against Inter looming. And Greaves was in hot water with the club.

Brother-in-law Tom Barden had arrived to see him before the Sampdoria game, having just driven from England to deliver some family items to the lavish apartment on Via Giovanni da Procida – about three miles across town from the San Siro – that Irene and Jimmy were moving into. Having driven north to the hotel in Como where the team were staying, Tom sat on the veranda outside Greaves's room and the two men shared a few bottles of beer. They talked into the early hours.

Returning to his room after breakfast the following morning, Greaves was aghast and insulted to find that a carpenter had been sent into his room to board up the doors to the veranda, from the inside and outside. His anger overrode any sense of risk as he climbed out to rip down the planks. After the match the next day, Greaves was anxious to get an early start on a trip to Venice with Irene, Tom and his wife, rather than spending the night shut away in the team hotel, as was the club custom. After an aborted attempt to exit via the balcony outside his room – it led to a dead end – Greaves got Tom to create a diversion to distract Rocco, who was sitting in wait in a position from where he could see his English star's bedroom door in a mirror. Shortly after midnight, Tom made an ostentatious show of ordering drinks from the bar and Greaves slipped past his manager like a public schoolboy evading his housemaster to sneak out for a cigarette. He and Tom were able to meet their wives and make an early getaway for Venice.

When Rocco realised what had happened he instantly announced that Greaves was being fined the equivalent of £287 for leaving camp and breaking city limits without permission. Greaves claimed he was the last to find out about it, the club having told the local media first. 'I do not know anything about what is supposed to be going on,' he said. 'So far as I know I will be training tomorrow morning at 9.30.'

Team-mate Maldini, who had made his Serie A debut under Rocco at Triestina and followed him to Milan, recalled another occasion when team-mates were aware of Greaves escaping the team hotel before a game. 'It was past midnight, we heard a low noise and we saw a shadow across the blade of light that was filtering under the door. We opened the door and saw Greaves sneaking out, fully clothed and carrying his shoes.' According to Maldini, Greaves was seen later in a nearby nightclub and was summoned the following morning to *Assassino*, Rocco's favourite restaurant. Greaves walked sheepishly across the dining room to where Rocco was seated and muttered an apology. 'Then the hell we had been expecting from Rocco broke loose at last,' Maldini related in a biography of the coach known as the *Paròn*, north-eastern Italian slang for 'boss' or 'master'. 'We had a hard time keeping a straight face, as Rocco's outbursts were so funny that one was tempted to stand up and clap instead of staying serious.'

Greaves felt that the Milan media were happy to seize upon such events as opportunities to present him in a bad light. His return to England the previous month and his obvious reluctance to be in a Milan shirt had not gone down well with local news outlets, and he felt he was being made the scapegoat for the team's indifferent form. His perceived moonlight flits helped them build a picture of a petulant figure for whom nights out and breaking the rules were of greater interest than winning games and scoring goals. 'To hear and read some of them you would have thought I was living it up like the king of the playboys,' he remembered. 'I was the club's top scorer but that wasn't good enough.'

The media in Milan and the fanatical support for the club fed off each other, creating a demand for stories and gossip that Greaves's transfer and subsequent unhappiness helped to satisfy. Greaves felt he had the weight and eyes of the world upon him as he walked around the city. 'I reckon the Milan newspaper industry must have gone through a slump after I left,' he said. One story that particularly irked him was a report that said he drank four bottles of Scotch on a single night out. Rocco quizzed him about the report, failing to see the absurdity of it. 'Then, of course, there were the sex orgies,' Greaves noted with sarcasm, having had to endure cameras lurking outside the flat to take pictures of him in his underwear.

Refuge, if it could be called such, came in the occasional companionship of England colleague Gerry Hitchens, who had been transferred from Aston Villa to Milan's Internazionale for £85,000, largely on the strength of his two-goal performance in England's 3-2 win in Italy in May. With glances over their shoulders, they would meet in a bar at Milan's train station. 'It was so busy that nobody would notice us tucked in a corner having a natter over a couple of pints,' Greaves said in his foreword to *The Gerry Hitchens Story*. Inevitably, they were eventually spotted by a press photographer and exposed in print. Their respective clubs approved neither of public drinking nor fraternisation with the enemy and, like Trevor Howard and Celia Johnson in *Brief Encounter*, they realised that their trackside socialising would have to stop.

The two big-name British forwards who had begun the season with Torino, Scotland's Denis Law and England's Joe Baker, signed from Manchester City for £110,000 and Hibernian for £75,000 respectively, encountered a similar attitude in their new home city. Welshman John Charles, a Juventus legend, was proving to be the kind of valuable ally that Greaves felt was absent in his life, although Law and Baker had to meet Charles covertly in restaurants beyond the city limits to avoid prying eyes. Those dinners offered a welcome break to monotonous evenings stuck inside their shared apartment.

Greaves, who would have been inclined to tell the clubs to stick their regulations, recognised that the greater years and maturity of Hitchens enabled him to adjust more easily to the demands of the lifestyle of Italian football. Despite his initial discomfort at being photographed whenever he ventured out with his family, Hitchens settled sufficiently to play in Italy for eight years. Maybe Greaves could have become accustomed to the pressures had the football on the field been fulfilling. In that, his dissatisfaction was in common with Law and Baker.

'It is all right for John Charles and Gerry Hitchens because they are powerful players who can play physical football,' Greaves said at the time. 'I never played this hacking, shoving football in England. I am not capable of playing it.'

Greaves's comments received a sympathetic hearing back home, reinforcing the stereotypical image that most English football followers possessed of the cynical, sly and often brutal world that existed beyond the Channel. In the early days of European club football, before the cross-pollination of styles fostered by the more open transfer system of future decades – and long before the advent of regular television coverage from other countries – such comments were seized upon as gospel. Of course, the approach of safety-first coaches such as Rocco did little to create an alternate vision.

Law reinforced the impression by lamenting, 'Every time I play I am followed by my shadow. He's not a wing-half but an inside-forward.' He would end up admitting that 'I found myself wondering why they came to watch this garbage', adding that 'at home you had to get past nine people just for a sight of goal'. Like Greaves, he was already hankering for a return to England. 'I wasn't happy. What really got me down in Italy was the negative football. Nobody wanted to play, everybody sat back grinding out results like 0-0, 1-1 and, very rarely, 2-0.'

Future Spurs team-mate Tony Marchi was already back in England after leaving White Hart Lane for a two-year stint in Italy, where he played for Vicenza and Torino on loan from Juventus. 'I went there playing like I did at Tottenham and they said, "No, you can't play that way." Wing-halves weren't allowed over the halfway line,' he told Ken Ferris in his book *The Double*. 'They played with five-man defences all the time and had another two players who always came back.' He described the play in the penalty area as 'a war zone'.

Greaves became frustrated that the claustrophobia and temperament of the Italian game led to fights in virtually every match. 'I just amble away and sit on the ball,' he said. 'The crowd say I am not interested because I do not join in the free-for-all. I didn't come here to be a fighter.'

Rocco had a rather different view of his player's reluctance to brawl his way through games. 'This idiot of an English,' he said at one point, 'He's good when things are going our way. But as soon as you have to struggle to get a result, he sails off to his own island.'[9]

Meanwhile, Irene – routinely described whenever she appeared in print as the 'pretty blonde wife' – sounded exasperated when she made a return visit to London. 'As far as Jimmy and Milan are concerned I'm not sure what is happening. Everything gets a bit technical for me. But I do know that life isn't easy for my Jimmy. He's on his own. You can't realise how difficult it is when you are surrounded by people who don't understand what you are talking about.' She continued, 'It's so different for Denis Law and Joe Baker. At least they can talk to each other.'

The money; the luxury home; the Jaguar – they were simply not worth it. With the biggest game of Milan's season approaching, against Inter, Greaves decided to make a plea for his freedom. 'They do not play my kind of football in Italy,' he told the group of English reporters who had travelled to see his greatest test since the transfer. On the day that those comments appeared, Greaves visited Andrea Rizzoli and was surprised and heartened at the hearing he received. The club president, it appeared, was as sick of the saga as Greaves was himself. 'Play well,' Greaves was told, 'and I will get things going for a transfer inside a couple of weeks.'

In the cosiness of truce, Greaves now told the Milan journalists, 'I am staying and I am happy to stay. I had a very pleasant and satisfactory talk with Mr Rizzoli. We sorted out some of the main difficulties I have faced since coming here.' Greaves didn't let on that there was more to the story than he was revealing, although he did tell his old confidant Desmond Hackett, 'I should have said that I was happy to stay for the meantime.' Hackett feared for Greaves when his deception was made known, warning, 'When

---

9   The word Rocco used for idiot was 'mona', a common vernacular in the region in which he grew up after being born in Trieste in 1912. The word can be used affectionately and one of Rocco's players recalled, 'In one way or another, we were all *mona* in his eyes.' In relation to Greaves, however, Rocco undoubtedly meant it as a derogatory term.

the Italian newspapers discover that Greaves did not tell them the whole story, he will be bitterly attacked.'

Events in the San Siro a couple of days later earned him some breathing space. Having scored four goals in a practice match to ensure his place for what was an away game against their co-tenants, Greaves struck in the 53rd minute to put Milan two goals up on their way to a 3-1 victory. Ending a three-man move, he found himself in enough space in the penalty area to score with a neat finish. Even a beaming Rocco embraced him after seeing him manfully soldier through a solitary role in the centre of a Milan attack playing without its Brazilian-born talisman José Altafini. 'He was wonderful fighting out there alone,' Rocco declared.

'Millionaire vice-presidents of the club came to shake his hand,' Hackett reported, adding that his fine for disappearing was likely to be waived. 'Thousands of chanting, dancing, flag-waving Milan supporters waiting for the players to drive away made Greaves a target for their ear-bruising cheers.'

Greaves, with Rizzoli's promise ringing in his ears as loudly as the cheers of the Milan *tifosi*, said of his first *derby della Madonnina*, 'Once you get out before 100,000 people the atmosphere is terrific. It really whips you into action.'

So now it was down to Rizzoli to live up to his word. It was not to be a quick and easy process. Twice more Greaves would be fined by the club, first for 'playing badly' in an Italian Cup defeat against Second Division Modena, and then for being late for training after being caught in a traffic jam. 'Unless you buck up your ideas and arrive on time you will remain a Milan player forever,' Rizzoli warned him, before announcing publicly, 'I absolutely refuse to discuss his transfer for any price whatsoever until he comes into line and starts behaving properly.'

Nor were Milan about to relent on their policy of not releasing Greaves for every England game, denting his hopes of being selected for late October's World Cup qualifier against Portugal.

By that time, though, Milan had a new star on his way to the club in Brazilian midfielder Dino Sani[10] and sufficient progress was being made in Greaves's escape plan that newspapers had been alerted that negotiations had been opened with English clubs. Yet even journalists who were following his every move appeared to be growing tired of the narrative. 'The latest yarn – or yawn,' was the way the *Daily Mirror* introduced the story of yet another fine. In the same publication, columnist Marjorie Proops devoted a page to telling Irene to stop complaining about the difficulties of life in Italy and to embrace the opportunity for an adventure.

As the end of October approached, it appeared that Greaves would either return to Chelsea or sign for Tottenham, the League champions and FA Cup holders. Joe Mears, his former chairman, said Chelsea were prepared to pay £90,000. 'We think Greaves would be worth it to us,' he said. 'He has not been doing well out there, but I feel a week or two at home would make all the difference.' Chelsea flew out to see him the day after he scored his seventh Milan goal in a victory against Roma, and after Spurs manager Bill Nicholson had said, 'We have not made a definite offer and in due course an appointment will be made for me in Milan.'

But it quickly became apparent that getting their bid in first was all that Chelsea had running in their favour. It was not enough; nor was the suggestion that they would pay Greaves £120 per week. His own admission that there was 'an emotional pull' towards Chelsea, in spite of the way they had treated him at the end of his time at Stamford Bridge, could also be disregarded.

Greaves felt that the club had known all along that their attempt to re-sign him was doomed to failure and were secretly relieved, suspecting that they simply did not have that kind of

---

10 Even that transfer did not completely satisfy Rocco, who had wanted Viani to sign Humbert Rosa, his former Padova player. At seeing Sani, who was balding and not as physical a specimen as Rocco preferred, the coach complained, 'We just bought a post office clerk. Viani did not bring back from Brazil the real Dino Sani, but his grandfather.'

money to spend. At least they could convince their fans that they had made an effort to bring him home. Greaves knew in his heart that he would end up at the club for whom he had felt most affection growing up. Chelsea director Brian Mears insisted, 'I was determined to bring him back to Chelsea but his mind was set on a move to Spurs. Perhaps the whole thing was a set-up. Chelsea offered him far more to return to west London than the salary paid by Spurs.'

Tommy Docherty suggests that had he been given the chance to outline his plans for reinvigorating Chelsea to the England forward, rather than leaving negotiations to club officials, he could have convinced him to choose Stamford Bridge over White Hart Lane. 'I was told by one or two younger directors that John Battersby was told to go out to Milan but "don't bring Greavsie back". In other words, make him an offer that he won't accept because Chelsea needed the money they'd got for him.'

To complicate matters, it now emerged that the Football League was considering delaying Greaves's re-registration. It appeared to be some kind of retaliation for the manner in which he had departed England, founded more on pique than legal precedent and likely to be dressed up in accusations of writing unauthorised articles for newspapers. League secretary Alan Hardaker had remarked, 'I'm sick of hearing the name Jimmy Greaves.'

But Tottenham fans weren't. They were energised and excited by the thought of England's sharpest shooter joining its dominant club. Nicholson – who had admired Greaves since noticing 'the natural instinct of the born goalscorer, which cannot be coached' while watching him play for London Schoolboys years earlier – flew to Milan for an initial, fruitless, meeting with AC officials. A second get-together in London saw some progress being made, before Nicholson was invited to discuss personal terms with his target. It was hardly the most complicated of negotiations. Greaves had played for Nicholson when he was in charge of the England Under-23s and could not wait to get to north London; to a club that offered him the chance of playing for the English game's biggest prizes. The kind of team he'd set his heart on several months earlier until his head had been turned by Italy.

When Greaves became Serie A's leading scorer with nine goals by netting twice in Milan's 5-2 defeat at Fiorentina, it was his final act as a Milan player. By the time he was dropped for the next match at Juventus, his transfer fee was moving slowly towards an amount that was agreeable to Spurs and Milan. Frustrated by the halting progress of negotiations that had been detailed in almost minute-by-minute diary form by the English press, and believing that Milan were merely using Chelsea's interest to force up the price, Nicholson decided on an offer he felt they would not refuse. He tabled a bid of £99,999, ensuring that Greaves did not become English football's first six-figure transfer. Greaves always insisted that the extra pound would not have bothered him in the least, especially not when he had the ball at his feet with the goalkeeper to beat. Yet the sum was arrived upon as much to protect Nicholson as his new signing. 'To many people, it would seem prestigious to go into the record books as the man who engineered the first £100,000 transfer,' he would explain, 'but I did not want that reputation.'

Yet while the transfer was being finalised, questions were being asked in Downing Street, where the Chancellor of the Exchequer was required to give his sanction to the deal. A Treasury memorandum pointed out the necessity for government to approve large movements of sterling out of the country in order to protect currency reserves. The Bank of England was awaiting the go-ahead to release the funds.

There were those opposed to such a move. The Treasury received a letter from an Ian Lacey, from Hove – clearly not a Spurs fan – who said, 'In all the newspaper talk about the transfer back to the UK of this footballer Greaves from Milan for about £100,000, no word has been uttered about exchange control. The Italian lira is pretty good nowadays and is this person worth, in the national interest, the transfer of so many million lira from our reserves? I say no, especially as he is a spoilt puppy.'

Yet Anthony Barber, economic secretary to the Treasury, concluded, 'As far as the balance of payments is concerned, it is more sensible to regard this as a payment made for luxury goods, which would not be refused. I gather that transfer payments for footballers work overall to our advantage.' In other words, the government recognised that there were more players leaving the country than were being imported.

At last, the deal was finalised and Greaves was on his way. Or not quite. With fog having closed the airport, he jumped in his Jaguar – and instantly ground to a halt as that same fog settled on the roads that were supposed to be leading him home. Two days later he arrived on the French coast, having been lost for a few hours in the mountains after heading south instead of north-west. Relieved, he made the ferry crossing to Dover, where he was ordered to pay £400 tax on his Jaguar before he could complete his journey to London. Without that amount of cash in his possession, he spoke to the *Sunday People* newspaper and they agreed to settle the bill as part of the fee they were paying him. It was fitting that a torturous period of his career should end with such a tortuous journey home.

He could afford to laugh about it all, especially with his new salary and commercial opportunities expected to earn him £10,000 per year, 10 times what he had been earning the previous season. Most importantly, after four months and nine Serie A goals, he was relieved to be away from a country that he said was fine for holidays, but offered a style of football for which he was clearly not suited. 'I had been slandered, libelled, maligned in every conceivable way, jeered, cheered, played out of position, had my heart broken in the most defensive football in the world, been bullied, coaxed and in general made to feel I had been living on a supersonic roundabout.'

5

PARADISE FOUND

*'However good a player I become, I still want my
quota of goals. I must have those goals because
for me they are the essence of football. I get more
satisfaction from playing badly and scoring than I
do from playing well and not scoring.'*

BILL Nicholson greeted Jimmy Greaves with a question. It should have been the easiest one he'd been asked in his life. 'You're now a Tottenham player – are you happy?' Greaves had felt like 'swinging from the chandelier' in the offices of the Italian League a few days earlier when the Spurs manager emerged from his meeting with AC Milan officials to tell him, 'Well, that's it.' Ordering Greaves to call him 'Bill', Nicholson further endeared himself to his new signing by adding conspiratorially, 'They're hard, this lot.' Greaves would remember that he 'curled up laughing when [Bill] let fly at the Italians about their unsporting delaying tactics'.

But now his joy at his transfer to Tottenham had been replaced by nerves. Here he was paying his first visit to White Hart Lane as a Spurs player, about to meet his new team-mates and watch the champions take on Leicester City, and he was more jittery than if he had been making his debut.

He was conscious of the publicity that had followed his every move in Italy; aware that he had not always been portrayed positively by the media; fearful that he might be thought by some to be a spoiled prima donna, determined to get his own way and to hell with anyone else. The December issue of *World Sports* magazine featured Greaves on its cover and ran a three-page feature, headlined, 'What now for the wonder who blundered?' Doug Gardner's article suggested that Greaves had gone from being 'everybody's favourite son' to a player who would 'have to prove himself all over again'. The writer accused him of 'indecisive immaturity' and – because of his friendly, outgoing nature – being susceptible to outside influences that were not always in his best interests.

The Times wondered, 'What will be the effect psychologically on Greaves himself; or his reception when he treads on an English field again? The whole thing might have been regarded as pure burlesque.'

And the paper's 'Football Correspondent', unnamed in those days but in reality the highly respected Geoffrey Green, was another who concluded that Greaves had proved himself to be 'prone to listen to too much ill-advised opinion' and cited his 'nervous nature, which has with it a certain stubbornness'.

Walking into his new home stadium with such thoughts occupying his mind was, Greaves admitted, the worst moment in the whole saga. Now he would discover the extent of the damage caused to his career. If his new team-mates did not accept him – if they thought too high a price had been paid for a man of questionable character; and resented that he was now one of only three or four players on the top salary band at the club – he would be no better off than in Milan.

The first player he encountered was a youth teamer, defender Phil Beal, who happened to be crossing the car park when Greaves arrived. They exchanged nodded greetings and, while Beal went off to join the juniors, Greaves headed into the stadium. Nicholson met him, took him into the dressing room and introduced him to club captain Danny Blanchflower.

The manager and his skipper made an interesting couple: the former a stereotypical dour and serious Yorkshireman who had grown up in hardship as one of nine children in Scarborough; the latter a romantic and whimsical Northern Irishman who spoke of the 'glory' of the sport and who was already carving out a career in journalism. Their contrasting view of football and outlook on life had created an unlikely partnership that had been the cornerstone of Tottenham's achievements since Nicholson had stepped up from the coaching staff to become manager in October 1958. 'He thought a lot of himself,' said Nicholson, discussing Blanchflower with author Ken Ferris in *The Double*. 'And I thought a lot of him. He had imagination. He perceived what was happening and provided answers.'

To his great relief, Greaves was immediately made to feel at home among the banter and buzz of the pre-game rituals. As kick-off approached he felt so at home that he half expected to be suddenly told to get changed into his kit. 'There was never a problem,' says winger Terry Dyson. 'We knew his history and what Jimmy could do as a player and he was a brilliant, lovely lad. He got on with all the players.'

Cliff Jones adds, 'I suppose to a certain extent some were wondering what would happen – someone like Les Allen who in a way was the one who made way for Jim – but we knew that Bill knew what he was doing. And Jim was a great lad. He was immediately one of the team. We were all mates and would go out with each other off the field and Jim was quickly part of that.'

After that initial brief encounter, Beal would quickly discover the kind of individual Spurs had acquired. 'You never felt in awe of Jimmy,' he explains. 'He never acted like a star and he never treated anyone differently. If he had any nerves he kept them to himself. When I got into the first team, we had a little bit of a fight about who went out last on to the pitch because we both liked to.

He gave in and let me go out last. He said he wasn't that fussy. That was how easy-going and laid-back he was.'

So much for his team-mates – what of the paying public? People, he had been led to believe, had grown weary of his constant whining from across the Continent. As he worked his way to the seats he and Irene had been allocated in the directors' box, he received nothing but cheery waves, pats on the back and general messages of goodwill from the fans. It was a hero's welcome. That Greaves's new club lost to Leicester did nothing to spoil the day. He had only one regret. 'I should have done it years before.'

The fact that Greaves was now at the club that fate seemed to have picked out for him from an early age was a source of concern for the authorities, however. The Football League would not ratify his registration to play for Tottenham until they had completed a full inquiry into the circumstances and details of his transfer. 'There are still things we want to clear up,' said League secretary Alan Hardaker. Chelsea, AC Milan and his new employers were all called upon to outline the events that had taken him from west to north London, via Italy. It was probably just as well that they did not know about an exchange between Nicholson and Greaves in the men's room at a banquet during the summer.

'Why didn't you join a better club than Milan?' Nicholson teased. 'You should have come to Tottenham.'

'I think I will next time,' Greaves chuckled back.

Not exactly the Watergate tapes, but it could feasibly have been construed as an illegal approach rather than innocent chit-chat had it surfaced at the wrong moment.

In the meantime, the Football Association had no such reservations and Greaves, pictured in the papers wielding a pair of pistols in the White Hart pub next to Spurs' stadium, was given the go-ahead to play his first game in a Tottenham shirt for the reserves at Plymouth Argyle. Dyson, who would also be playing, recalls, 'Bill's idea was always that if you didn't play for the first team you played for the reserves; no sitting around waiting. The reserve league [Football Combination] in those days was very good, so you were up against strong players.'

Despite having quickly been made to feel one of the lads during his first few days' training, he again experienced uncharacteristic nerves, describing himself as a 'very worried man' as he and his new colleagues made the journey south-west from Paddington. The train was packed with journalists and cameramen, yet it was the reception he would receive from the spectators, rather than what was said about his performance, that caused him concern. How much would public opinion be weighed against him after what the *Daily Mirror* called 'a saga that has sickened soccer'?

In a separate article in the same newspaper, influential columnist Peter Wilson wrote:

> Nothing succeeds like self-interest. That is obviously the conclusion you have to come to when considering the case of Mr Jimmy Greaves, who has been the centre of the greatest whitewashing job since the emergence of the White Cliffs of Dover. I am prepared to admit that Greaves may again prove himself a great player. For my money he hasn't proved himself a great sportsman or an admirable sporting representative of Great Britain.

Yet a crowd of 13,000 turned up at Home Park to greet him, and not even a packed White Hart Lane could have been more generous in its welcome. Argyle chairman Ron Blindell even grabbed the microphone as the teams took the field to announce, 'On behalf of Plymouth Argyle, Devon and Cornwall and, if I may be presumptuous enough, the whole of England, I would like to bid you welcome. We are delighted to have you back.' The crowd cheered and Greaves could have kissed every one of them. 'It was they who assured me that everything was going to be all right now that I was back in English football.' It didn't stop him sticking a couple of goals past their team, of course. The happy mood of the day was rounded off by 'a party to beat all parties' on the return train. Dyson adds, 'Back then we used to have to wait until midnight and get the overnight train back to London. We got back at six o'clock in the morning.' One reporter managed to lose most of his clothing somewhere along the way.

Greaves was back on a train, northbound this time, on Thursday, 14 December. Alongside him were Nicholson and Spurs chairman Fred Wale; their destination the Football League's final deliberations in Sheffield over the legalities of his transfer. It was a more relaxed journey on this occasion. Greaves was sure that Chelsea and Tottenham had conducted themselves in a manner beyond reproach and, as for AC Milan, well, he didn't care too much about them.

After much waiting around, Nicholson and Wale were finally invited to speak to the Football League's martinet secretary, Alan Hardaker, and his colleagues, after which Greaves was summoned to answer some questions – 'none of them too antagonistic'. Then Hardaker delivered the verdict that Greaves was free to resume his First Division career. It was such a brief encounter that the Spurs contingent wondered if it had just been an excuse for the Football League executives to get together for a decent lunch.

Reading from a statement, Hardaker told reporters, 'The Football League have delivered their inquiries into the transfer of J.P. Greaves from Milan to Tottenham Hotspur. Full consideration of the details furnished by all parties has been given and did not reveal any calculated irregularities. The commission are satisfied with the explanations given and accept the registration forthwith.'

Quite why such a procedure had been deemed necessary in the first place was never explained and Hardaker said that the details were being kept secret 'for the good of the game'. Greaves felt it was because certain administrators believed he had given English football a bad name with his antics in Italy and were not prepared to allow him and his inflated bank account, as they saw it, to breeze back into their game unchallenged. He also sensed people's suspicion that the whole Italian diversion had been his way of ensuring the Chelsea to Tottenham move that Joe Mears would never have sanctioned. Nicholson was prepared to let bygones be bygones, posing for pictures with Hardaker and even accepting a cigar from him before handing it back with the explanation, 'Sorry, I don't smoke.'

The treasurers of Spurs and Chelsea could have been excused their own celebratory Cuban once news broke of Greaves's imminent arrival. Every reserved seat at White Hart Lane was instantly snapped up for his debut against Blackpool, while his former club reported a similar situation for his return to Stamford Bridge on Boxing Day.

Greaves did not disappoint the 42,734 who saw his first game back in Division One; nor the pressmen in attendance. 'Jimmy always scored on his debut,' Blackpool goalkeeper Tony Waiters recalls. 'We went out for the warm-up and then the coin toss. We had to change ends once we had decided which direction we were going and the photographers all came round behind my goal. They were stretched from corner flag to corner flag! It didn't fill you with confidence.'

Blackpool manager Ron Suart had told his players, 'Greaves hasn't played for weeks and weeks so he can't really be fit, can he? Surely he won't be much of a problem if he isn't match fit.' At which point England colleague Jimmy Armfield had warned his boss, 'Greaves doesn't need training. I know Jim and I know what coming back to London will mean to him. He has a point to prove.'

Waiters continues, 'Ron came up with a masterplan that we would man-mark Jimmy. We had a player called Bruce Crawford, who was a bit of a character and a Jack the lad, but he had very good endurance so he was assigned the task of marking him. We had been going quite some time, maybe 30 or 40 minutes, and Bruce came back into the penalty area and said, "How am I doing boys?" and was giving it the thumbs-up. Suddenly there was a cross and Jim went out and volleyed it into the net.'

Greaves's own understated verdict was that 'I had a funny sort of match', although Blackpool weren't laughing. He ended up with a hat-trick. 'Every time I kicked the ball it seemed to end up in the net,' he said.

'Yes, he's worth the fee' was among the headlines the next day. Another, in *The Times*, read, 'A blur of white and an unforgettable goal: Greaves revitalises Spurs'. Greaves was never one to remember many details of his goals, but his first in a Tottenham shirt would remain one of his favourites. Mackay, one of the earliest players to make use of a long throw as an offensive weapon, hurled the ball into the area, Terry Medwin headed on and Greaves, feinting to escape the attention of a cluster of Blackpool defenders, connected with a scissors kick at chest height. It flashed past Waiters and White Hart Lane had a new hero. 'I'll always remember his first goal,' Mackay recalled. 'I thought to myself, "Aye, he'll do for us."'

The Times report observed, 'No one scores four goals as a farewell gesture, which he did for Chelsea last April, and then returns with the explosive effect of Saturday without possessing some deep indestructible quality.'

Mackay would come to believe, 'Greavsie was without doubt the most natural goalscorer that I played with during my career. Jimmy had a tremendous balance, anticipation in the penalty area and finished clinically. We knew that when Jimmy was one-on-one with a goalkeeper it was a goal. Other players, if they were through on a keeper six times, maybe would score four. Jimmy would score … all the time.'

Greaves felt he had played much better without scoring. And his first 90 minutes had proved what he had expected; that playing in the finest team in English football would be 'paradise'.

He had joined a club that, under Nicholson, had discovered the elusive formula of winning matches as well as capturing hearts and minds with the manner of their success. The manager had been a disciple of Arthur Rowe, playing in his Spurs team that won the League Championship in 1950-51 with its then revolutionary 'push and run' style. Rowe's methods were considered the first real tactical advance in English football since Herbert Chapman introduced the stopper centre-half at Arsenal in the mid-1930s; a game that relied on short, accurate passing and the ability of players to move quickly into space rather than standing around waiting for the ball to be delivered to feet. In the *Sunday People*, Ralph Finn described 'an integrated, flowing pattern-work of football that sent opponents dizzy'. Rowe had opened his mind to such concepts while coaching in Hungary and Nicholson, his centre-half, embraced the philosophy eagerly.

It required a great level of fitness, however, and Rowe found that, after finishing as runners-up in Division One in 1951-52, his team's effectiveness faded quickly as players aged and new ones proved unable to adapt to the system. Ill health saw Rowe vacate the manager's position, as it later forced his successor, Jimmy Anderson, out of the role early in the 1958-59 season. Nicholson took over and his team recorded an astonishing 10-4 win against Everton in his first game in charge, although it was the goals conceded that were considered by most to be more significant than those scored. 'It can only get worse,' warned Blanchflower, whose habit of changing tactics and formations during matches had brought him into regular conflict with Anderson.

Yet Nicholson, who had learned the art of managing men as an army PT instructor during the Second World War, was able to identify the kind of players he needed to add a touch of pragmatism to the best aspects of Rowe's approach. Mackay, an anvil of a wing-half, was signed from Hearts; Maurice Norman was converted from a right-back lacking in pace to an effective centre-half. Further forward, the whispy genius of John White, 'The Ghost', and skilful winger Cliff Jones arrived from Scotland and Wales respectively to add attacking flair. Blending it all together, and adding the idealism to balance Nicholson's realism, was skipper Blanchflower, given the licence to organise that he had been denied by Anderson. Additionally, Nicholson had ensured his own line of communication from the place where he sat impassively in the directors' box via the installation, in February 1961, of a telephone link to trainer Cecil Poynton on the bench. From his elevated position, Nicholson watched his team uphold the principles of Rowe, albeit executed at a slower pace, allowing for the thoughtful Blanchflower to flourish and the play of White and Jones to find its head.

In 1960-61, he saw them achieve what no English team had managed since Aston Villa in the previous century, winning the League and FA Cup in the same season. The title was wrapped up with games to spare; the Double clinched in a relatively mundane 2-0 victory over Leicester at Wembley, where Nicholson's immediate emotion was dissatisfaction that his team had not demonstrated to the watching nation the kind of football of which they were capable.

By the time the Football League decided that the game would not come grinding to a halt if Greaves was allowed to play for Spurs, the champions' defence of their title was going along in fits and starts. Apart from a couple of three-match streaks, they had struggled to string consecutive wins together, a trait that continued when they lost at Arsenal in Greaves's second game. He ended the contest with a swollen and bloodied left eye after a collision with the Gunners' John Snedden. Then came his return to Stamford Bridge, where, despite being grateful for the warm welcome he received from the Chelsea crowd, he felt no sentiment as he scored the first goal in a 2-0 win. Mackay, among others, 'became more convinced' that Tottenham's bid for three trophies was realistic after the signing of Greaves. 'During the second half of the season he was like a man possessed,' he remembered.

As 1962 began, Tottenham's attempt to retain the FA Cup opened at Birmingham City, where Greaves scored twice as a 3-0 lead was built inside 33 minutes. Yet, consistent with Spurs' inconsistency over the previous months, they allowed the home team to secure a 3-3 draw. Then they went behind in the first minute of the replay before running out 4-2 winners, Greaves among the scorers. Before Spurs' fourth-round visit to Home Park, Plymouth manager Ellis Studdard claimed that if his Second Division team failed to pull off an upset it would be because 'everything we've got, everything we've done is not enough'. He added, 'During tactical talks we've thrashed out every point, and that includes the way to stop goal master Jimmy Greaves.' Studdard was right; it was not enough. Spurs won 5-1 and Greaves scored twice. A 4-2 win at West Bromwich Albion saw them negotiate the fifth round safely, despite an ankle injury suffered by Jones midway through the first half. Greaves made it 3-1 after rounding the goalkeeper and then recovered from a painful blow on the jaw to settle the game with almost the last kick after the home side had pulled a goal back.

Greaves was proving to be everything his new employers had hoped for, and more. 'What I liked about him was his attitude,' Nicholson recalled. 'He was friendly and interested.' The manager noted with approval how engaged Greaves was with the details of the club; for instance, reading thoroughly the travel information pinned on the noticeboard and never turning up late.

He could occasionally be awkward, however, especially if he didn't like the direction that training was taking. Nicholson remembered a row over 'something he had failed to do' in the indoor training area. 'He responded angrily and there was silence as the other players stopped to listen. It was one of the most explosive moments of my career.' Greaves breezed in the following morning as though nothing had happened and bearing no hint of a grudge.

Quite simply, he was enjoying life too much to let any small moments of frustration linger. As well as joining a club able to fulfil his ambitions on the field, he found himself embedded with a group of team-mates whose company was a delight and whose appetite for a drink exceeded even his own.

Ever since the beginning of his career, Greaves had enjoyed what he called 'the camaraderie and companionship of the barroom', even if wages in his early years as a professional had provided a natural control over the amount he consumed. The pattern of drinking into which he settled during his Stamford Bridge years 'was never a problem'. In Italy, alcohol had assumed a more important, somewhat darker, role in his life, an escape from the miserable existence to which he had condemned himself.

Back in London, alongside his new Tottenham buddies, drinking was once again 'my pleasure'. And he was given plenty of opportunity to please himself. 'I knew he liked a drink,' says former Chelsea team-mate John Sillett, 'and we would always have a drink when we would meet up. Tottenham were a bigger drinking club than Chelsea, which I didn't know until one day Jim told me, "You think we used to drink at Chelsea? We were amateurs compared to the boys at Tottenham. If you don't drink, you are not in at Tottenham."'

After home games, the Spurs players would head out into Tottenham High Road and gather in the Bell and Hare or the Corner Pin. 'Our saying was "win or lose, on the booze",' Jones confirms. 'The fans would be in there and it was a time when there was more of an attachment between the supporters and players.' The team was given its own assigned area in the back room of the pubs and fans would pass in pieces of paper for their heroes to sign.

At Hearts, Mackay and his colleagues had been barred from drinking within two miles of their home ground. Given greater freedom at his new club and, with skipper Blanchflower being a non-drinker, Mackay revelled in being able to hold court on his seat at the bar, insisting on ordering the first round. Yet there was plenty of time for others to get the drinks in as the events of the afternoon were dissected and, eventually, consigned to history. The collective philosophy was that no player should be allowed to drift off home after they'd had a bad game. Better for mistakes to be discussed and forgiven, grievances to be aired and successes celebrated, so that everyone reported to training on Monday with a clean slate. On some Saturdays, the players would move on to greyhound racing at Walthamstow or find themselves in a West End club.

Bobby Moore would recall, 'You were always hearing stories of Dave [Mackay] being picked up off the pavement up and down Tottenham High Road every night of the week. It didn't stop him being a great player for Spurs every time he went out on to the pitch. As long as you don't really drink to excess, the problem is mental rather than physical ... the whole business is just an attitude of mind.'

The relationship that football journalists of that era enjoyed with those whose feats they reported meant that Greaves's close friend, Norman Giller, was able to witness – and participate in – the Spurs drinking sessions. 'I moved on to the *Daily Herald* and then the *Daily Express*, with Jimmy as a pal while I was reporting on his career,' he recalls. 'Back in those days we had free access to the players. I have an old contacts book with telephone numbers of every major player and manager of the time. I could call any of them at home. Can you imagine that happening today? It was like another planet.'

Giller's bond with Greaves had strengthened when his wife, Eileen, became best friends with Irene. 'We socialised and got our tickets for the best concerts in town from football ticket spiv 'Fat Stan' Flashman. The one area in which Jimmy and I always bantered and battled was politics, with me left of centre and him on the right – often the far right. Jimmy was happiest out of the public eye.

'He and Irene were busy bringing up their kids after the heartbreak of losing Jimmy Jr. They were comfortably off and had a beautiful house with a tennis court in the grounds. Jimmy was brilliant at all sports and could bat and bowl left- or right-handed. He used to beat me easily at table tennis and I would not dare challenge him at lawn tennis. He could also throw a nifty dart. They were heavy drinking days, but it was nothing he could not handle. It was the culture in the game at the time; a good performance rewarded with a good drink.

'The writers used to drink with the players regularly after matches. Dave Mackay would always be king of the court and the only two rules for the few pressmen allowed into the inner sanctum were: one, that everything was off the record; two, more important, that you got a round in. Jimmy could sup with the best of them, but the man who could really put it away was [future signing] Alan Gilzean, who hardly said a word but got through his Bacardi and Cokes at a rate of knots. Dave ruled the roost, but Jimmy was always getting into the conversation with wisecracks. His wit was as fast as his feet.'

Nicholson and Eddie Baily, who would shortly be joining the club as first-team coach, were well aware of the players' social habits, but would remain tolerant of them because they rarely, if ever, witnessed any detrimental effect in the workplace. 'There is a lot of free time in football and a lot of energy expended,' Nicholson accepted. 'It is normal to drink and I let them get on with it as long as it was done in moderation and didn't affect their performance.'

Greaves suspected that Nicholson never truly appreciated the extent of the team's drinking, but insisted that 'there was not a single passenger or slacker'. Besides, he said, 'A good drink was our reward for a job well done.'

Back on the field, it was becoming increasingly clear that if there was to be a domestic trophy to toast at the end of Greaves's first season at Tottenham then it would have to be the FA Cup. Only one win in their first nine League games of 1962 meant they had lost their aspirations of retaining the title. By the middle of March, they were one game away from a return to Wembley, having seen off Aston Villa 2-0 at White Hart Lane in the sixth round. And they were ready to welcome Greaves into the team for the European Cup semi-final.

Their Continental campaign had begun with a spectacular overturning of a 4-2 first-leg deficit against Polish team Gornik Zabrze, Jones scoring a hat-trick in a 10-2 romp when the tie returned to north London. It was the first game that effectively settled their second-round tie against Feyenoord, a 3-1 victory in Holland being followed by a 1-1 draw. February's quarter-final encounter with Dukla Prague, champions of Czechoslovakia, was too soon for Greaves's participation. Instead, he watched enviously as Spurs, a goal down from the first leg, won 4-1 in front of more than 55,000 ecstatic fans, Mackay and Smith scoring two goals each.

When the draw for the final four paired Tottenham with holders Benfica, Bela Gutman, the Hungarian coach of the great Portuguese side, announced, 'This is the European Cup final. No one else matters.' Even the reserved Nicholson remarked, 'As I have said before, the team that beats Benfica wins the cup.'

An FA Cup semi-final against Manchester United; a European semi-final against Benfica. These were the games Greaves had dreamed of when he had gone to his Chelsea bosses and asked for a transfer; the kind of matches that were making the pain and pressure of his time in Italy fade into the past – even with AC Milan threatening to sue him for comments he had made since his return to England. Thanks to the financial support of his new club, he and Irene had moved into a four-bedroom detached house in The Fairway, Upminster, overlooking a common and a golf course. This was the luxury life he had sought and which had been here for him all along, without the need to seek out the Italians' lira.

Even training, something with which Greaves had never had a close relationship, had a new dimension at Tottenham. What happened between 10am and 1pm in the Hertfordshire countryside at Cheshunt was very different to what Greaves had experienced at Chelsea's Welsh Harp ground. Nicholson was not averse to making his players run, especially at the start of every season, as fitness was a key attribute he required of his team. Yet

Spurs would discuss tactics and work on dead-ball strategies in a way that was unfamiliar to Greaves.

As well as working out how to make best use of Mackay's long throws, Spurs were among the first teams to push central defenders forward for corners and devise a series of planned moves for free-kicks. Defensively, the full-backs worked during training on positioning themselves near their goalposts for opposition corners and work was even done on defending at throw-ins. They employed 'ghost football', where the first team enacted sequences of play without a ball in order to become accustomed to moving into the right positions. According to Jones, it 'built up rhythm, helped us improvise and enabled us to work out 101 little routines'. Greaves marvelled at the attention to detail, acknowledging that his own purchase had been merely another way in which Nicholson was always striving for improvement. Tottenham had long since proved that they could find goals from anywhere in the team. 'They just fancied a few more,' Greaves noted, 'so they sent for me.'

It was that ability to find the net that clearly worried Benfica. Goalkeeper Costa Pereira approached the first leg of their semi-final with the warning that his team 'must beat Tottenham by four clear goals if we are to survive. Such a margin in our favour will be essential when we play the return match in England. We have heard what it is like to be the visitors at White Hart Lane.'

Years later, Nicholson would recall that he'd been 'reasonably confident' that, with Greaves now eligible, his team could overcome the Portuguese side by 'playing our usual attacking game'. However, he had been pragmatic enough at the time to acknowledge a likely Benfica onslaught in the first leg at the Estádio da Luz. He selected a more defensive formation than usual, leaving out winger Medwin and packing the midfield. It was the first time since arriving at Spurs that Greaves had disagreed with his manager's actions. Two goals in the first 10 minutes undermined the strategy and meant that Pereira's ambitions looked like being realised, although

Smith's late goal meant that Spurs eventually returned home with only a 3-1 deficit to overturn.

Greaves had been disappointed, even disillusioned, with his first experience of European football. By the end of the night he had seen Danish referee Aage Poulsen make a series of decisions that 'left me feeling downright suspicious'. This included disallowing efforts by Smith and himself while a string of brutal challenges on Tottenham players went unpunished. 'We were obviously disappointed,' Dyson recalls. 'We were unlucky out there to have two goals disallowed that were diabolical decisions. We knew the referee wasn't crooked, but it seemed like it.'

Ten days later, Spurs faced Manchester United in the FA Cup at Hillsborough, Greaves putting them ahead with a low, first-time finish with his left foot after the ball arrived from the left. Jones headed a second goal and Spurs survived a second-half hailstorm and a strike by United centre-forward David Herd before Medwin secured their Wembley return with a late header.

The following Thursday, 64,448 fans took their place under the White Hart Lane lights to see if Tottenham could make it to two finals by achieving a three-goal margin of victory over Benfica. Yet, as in Lisbon, they began slowly, conceding after 15 minutes when José Águas slid the ball in at the far post. Greaves had already brought a low save out of Pereira with a header and within minutes of Benfica's goal he was celebrating with his team-mates after clipping the ball in from the edge of the six-yard box after a volleyed delivery by Smith. Yet Poulsen consulted his linesman and ruled out the goal as Spurs players circled angrily around the officials.

There was no dispute, however, when Smith controlled White's lob on his chest and banged home a goal that made the score 4-2 on aggregate. And two minutes after half-time, Poulsen endeared himself a little more to the home crowd by deciding that White had been pushed over as the ball was centred into the box. Blanchflower's calm penalty kick left Spurs with what appeared to be plenty of time to get the goal they needed to take the tie into extra-time. Yet the referee was back in Tottenham's bad books when he failed to see that Medwin's effort had been blocked on the line by a defender's arm. That was how the Spurs luck was to run for the rest of the night. Despite the deafening support from the stands, the strains of 'Glory, Glory, Hallelujah' that rolled down to the field from all corners, they could not score again. Jones evaded the increasingly cynical attention of his markers to fire a long-range effort at the keeper, Smith hit the post and Mackay saw a header drop against the top of the crossbar.

After the game, while Greaves debated the offside decision with reporters and Benfica coach Gutman predicted that Spurs would one day win the European Cup, Nicholson focused on his team's failure to turn their dominance into the goals they'd required. His acknowledgement that the holders had been lucky to survive could not prevent him complaining, 'My players' enthusiasm ran away with them. They should have slowed the game down a little. They lacked control.'

Nicholson's response would not have been a great surprise to his players. Les Allen remembers that he was inscrutable at the best of times. 'You'd think you had played well and he would tell you that you'd played badly,' he says. His men were used to it, and expected it. Only Maurice Norman was regularly immune, Nicholson recognising that a gentler touch was required with his centre-half. 'If Bill had kicked him up the arse, he'd have started crying,' Jones recalled.

Trying to put their disappointment behind them, Spurs put four goals past Sheffield Wednesday two days later – Greaves bagging a pair – and lost only once in the final eight games to finish third in the table, four points behind surprise champions Ipswich Town. Greaves had 21 goals in 22 games to show for his first part-season in Tottenham colours. Add his eight goals so far in the FA Cup and nine for AC Milan, and 38 club goals in a season that began in such turmoil was not a bad return. And he was not done yet. There was still the Cup final against Burnley to come.

Burnley, League champions as recently as 1960 and runners-up a point ahead of Spurs in this latest campaign, offered the prospect of a final for lovers of fine football. Footballer of the Year Jimmy Adamson, their thoughtful skipper, now bound for the World Cup as England's player-coach, announced, 'I want Burnley to win, but I hope it won't be a dull game as many finals have turned out to be.'

In the Spurs camp, a determination to ensure more European football and the desire to put on a better performance than they had a year earlier at Wembley never translated into tension. Greaves recalled calmness in the dressing room before the game. For him, the stakes were highest of all; his first shot at a winner's medal. Yet experience of playing at Wembley for England, and confidence in team-mates who had achieved so much in recent seasons, relaxed him to the point where he could not see 'any possibility' of losing.

Film cameras allowed into the dressing room to record the build-up captured the bare torso of Greaves rising and falling as he inhaled and exhaled, his breathing and the clacking of studs the only sound. Players such as Blanchflower and goalkeeper Bill Brown ensured that their hair was immaculately combed and parted, ready to meet the Duke of Edinburgh before the game.

'This is Greaves,' said Blanchflower formally as he led the Duke down the Tottenham line-up.

'Ah,' said the royal guest, adding after a pause, 'I thought you were in Italy.'

'No, sir,' Blanchflower chipped in. 'We brought him back. And he cost enough.'

The inclusion of Greaves for his old Chelsea colleague, Allen, was one of only two changes from Tottenham's final team of a year previously. Nicholson would describe dropping Allen as 'one of the saddest things' he had to go through with while a manager. 'I felt sorry for him. He had done nothing to deserve being replaced, but a football manager cannot afford sentiment. Greaves was the best goalscorer of his day and I had to get him.' The preference of Medwin over Dyson on the wing was the other difference in Wembley line-ups, meaning Spurs took the field, in numerical order, like this: Brown, Baker, Henry, Blanchflower, Norman, Mackay, Medwin, White, Smith, Greaves, Jones.

Greaves needed only three minutes to prove to the Duke that he had been worth the money Spurs had spent on him. Receiving the ball about 30 yards out, via a nod-down by Smith, he probed the right side of the penalty area before checking, turning 90 degrees to his left to evade two defenders and then cutting the ball back across Burnley keeper Adam Blacklaw with his left foot. 'Greaves showing superb control with that one,' Kenneth Wolstenholme confirmed for the BBC viewers.

Greaves would dismiss newspaper descriptions of it being a 'wonder goal', explaining that the reason he'd had to screw the ball back so far was that he had overrun it in the first place. But he admitted that it was the most important in his career so far. He could have set up a second 10 minutes later, gliding forward and laying the ball to his right, only for Smith to be somewhat tentative in getting on the end of his pass. Then Greaves lashed in a left-foot shot from just outside the box and saw Blacklaw parry it away.

Quick to drop men back behind the ball when not in possession, and with Mackay never straying too far from the creative threat of Jimmy McIlroy, Tottenham offered Burnley few openings, a low shot from distance by centre-forward Ray Pointer and an attempt on the turn by Jimmy Robson their most noteworthy efforts of the first half. But five minutes after the interval left-winger Gordon Harris got outside Peter Baker and crossed low for Robson to turn in an equaliser. Within a minute, Tottenham were back in the lead as White manufactured space for himself on the left to feed the burly Smith – socks round his ankles – who turned and fired in from close range.

As the game settled into a pleasing end-to-end rhythm, White's slight frame rose to head just over and Burnley could have done more than force Brown to save low from Harris had they not frequently wasted their final delivery, or been denied by Norman and Mackay. Referee Jim Finney had barely had to blow the whistle since half-time, but with 10 minutes remaining he saw his linesman flagging for a foul by keeper Blacklaw under White's cross from the left.

'I'm done in,' said Greaves to Burnley skipper Adamson as Blanchflower placed the ball on the penalty spot.

'So am I,' replied Adamson. And so were his team's hopes as Blanchflower scored low to the keeper's left, prompting the first chorus of 'Glory, Glory' from the Tottenham fans. They kept up their signature song until the end of the game.

Greaves greeted the final whistle by standing close to the centre spot with both arms thrust skywards before making his way around his opponents to shake hands. Unused to the post-game formalities, he stood aside and let all but one team-mate, Jones, go up to collect their medals before him. And then it was the lap of honour, communal bath and off to The Savoy for a banquet. When the players were dropped back at White Hart Lane at half-past midnight, they were astonished to find hundreds of fans waiting to cheer them off the team coach. The party mood of the fans spread to the team, who decided they would head to Nicholson's house, close to White Hart Lane, put on some records and continue the celebrations until early morning. The manager, however, had no idea that his home had been turned into a nightclub until he returned separately from a visit to the Burnley team dinner. 'Once he'd picked himself up off the floor, he took it like a man,' Greaves recalled.

It was the kind of party that Greaves had never imagined he would be enjoying when he was drinking beer on his own in Milan, wondering what reporters and club officials were saying about him and feeling as though he was trapped in a nightmare. But there were more dreams to chase before this season was over. Jimmy Greaves was off to the World Cup.

6

LATIN LESSONS

'We had to slink back into England after the World Cup. We'd lost, and you're not easily forgiven for doing that.'

W HILE Tottenham Hotspur had been spending the early weeks of the 1960-61 season laying the foundations of their League and FA Cup Double, Walter Winterbottom was putting in place two significant developments that he believed could give England a better chance of winning the World Cup for the first time in Chile in the summer of 1962.

After 14 years of having an unwieldy group of FA officials determine which players he would have at his disposal, the England manager had at last forced the Football Association to allow him the final say – even if he would still have to work as part of a collective selection committee. Momentum towards such an outcome had built after Winterbottom's team returned from the South American tour that had seen Jimmy Greaves make his international debut. Comments by observers such as former England forward David Jack did no harm to that cause. 'The selectors have much to answer for,' he'd written in *Empire News*, 'and the abject failure of this tour brings into question their very worth as decision makers regarding the composition of our national team.'

Now Winterbottom was determined that his increased power would bring greater continuity than he had known since becoming the first man to be appointed manager of the national team in 1946. With a group of 18 players, including Greaves, huddled in front of him on a cold October morning at the Lilleshall national recreational centre in Shropshire, Winterbottom promised that the days of random, indiscriminate team changes were over. This, he promised, was the nucleus of the squad that would challenge for the World Cup.

A thoughtful tactician who saw strategy and patterns on a football field where someone like Greaves merely noticed talent and effort, Winterbottom also informed his players of what he hoped would be a further advancement in their on-field ambitions. Beginning with the upcoming game against Northern Ireland, England would be employing permanently the kind of 4-2-4 system being used more frequently by sides in Europe and South America and with which they had been dabbling over previous games. The old WM formation was being discarded like a couple of worthless Scrabble letters.

In the home game against Yugoslavia five months previously – a 3-3 draw in which Greaves had scored – the attacking intent of the visitors had forced wing-half Ron Flowers into a deeper, more central position. Increasingly, the Wolves man found himself covering centre-half Peter Swan rather than venturing forward, inadvertently giving England a back four. 'A few days later, shortly before England met Spain in Madrid, Walter asked me if I'd stay around and cover the middle as I had done against Yugoslavia,' Flowers recalled.

It was hardly a resounding success. England lost 3-0 to a Spain team inspired by Alfredo Di Stéfano and then, with Greaves left out, were beaten 2-0 by Hungary in Budapest a week later. 'I personally hadn't much idea what our defensive system really set out to try to achieve,' Flowers admitted. 'I began to wish I was not being included.'

Yet Winterbottom had seen enough to convince him to persevere. Besides, the formation was not merely about being stronger in defence, even if it did require the men on the attacking flanks to drop back and help the two central midfielders rather than kicking their heels at the intersection of touchline and half-way line in the manner of the old-fashioned wingers. The two men at the heart of the formation would be the creative force, while someone such as Greaves now had even greater freedom, as an out-and-out striker, to concentrate on scoring goals rather than worrying about the covering work traditionally undertaken by inside-forwards in the WM system.

Not that Greaves had ever worried too much about all that stuff. Nor would he suddenly allow his head to be filled with Winterbottom's strategies and schemes. 'If I had been clever enough I might have learned a great deal from Walter Winterbottom, but I could never understand him,' he would admit a few years later. 'I don't think any of his words of wisdom rubbed off on me. Football theories are a little above my head.'

Greaves had yet to make himself a permanent presence in Winterbottom's team; few did in the days of the selection committee. After winning his first senior caps on the summer 1959 tour, he scored in a 1-1 draw in Wales the following autumn – converting after John Connelly's effort was saved – although reports of the game suggested he displayed a lack of interest and that his place was under threat from a more creative inside-forward such as Johnny Haynes. He was disappointing again in his first home game for England, a 3-2 loss to Sweden; then missed the next two matches, before reappearing in the end-of-season games in which Flowers had been asked to learn new defensive duties.

Winterbottom was confident that his players would adapt successfully to a new system, but warned them that their touch and movement would have to improve. Private practice matches against club sides such as Bolton, Arsenal and Liverpool were used as further road tests, with Haynes and Bobby Robson as the midfield pivots, and now Northern Ireland offered a public examination in the first international of the 1960-61 season. 'The old guard had gone and Walter had created a young England team that was finely balanced and in tune with another,' was how Greaves looked back at this period, a season in which England rattled up goals and victories and created a mood of high optimism with one year remaining until the World Cup. 'We were not just beating teams, we were steamrollering them.'

In Belfast, the Irish made a game of it until the interval, by which time Greaves had put England 2-1 ahead. Bobby Charlton scored shortly after the interval and, although the home team pulled another goal back, Greaves scored one of the two late goals that made the final score 5-2. Blackburn winger Bryan Douglas, back in favour after playing in the 1958 World Cup finals in Sweden, also found the net, although it is the contribution of the man he was supplying that he recalls more vividly. 'If you put the ball around the box, then nine times out of ten, Jimmy would be there,' he says. 'He was absolutely fantastic. He didn't have to smash the ball in the back of the net; he would place it time and time again. He just had that natural instinct and would appear from nowhere. As a goalscorer, I don't think there has ever been anyone to compare with him. Even folks like Messi.

'He was a great person as well as being a great player; modest, no big ego. He was like a big kid at times. When we trained, we would usually start off by jogging round the pitch and I would turn and there he was kicking balls into an empty net. He got told off for it at times. But he was that sort of person, easy going.'

Less than two weeks after smashing the Irish, England's campaign to qualify for the World Cup began with a 9-0 romp in Luxembourg, these being the days when there really were easy games in international football. Charlton and Greaves both scored hat-tricks.

A further week on, England returned to Wembley in pouring rain to avenge their summer defeat against Spain. In his book, *World Cup 1962*, Donald Saunders described the atmosphere as 'the most electric' since the visit of Hungary in 1953, adding that 'the crowd seemed to sense that English football was on trial'. In the second minute, Bobby Smith passed from the right and Greaves sprinted on to the ball. He took a couple of touches without breaking stride and then opened his body to steer a delicate left-foot finish inside the left post. 'This little genius has scored many a fine and important goal, but I doubt any has been more welcome to his England colleagues and supporters,' Saunders noted. Twice Spain came back before Smith's two second-half goals sealed a 4-2 win on a day when Haynes had been outstanding in his first game as captain.

Observers across Europe acknowledged that England might be ready to take on the best in the world.

Greaves loved playing alongside Haynes as much as any other player in his career, even though he felt compelled to deny the full extent of his team-mate's genius when writing a column for *The Sun* many years later. 'It was one of those clichéd columns where the desk had asked Jim to name his best England XI,' recalls Martin Samuel, his collaborator. 'He came to a position and said, "Johnny Haynes was the absolute best I ever played with." He said he would try to find you with a pass, whereas Bobby Charlton was a lovely footballer, but he switched the play too much. "He would be on the right and he would hit it 40 yards left and it looked fantastic. But if you are the striker and you have made your run and got your yard of space, then, fucking hell, now you have got to come back out again and now you are marked and you have got to lose your man again." He said Haynes would try to find you through this forest of players, with an eye-of-the-needle pass. If he could get you, and he usually did, then you were away and you had left everyone for dead. He said, "I would always have Johnny Haynes, he was the best. But obviously everyone will go bananas if I don't put Bobby Charlton in there, so put him in instead. I don't want to be answering phone calls all week.'"

Greaves took his international record to 11 goals in 11 games when he scored twice in November's 5-1 Wembley win against Wales. Again he was up and running after two minutes, a quick strike under the body of goalkeeper Jack Kelsey after being fed by Smith. 'He was particularly delicate about laying the ball off,' Greaves would say of Smith, a man who looked more like a blacksmith than an artist. 'We dovetailed beautifully.' Greaves added the fifth when he skipped out of a challenge to score from close range from the left side of the box.

Four wins in less than two months, with 23 goals scored. Here at last was an England team ready to experiment and modernise in a manner that reflected a changing society. It would be almost five months before they would play again, against Scotland, but such was the mood of enlightenment temporarily inhabiting football's corridors of powers that clubs were told to release players for England gatherings, where Winterbottom would show films of matches and discuss tactics. There was little dispute about the efficacy of his methods after Scotland departed Wembley on 15 April, 1961. Even the Queen, watching her first Auld Enemy contest, cannot have failed to recognise the superiority of the England team.

Greaves, also enjoying his first England-Scotland game, set up Robson for the opening goal after nine minutes. By the half-hour mark he had scored two of his own, running through the middle on to Haynes's pass before lifting the ball in for his first, and then devouring an easy tap-in. Winterbottom warned his players to keep the game tight in the early stages of the second half, but Scotland, with enormous support in the Wembley crowd, narrowed the deficit to 3-2. Then Greaves took a quick free-kick to help Douglas get a fourth England goal and Smith added a fifth. After two from Haynes, Greaves used some neat footwork in the box to create space to push home the eighth goal with the outside of his left foot.

Smith scored his second before a late Scottish consolation made it 9-3. It was a remarkable victory, taking England's tally of goals for the season to 32 in five matches. Skipper Haynes, once thought to be a conceited, self-interested distraction in the England dressing room, was carried off on his team-mates' shoulders. The *Evening News*, in a foretaste of modern statistical studies, revealed that he had succeeded with 51 of his 56 attempted passes, while Frank Butler in the *News of the World*, wrote, 'There are some who will say Jimmy Greaves is worth £200,000 after the way he strolled through this humiliation of Scotland.'

With Greaves missing because of his post-season Chelsea suspension, England scored eight more against Mexico. Then, in the heat of Lisbon, a late Flowers goal gave them a creditable 1-1 draw in their World Cup qualifier against Portugal. Greaves was back for that game, also playing in the subsequent friendlies in Italy and Austria. The latter of those contests represented England's one setback of a season in which they developed a settled team that looked capable of mounting a serious challenge in Chile a year hence. With Swan a forceful presence at the heart of the defence, the Haynes-Robson partnership an imaginative influence in midfield, and Greaves and Smith a productive strike force, England's team possessed that all-important spine. Yet within a few months, the backbone would have been ripped out. 'That 1961 team came to the boil too early,' Greaves would recall. 'We were past our peak by the time the 1962 World Cup came around.'

While Greaves was living his Italian nightmare, England began their 1961-62 campaign without him, clinching their place in the World Cup finals by beating Luxembourg and Portugal at home. Less impressive were draws against Wales and Northern Ireland before the turn of the year, results that exposed England's lack of attacking threat without Greaves, fellow Italian exile Gerry Hitchens and the injured Smith.

After a winter break, with Greaves now safely back in England, the national selectors reintroduced him to international football in an Under-23 game against Scotland at Aberdeen. He scored twice in a 4-2 victory and made an indelible impression on someone who would come to oppose him in numerous north London derbies. 'Greavsie ran us ragged,' remembered Leicester wing-half and future Arsenal captain Frank McLintock. When Greaves bore down on goal, McLintock hoped that he had carried the ball too close to goalkeeper John Ogston. 'He got to within 15 yards of the goal … and leaned to his left. The goalkeeper followed suit and Jim just opened his body slightly and slotted the ball a foot to the keeper's right; he didn't have enough time to shift his weight back to make a save. "You jammy sod," I thought, but after seeing him execute the same trick at least another 50 times in his career I had to recognise the intelligence, economy and cruelty of Greavsie's finishing.' McLintock would come to recognise that 'for all his outgoing, jocular personality and genuine levity at times on the field … Jimmy Greaves was the slyest and most merciless forward England has ever had'.

When England's seniors resumed action with a 3-1 home win against Austria in April, Tottenham's European commitments meant Greaves remained absent. But at last, having missed five matches, he was in an England shirt once more on 14 April, with the World Cup less than two months away and the squad to be announced in a few hours' time. Haynes was relieved to be able to welcome him back, despite initial concerns about adverse effects from his experience in Italy. 'I saw him play three or four times after his return and thought that his general play had improved and wondered if this was a good thing and whether it might blunt his scoring ability,' the England captain confessed. 'But he soon recovered his scoring touch with the Spurs and I soon stopped worrying.'

Yet, despite having their successful forward line of the previous season reassembled, England lost 2-0 in Scotland. When the 20-strong party for Chile was announced it was Smith who paid the highest price, not even being named as one of the two players who would remain at home to be called upon if required.

England now had only a home game against Switzerland before they headed to South America. It was hardly the most rousing of send-offs. A midweek afternoon crowd of only 35,000 saw a lacklustre 3-1 win against understrength opposition, Greaves hitting the post from close range. 'How different was the atmosphere surrounding the team now from the spirit of elation in their camp 12 months earlier,' Saunders wrote, adding that the season had 'deprived them of the right to call themselves one of the finest sides in Europe'.

England departed for South America on two planes; the starters against Switzerland, plus Winterbottom, player-coach Jimmy Adamson and two others on one plane; the rest of the party on a later flight. Seventeen hours later, after stops in New York and Jamaica, they arrived in Lima, where they would play a final warm-up game against Peru. Winterbottom announced two surprise selections; Swan replaced at centre-half by the uncapped Maurice Norman – a change he was thought to have been planning even if Swan had not been suffering from tonsillitis – and Robson, who'd injured an ankle in training, making way in midfield for the young West Ham player Bobby Moore. Like Norman, Moore was winning his first cap; like Norman, he was told by the manager that a place in the World Cup line-up was there to be won if he performed well. Regardless of Robson's fitness, Moore's defensive qualities were thought to fit Winterbottom's philosophy for the tournament more comfortably than the West Bromwich Albion man's ingenuity; never mind that perhaps the manager might have come to that conclusion earlier than 11 days before the tournament kicked off.

Norman and Moore both had a busy opening few minutes before Flowers gave England the lead with a penalty. Then Greaves took over, completing a hat-trick before half-time and prompting Saunders to record that he 'had not only become again the ace marksman of old but had worked with a willingness missing in recent games'.

This being the eve of the World Cup – and the English press no less reactionary back then than they would become before future tournaments – the 4-0 win created a widespread feeling that the cup could perhaps be won after all. Even the more restrained *Times* suggested, 'The skill they showed here today suggested they will get farther than recent performances had led even their most devoted supporters to believe.'

'That performance started a tidal wave of optimism back home,' Greaves remembered. Yet, he added, 'We didn't kid ourselves that we were suddenly world beaters.' In fact, Winterbottom appeared to be trying to dampen expectations by telling journalists, 'If we strike it happy – by that I mean hitting our best form at the right time – England can go all the way to the semi-final.' But by concluding that 'we are quite capable of reaching the final if we start well' he probably re-fuelled high hopes.

England's final preparations were carried out in the small village of Coya, 2,000 feet up in the Andes. It was home to a mine owned by the Braden Copper Company, and not much else. The setting was either 'an ideal spot for licking footballers into shape for the most important task of their careers' – the opinion of Saunders – or 'cold, bleak and barren' when viewed through Greaves's eyes. With the Chilean-born former Newcastle United forward George Robledo acting as interpreter,[11] the squad lived and trained at a complex kept by the mining company for its employees and families. It had been offered to the FA free of charge. A golf course, cinema and bowling alley offered some distractions and a grey-haired English lady, Bertha Lewis, had been brought from her home in southern Chile to cook for everyone. 'I am giving these lovely young men steak and kidney pud, roast beef, Cornish pasties, ham and eggs, Irish stew and home-made cakes,' she

---

11 Fluency in Spanish was a recently acquired skill for Robledo, who had a Chilean father and English mother. Living in Yorkshire from the age of five, he spoke no Spanish when selected for the 1950 World Cup and had only picked up the language after a transfer to Colo-Colo in Macul, Santiago, in 1953, a year after scoring the winning goal in the FA Cup final.

boasted. 'They are going to get all they want four times daily.' Hardening of the arteries appeared a greater threat to England's chances than playing at altitude.

'We were distributed around the buildings,' Douglas remembers. 'I shared a house with Jimmy Armfield, Bobby Moore and Jimmy Greaves. The other lads were scattered around and they all came to our house for their meals. There was a little train into the town, or should I say village? It was all dust streets. I remember we had a little table tennis table and a little bowling alley. It wasn't automatic; some of the local kids would put the skittles back up. Compared to today it is hard to explain. We were miles from anywhere.'

According to the *Daily Mirror*'s Frank McGhee, 'everything in their garden paradise is wonderful, magnificent, marvellous!' But Greaves found the remote location as oppressive and restrictive as the endless training camps he'd endured in Milan. 'Locking a team up away from the bright lights might be all right for those countries where the individual doesn't have as much freedom as he does in England,' he wrote in the autobiography published shortly after the World Cup, 'or where the players are likely to go on a bender as soon as the team manager is out of sight.'

Flowers spoke for many when he said that the boredom was difficult to ignore and felt that England were in their camp for too long. 'No one seemed to stop writing home,' he said. Hitchens had packed 19 Italian suits, yet found that he barely ever had the opportunity to change out of his tracksuit. Even Roger Hunt's status as team bingo champion failed to lighten his own feeling of homesickness. One comment by right-back Armfield reveals much about the manner in which England's players were viewed by their employers and about their own sense of place in football's hierarchy. Whereas England's modern stars are ensured five-star treatment at every World Cup, both for the sake of preparedness and because there would be a revolt if they were not, Armfield accepted that 'we were there to represent England in the World Cup and for that privilege we were prepared to put up with a few hardships'.

England's group games were played in Rancagua, an hour from their headquarters, in a 25,000-capacity stadium that the benevolent mining company had renovated. It would still not have rated as much more than a decent non-League ground in England. 'There were more people watching Accrington Stanley on a Saturday than there were at our games,' says Douglas. Needing to win their group to avoid a probable quarter-final meeting with holders Brazil, it was imperative England achieved a positive result in the opening match against Hungary, the nation that had informed so much of Winterbottom's – and English football's – thinking over the previous nine years. They failed to achieve it, primarily because they lacked the guile and penetration to break down the opposing defence. And because Flowers fell over at the wrong moment.

England went behind to a strike from distance by Lajos Tichy after 17 minutes; equalising just before the hour after Greaves saw his goalbound shot from inside the six-yard box handled by left-back Laszlo Sarosi. Flowers converted the penalty. Yet Greaves was rarely a threat and Flowers was less assured with 19 minutes remaining as he closed in on Hungary's star forward Florian Albert. Reportedly hearing a team-mate shouting 'let it go', Flowers hesitated and lost his footing, leaving Albert to advance into the area, slip past goalkeeper Ron Springett and slide the ball into the net. 'I left the centre-forward and moved towards the ball,' Flowers explained. 'At the crucial moment, however, I slipped.'

Greaves felt that England had played reasonably well and had only lost because of his colleague's unfortunate accident. The reporters covering the game for the English press were less generous, critical of the overall performance against a workmanlike team that was a mere shadow of the 'Magnificent Magyars' who had preceded them. Yet Greaves felt the journalists had fallen prey to their own undue optimism on the eve of the tournament and the patriotism that can afflict Englishmen on foreign soil. 'The soccer writers get bitten by this national prestige bug,' he argued, 'and when things go wrong they start lining up the scapegoats.'

The condensed nature of the tournament meant that England were back in action only 48 hours later, rebounding with a 3-1 defeat of Argentina. Two up at half-time through another Flowers penalty and a fierce Charlton strike, Greaves scored the goal that made victory safe after 67 minutes, a simple tap-in after Douglas's low shot was saved. It was a rare moment of freedom during a frustrating 90 minutes in which he rarely escaped the merciless marking of Raúl Páez.

England now needed only a point to secure second place in Group Four and a place in the quarter-finals. They achieved that and nothing more, slogging their way to a goalless draw against a Bulgaria team that had just been thrashed 6-1 by Hungary. Yet, having seen Bulgaria lose 1-0 in their opening game against Argentina in what he called 'a first-class clogging match', Greaves anticipated the kind of contest this was likely to be. He and Hitchens had recognised it as the type of game they'd become accustomed to in Italy. Sadly, it proved typical of the manner in which the entire competition would unfold. In his account of the finals, Saunders wrote of the early stages:

> It became clear after only two days, during which eight matches were completed, that most teams were so anxious to avoid an early return home that they had forgotten football was only a game and the World Cup its greatest shop window. From all four centres came reports of violence, ill temper, serious injury, and precious little of the artistic football to be expected from the world's leading professionals.

The encounter that would be written most prominently into the tournament's infamy came in the second set of games, when hosts Chile took on Italy in what became known as 'The Battle of Santiago'. David Coleman's introduction to the BBC highlights of the game has gone down in the lore of televised sport. 'Good evening,' he began, his folded arms and concerned expression giving viewers a hint that this was going to be no light entertainment offering. 'What you are about to see is the most stupid, appalling, disgusting and disgraceful exhibition of football, possibly in the history of the game. Chile versus Italy. This is the first time the two teams have met. We hope it will be the last.' What followed was an edited version of events that would not have looked out of place in a modern-day UFC octagon. Punches and kicks were thrown; blood was spilled and bones were broken; and even the police were called upon to restore order. English referee Ken Aston sent off two Italians, but with the thuggery spiralling beyond his control that fell well short of an appropriate level of justice.

Against England, the Bulgarians mixed cynicism with well-drilled massed defence. Greaves admitted that England's resolve to qualify with a victory was exhausted long before the end of proceedings. 'You can only run into a brick wall so many times. After that you lose heart,' he said, conceding that England had settled for a draw with around 10 minutes remaining.

Greaves himself had been disappointing once again, wasting a pair of early openings. He 'continued to dismay' according to one newspaper report, while his strike partner, Middlesbrough's Alan Peacock, again preferred to Hitchens after making his debut in the previous game, looked out of his depth. In the *Daily Mirror*, Frank Wilson joked that six cups of coffee had barely kept him awake while watching the match.

England might have reached the quarter-finals, as demanded by the press and the public, but their contribution to the global game was being questioned for the fourth World Cup running. The debate about whether they should embrace overseas influence and methods in order to maintain relevance in the international community echoed the ongoing discussion over the Conservative government's plans for Britain to step into the future by joining the six member nations of Europe's Common Market. Such a move would 'contribute to the political stability of Europe as well as its economic well-being', US President John Kennedy had said on the eve of the World Cup. His views on Winterbottom's 4-2-4 tactics went unrecorded.

With only two full days to rest, prepare and travel, England quickly found themselves in Viña del Mar for the quarter-finals. 'It was a seaside town,' notes Douglas, 'and it was a bit of much-needed luxury.' The payback was having to face Brazil, who had lost Pelé to injury but emerged top of their group anyway. The close proximity of the game and the fact that England had only needed to draw their final group match to qualify had persuaded many observers that important players should have been rested in preparation for the quarter-final. Greaves, it was suggested, could have benefitted from a few days off. Yet Winterbottom had preferred not to take qualification for granted and, therefore, 10 of his men were now facing their fourth game in 11 strength-sapping days. Hitchens, restored at centre-forward against Brazil, was the only team member to have had any respite.

Greaves was one of those causing the greatest concern. In the *Mirror*, McGhee called him 'the most disappointing player in the whole team' and noted that he 'still seems alarmingly disheartened'. The *Daily Express*, in its preview of the quarter-final, wrote, 'We must hope that Jimmy Greaves shakes off his mood of despair and indecision and doesn't loiter over scoring opportunities.'

Haynes admitted to feeling 'conceited enough to believe that we could beat Brazil' and optimistically considered that 'the livelier imagination of the Brazilians was perhaps equalled by the solid collective play of the English'. It wasn't. English collectivism was overshadowed by a virtuoso performance by Garrincha. Emerging as Brazil's star turn in the absence of Pelé, the brilliant winger tormented the England defence. If he was not propelling his stooped, frail-looking figure down the right flank, he was twisting and turning his way infield, leaving panic in his wake.

Prepared to dribble past anyone and unafraid to shoot from distance, it was he who rose to head Brazil into the lead from a 31st-minute corner.

After Hitchens headed an equaliser before half-time, it was no great surprise that Garrincha was at the heart of Brazil's second goal after 53 minutes, Springett only able to knock his driven free-kick into the path of centre-forward Vavá. Ray Wilson, one of the world's finest left-backs, was powerless to turn back Garrincha's relentless surges into the England box. Even a corner on the right was a scoring opportunity, forcing Springett to parry the ball as he swerved it under the crossbar with the outside of his right foot. 'This man can do everything,' cooed commentator Kenneth Wolstenholme. As if to prove him right, Garrincha picked up the ball 30 yards out and curled his shot beyond Springett's left arm into the top corner of the goal.

In the best game of the tournament so far, the 28-year-old winger was the most obvious difference between the two teams in Brazil's 3-1 victory. 'At half-time we thought we had a chance,' Douglas recalls. 'But Garrincha was a terrific player, a bit like Stanley Matthews. Once they got in front, you know what they are like, we couldn't get the ball off them. To be honest, a lot of us were relieved to be coming home. We were bored out of our minds.'

Greaves was honest enough to admit that England would not have been good enough even disregarding the considerable influence of the man whose name translated as 'Little Bird'. Once again, his own contribution had been minimal. 'Greaves gave another unhappy display,' Brian Glanville wrote, 'especially in the second half when he seemed curiously shy of physical contact.' And a rueful Saunders concluded, 'If only Greaves, the one England forward capable of matching the Brazilian finishing, could have risen this day to the heights he has occasionally scaled at home.'

His lightest moment of a tournament heavy with disappointment occurred during the first half, when a small black dog found its way on to the field. It gave rise to one of his favourite after-dinner stories. 'I went down on hands and knees, being a dog lover, and called the dog over,' he would recall. The curious canine approached the England man and allowed itself to be caught in his grasp. Greaves handed him to a stadium official, but not before his all-white kit had been sprayed by the contents of the dog's bladder. 'He peed all down me. We never had a change of shirts in those days. After the game, Garrincha wanted the dog and he took it back to Brazil and called it Jimmy Greaves. I am famous in Brazil as Garrincha's dog-catcher.'

That Greaves's involvement in the World Cup should be remembered mostly for being urinated on by a stray dog says much about his tournament. 'The form of Jimmy Greaves was puzzling,' Haynes admitted. 'Jimmy said himself he felt he was doing everything as he always did it, but nothing would work for him.'

Many people's favourite to leave Chile as the leading goalscorer, he instead flew home with criticism ringing in his ears and frustration at the state of international football weighing heavy in his heart. Brazil had been the one team he'd seen who appeared to be interested in anything other than stifling the opposition, and he included England among those who had taken a disappointingly defensive approach to the competition.

He felt England 'threw away our natural inclination to open football' and wished Bobby Robson had been given an opportunity to help them unlock opposition strongholds. He was honest enough to admit, however, that he had contributed little, describing himself and Haynes as 'mentally jaded, physically tired' and stating that he could have had no complaint had he been dropped. Haynes, meanwhile, noted that Greaves told him he had not even thought about the World Cup until he boarded the plane for South America, so wrapped up in Spurs' season had he been.

Greaves's mood of disillusionment dictated a series of comments that would cause him to slip further in the esteem of the English football public when they appeared in his autobiography, *A Funny Thing Happened on My Way to Spurs*, two months after the tournament. Had deadlines not meant that his thoughts were captured by his ghostwriter Clive Taylor in the gloomy aftermath of the event – had he had time to consider how his words would be received – he might have shown some restraint. Certainly, the chapters covering the World Cup have a far more unguarded, honest feel than the light-hearted tone of most of the book.

He hinted at what was to come by saying that 'football loyalty now revolves around the clubs and not so much around England', describing the atmosphere of international football as 'poisonous with politics and prestige' and calling it an 'ordeal' for players from all countries. Examining England's performance, he conceded that playing an 'English style' of game might not have achieved greater success, but would have afforded the players a greater sense of pride. And he went on to say:

> I believe we would have fought harder had we been playing for our clubs. I don't know why it is, but the spirit and the fire that marks English play at club level doesn't seem to be so evident in the national side. When an Englishman plays for his club he's got the fire in his belly. But the flames lose some of their heat once he pulls on an England shirt. Maybe it's because we don't know each other in the same way. We're from different clubs and we are just brought together for the occasion. Then again, our club games are our bread and butter and as such we probably give them more thoughts...
>
> I think this thing will sort itself out – *because I believe that international football between representative teams is on the way out* [his italics]. Its days are numbered and it will disappear completely just as soon as we get a full programme of international football at club level. And surely that must come before very long ... European leagues, world leagues, whichever way the future of the game lies, the present system of international matches is doomed. And nothing I saw in Chile will cause me to mourn their passing.

Of course, Greaves was wrong. The monolithic rise of the Champions League might have tugged at the trouser leg of the World Cup in the 21st century but has not yet completely pulled it from sport's highest rung, as evidenced by the way the country unites behind the national team every four years. And his comments about club priorities against those of national teams have been echoed by plenty of modern players, creating the odd headline and plenty of shrugs before the news cycle rolls on to the latest managerial sacking or kiss-and-tell scandal.

In 1962, however, with the Cold War at its height and Kim Philby shortly to be exposed as the latest MI6 officer to have been spying for the Soviet Union, his remarks were regarded by some as treasonable.

They also became characterised over time as Greaves having indicated that he himself 'had no fire in his belly'. That irked him, even though his protests seemed like splitting hairs over his precise phraseology.

On 24 August, the *Daily Mirror* used Greaves's published comments as the basis for a full-page debate headlined 'Why Not Give England a Break?' It asked readers to vote on whether their greater loyalties lay with club or country. Chief sports writer Peter Wilson conceded that his recent mailbox had been full of letters supporting Greaves, claiming that the lack of passion among English supporters justified Greaves's controversial comments. 'I do really believe as far as soccer is concerned that we English are a codfish-like lot, as cold as fish fingers compared with the Scots, the Welsh and the Irish,' he offered. 'If you attend an international at Hampden Park, Glasgow, it's "Scots wha-hae" *(sic)* – and to hell with the invaders.'

Greaves would rehabilitate his reputation over the coming years. By the time England were preparing to host the next World Cup he was one of the most popular players in the country and perceived as a cornerstone of their bid to triumph on home soil. Yet the lingering memory of his remarks meant he found it necessary to address them when he published his next book, *My World of Soccer*, not long before the 1966 finals.

He said they'd been made when his 'head was full of romantic notions' and at a time when he had recently returned from Italy to find himself playing in what amounted to an international all-star side at Tottenham. 'So when I turned out for England it was like stepping down a grade,' he would write. 'I noticed that when playing with England there was a lack of inspiration about my game, but that was a long time ago.' He was 'older and wiser', he would explain. It was not the most cogent plea of mitigation, but the fact that he felt he needed to make it four years later demonstrates the disquiet his original remarks had created.

7

GLORY NIGHTS
AND DOG DAY
AFTERNOONS

*'It's a hard call, but Spurs against Atletico Madrid
is to my mind the greatest game I ever played in.'*

IF Jimmy Greaves needed a fast start to the season to polish his tarnished image after the World Cup, then he found it in Tottenham's 5-1 thrashing of Ipswich Town in the FA Charity Shield at Portman Road. 'Jimmy Greaves is going to be the game's biggest box office draw for his sheer goal-snatching flair,' raved the *Daily Mirror* after he scored twice and had a hand in three other goals against Alf Ramsey's League champions.

The game had been more than a pre-season showcase for a Tottenham side who believed that only the distractions of Europe and the FA Cup had prevented them denying Ipswich their unexpected title triumph. According to Dave Mackay, 'We felt we had something to prove.'

The opening of the campaign saw Spurs manager Bill Nicholson being touted by most journalists as the next manager of England after Walter Winterbottom's agreement to stand down as soon as a replacement was appointed. Nicholson's suitability for the role was further demonstrated in the eyes of many by the plan he hatched to deal with Ramsey's deployment of deep-lying wingers, a tactic that characterised his team's success in their first season after promotion from Division Two. Wing-halves Danny Blanchflower and Mackay went wide to deal with the wingers; full-backs Peter Baker and Ron Henry came inside to handle the inside-forwards; and Spurs were left playing the kind of 3-4-3 formation that would have had experts salivating as they admired the tactical flexibility of foreign coaches in the Premier League more than half a century later.

Once the First Division season began, Greaves found the accolades coming thick and fast. 'The executioner' one report called him after his goal in the opening game against Birmingham City. Then he 'plundered two of his most impish goals in five stunning minutes' in a 2-2 draw against Wolverhampton Wanderers. Four more goals were racked up in a 9-2 thrashing of a Nottingham Forest team that had been conceding only one per game until then; a hat-trick arrived three weeks later in a 6-2 beating of Manchester United – two games that formed part of the team's rush of 30 goals in five League matches.

Les Allen, who found himself battling for a place in the Spurs line-up in the wake of Greaves's arrival at White Hart Lane, believes he was witnessing a better player than the teenager he'd played alongside at Chelsea. 'Even though he didn't stay long in Italy, he improved while he was there,' he suggests. 'And then Bill Nick put the finishing touches to his actual contribution to the game. He got him working a bit harder than he normally did and, consequently, he got more chances.'

Even when not scoring, Greaves was earning rave reviews for his Tottenham performances. Embarking on their European Cup Winners' Cup campaign, Spurs were drawn against Rangers, who had just won the Scottish Cup and were setting off toward their own domestic double in the 1962-63 season. Before almost 60,000 at White Hart Lane on Hallowe'en, Tottenham won the first leg 5-2. 'Top honours last night went to Greaves, who showed the kind of fight and skill he rarely seems to produce for England,' wrote the *Daily Express*, presumably referring to his quiet game in a 1-1 European Nations Cup draw against France at Hillsborough earlier in October[12] – although he had scored in a 3-1 win in Northern Ireland since then. 'Three of the [Spurs] goals came from corner kicks he took on the right wing,' the report of the Rangers game noted. 'And it was Greaves more than anyone that gave Spurs a fighting chance at Ibrox.'

It was a sign of the open nature of the football of the era and the automatic advantage attributed to any home team in European football – even one from the same island – that a three-goal cushion was only considered to have offered Spurs a 'fighting chance'. Six weeks later, Greaves scored a clinical 10th-minute goal to silence a raucous 80,000 Glasgow crowd as Tottenham wrapped up the tie with a 3-2 win. Receiving the ball just inside the home team's half, Greaves used his speed off the mark to slip away from his marker, before converting with an early strike just inside the box as other defenders arrived too late to close him down. The truncated nature of European football in those days meant that they were in the quarter-finals by virtue of that one success.

In the meantime, Greaves scored the fourth goal in England's 4-0 win against Wales in Winterbottom's final game in charge. By the time England played again in February, Ramsey – Nicholson's old Spurs team-mate – had been summoned from Ipswich to fill the managerial vacancy.

One of Ramsey's last acts at Ipswich was to attempt, unsuccessfully, to overcome Greaves's old team in the European Cup. AC Milan, who had gone on to win the Italian League without their unsettled import, arrived in England with a 3-0 first-leg lead and

---

12 Despite his disappointing performances in Chile, Greaves was the only forward player to retain his England place for that first post-World Cup game.

with coach Nereo Rocco saying, 'I would like to see Jimmy Greaves while I'm here. I'm still upset over his departure from Milan and I would like to show that we can still be good friends.' Recovery proved beyond Ipswich, despite a 2-1 win at Portman Road, while reconciliation held little interest for Greaves.

Ipswich's defence, already unable to contain Greaves in the season's curtain-raiser, remained a far more enticing prospect for him. He celebrated Boxing Day by putting another three goals past them in a 5-0 victory at White Hart Lane, raising his total of League goals to 23. 'Three goals in the last eight minutes is in itself remarkable enough,' said *The Times*, 'but much of his play besides was equally so as he brushed through the defence himself and then split it wide open with well-conceived passes.'

The game had been played against a backdrop of heavy snowfall, the start of the most disruptive three months English football ever suffered at the hands of the weather. In parts of the country, snow drifts were measured at greater than 10ft and it took until March for temperatures to fight their way regularly above freezing. For a while it appeared that football would suffer more than just a fixture pile-up as smaller clubs around the country struggled to pay their bills without regular income from the gate. Remarkably, none went out of business, even though the weather remained so brutal that the season would be extended by four weeks. Tottenham played only one League game in each of January and February, but a third-round defeat against Burnley in a rematch of the previous season's final rid them of the problem of fitting in further FA Cup games and ended their two-year hold over the tournament. Meanwhile, some ties in the competition were scheduled as many as 10 times.

The freeze meant that Spurs went almost four months without losing in the First Division – nine wins and two draws in the 11 games they managed in that time. But their failure to win more than three of their last 10 games, while Everton were going through their final 11 unbeaten, would see them finish in second place, six points behind the Merseyside club, despite scoring 111 goals to the new champions' 84. Greaves finished with 37 of them, including another four-goal haul in an Easter win against Liverpool. Decisively, though, neither he nor any of his team-mates could find the net in their two games against Everton, who took three points from the games between the top two.

It was to Europe that Tottenham looked to continue their sequence of trophy-winning seasons, a run of success that was in jeopardy after a 2-0 defeat to Slovan Bratislava in the first leg of their Cup Winners' Cup quarter-final. 'It was the worst performance of any Spurs team I have played in,' Greaves declared as his team left Czechoslovakia, the nation that had finished runners-up in the most recent World Cup. Nine days later, he was part of one of the best.

The night was captured by John Moynihan in a chapter devoted to the game in his seminal book, *The Soccer Syndrome*, published three years later. Describing his approach to the ground after the game had already kicked off, he wrote that 'the noise had become mountainous, swollen, almost obscene'. It rose to bone-jarring decibels after 31 minutes when Mackay scored the first goal from long range. A few minutes later, Greaves evaded a challenge and lured keeper Wilhelm Schroiff before lashing the ball past him. Then White headed in and Spurs had turned a two-goal deficit into an aggregate lead in the space of 10 minutes. As Spurs continued to pass their way through an overrun Slovan defence, Greaves scored the first of their three second-half goals with a rare finish from outside the box, lifting the ball over a goalkeeper left stranded after he had punched away a Cliff Jones cross. A 6-0 win in front of a 61,504 crowd was, according to Moynihan, 'a night of absolute domination by an English side, a night of rejuvenation after so many years of humiliation'.

In Yugoslavia a month later, Tottenham achieved a different kind of triumph; one of resilience and resistance after they were reduced to 10 men in the first leg of their semi-final against OFK

Belgrade. It was Greaves – playing on the right wing because of Cliff Jones's absence – who didn't make it to the end of the match, sent off after 55 minutes of a game that had already featured one mass brawl. Bobby Smith had been fouled on the edge of the penalty area after 26 minutes and, when the home players felt he had attempted to deliver his own retribution against a now flat-out Maric, fists flew on both sides. From the delayed free-kick, Smith set up White to give Spurs the lead, but the home side equalised via a penalty a few minutes later.

The dismissal of Greaves came out of the blue. Away from the play, he felt he had been given one crack on the shin too many. 'I saw red and my only thought was to retaliate,' he admitted. Yet he was rather less deadly in combat than in front of goal. He kicked out – and missed. Hungarian referee Lajos Aranyosi noticed the retaliation rather than the original assault and sent Greaves to the dressing room.[13] Greaves felt that the official 'was gradually losing control of the game and had decided to make an example of me in an effort to cool down the rest of the players'.

The referee told English journalist Peter Lorenzo, 'I sent off Greaves for taking a kick at number five when he hadn't got the ball. I told Greaves this wasn't gentlemanly.' The first Spurs player dismissed since team trainer Cecil Poynton in 1928, Greaves felt he had been cast as the scapegoat in being the only one sent off. He did admit, however, that his intent was sufficient to warrant his punishment, especially after being reminded of that fact by Nicholson after the game.

Spurs regrouped, rolled up their sleeves, ignored the venom coming down from the terraces – and even a bottle thrown at Mackay by one fan – and ended up sneaking a late winner via Terry Dyson to take a 2-1 lead back to London. Goals by Mackay, Jones and Smith completed a 5-2 aggregate victory and gave England

---

13 By the time Greaves wrote his final autobiography 40 years later he recalled the incident as his opponent having missed with an attempted punch, to which Greaves himself responded with a haymaker that connected only with air. Contemporaneous reports describe the Belgrade defender making contact with a kick.

its first representative in a European final. Their opponents in the Dutch city of Rotterdam would be Atletico Madrid, bidding to win the competition in consecutive seasons.

Spurs set off for their seaside destination of Scheveningen, a district of The Hague, to prepare for the final. Greaves departed after being fined £9 for driving offences at Romford Magistrates' Court. Having failed to observe a 'stop' sign, he then neglected to produce his driving licence and insurance certificate for police. An England football star appearing in court two days before a European final might be expected to make front-page headlines and cause a tidal wave on social media in the modern era. Greaves's embarrassment was tucked away in two paragraphs positioned in the bottom left corner of page 23 of the *Daily Mirror*.

Those following Tottenham's fortunes were more interested in medical reports than motoring misdemeanours. If any one player appeared indispensable to a Tottenham team going into what was virgin territory for an English team it was the indomitable Mackay. Yet the Scot had suffered strained stomach muscles and was forced to admit as kick-off approached, 'Only a miracle will get me fit.'

There was no miracle. Mackay was not among the Spurs players who changed into the all-white kit the club had adopted for European football before sitting down to listen to Nicholson's final instructions. Greaves recalled Blanchflower interrupting Nicholson's warnings about the strengths of the team lying second in La Liga.

'Hang on a minute, boss,' interjected the Spurs captain, who'd also had the powers of assistant manager conferred upon him. Blanchflower proceeded to remind his audience that their opponents had no one to rival the likes of Norman at the back or Greaves up front; no prospect of matching the teamwork that had carried this Tottenham side so far. 'That pumped us up,' recalled Greaves, who acknowledged the strength of character that Nicholson demonstrated in allowing Blanchflower to hijack his team talk.

After 16 minutes, the belligerent Smith freed Jones on the right and Greaves met his flighted cross with a first-time finish, a half-volley with the inside of his right foot without breaking stride. Sixteen minutes later, Greaves crossed deep from the right wing, Dyson fed the ball back across the penalty area and White shot high into the goal to double Spurs' lead.

Madrid pulled one back from the penalty spot immediately after half-time, full-back Ron Henry having leapt on the line to turn a shot over the bar with his left hand. It inspired Atletico into sustained attack, Brown scrambling the ball away and Henry, struggling with strained knee ligaments, heading off the line. Yet the game turned inexorably back towards Spurs after 69 minutes when Dyson turned his marker and crossed high towards the near post. 'I watched as it curved in and thought, "Blimey, that's a bad cross,"' he recalled. Inexplicably, goalkeeper Edgardo Madinabeytia, completely unchallenged, fumbled the ball between his raised hands and into the goal. 'To be honest, it was a fluke,' Dyson confessed.

Now Spurs breezed forward, every pass carrying them closer to their destiny and further breaking Atletico's spirit. With 11 minutes remaining, Greaves's left-foot volley from six yards after Dyson's delivery allowed the Spurs fans to begin their victory celebrations. The outstanding Dyson made it 5-1 from the edge of the box after the disheartened Madrid defenders offered him a clear run from the halfway line. After Brown denied Atletico a late consolation, the referee grabbed the ball before the corner could be taken and blew his whistle.

Tottenham had become the first English team to succeed in this relatively new world of European football, a much-needed fillip for the national game after the disappointment of the previous summer in Chile.

It was all so new that BBC commentator Kenneth Wolstenholme fluffed his lines. 'Tottenham Hotspur have won the European Nations Cup,' he announced excitedly. He would have his moment of redemption three years later on a July afternoon at Wembley.

For now, Spurs players found each other to share congratulations among the smattering of fans who had made their way on to the pitch. Mackay was among them, hugged by Greaves as his eyes filled with tears, a mixture, Mackay explained, of 'delirium at our success and disappointment at having not been a part of the climax'. And then Blanchflower lifted their fourth trophy in three seasons.

'There was a lovely relationship I've never experienced before or since in a football team,' *Daily Mail* writer Brian James told the authors of *The Ghost*, the biography of John White. 'The warmth there was like being in a family.'

Allen argues, 'One of the main reasons why we did well was the fact that in the reserves there were seven or eight internationals, players like Medwin, Hopkins, Marchi. We had such a good bunch of players waiting to get in the team it kept everybody on their toes. When Jimmy arrived, it added to the strength and made it more difficult for the opposition. It happened a few times that Bobby Smith came back in and I was out – places were very hard to keep all over the pitch. Even when Dave Mackay, who was a great player, was injured and Tony Marchi took his place, it didn't upset the team too much. That was the case with more or less every position.'

Yet, even though this had been a first for a British team, it was also the end. Ken Jones warned *Daily Mirror* readers in his report of the Rotterdam triumph, 'Remember that four years at the top has sapped their stamina – and we may never see this side playing in big-game competition again.'

Mackay recalled lying awake after a night of celebrating and feeling 'a nagging sadness; a sadness that one feels at times of extreme happiness, a sadness that emanates from knowing that things may not be this good again. In my heart, I knew that the victory marked the beginning of the end of the Double side.'

By the end of the following season, Blanchflower, struggling for fitness, had finally accepted the inevitably of retirement, while Mackay, the pulse of the team, was on the sidelines after breaking his leg during a second-round Cup Winners' Cup defeat against Manchester United. Blanchflower would write in his *Sunday Express* column, 'Just last May we were holding triumphantly the European Cup Winners' Cup ... now the ranks are sadly diminished.'

* * * *

The three seasons after the European triumph might harshly be described as years of steady decline, Spurs finishing fourth, sixth and eighth in successive seasons. More charitably, the period can be viewed as a rebuilding phase that gave Greaves and Double winners Mackay and Jones the opportunity for a final Spurs triumph and laid the foundation for another mini-dynasty – in knockout football at least – a decade after the original Glory Glory years.

They began 1963-64 with eight wins in the first 10 games, although there had been an early gust of the winds of change when Phil Beal was given a first-team debut at Aston Villa, taking the No.4 shirt from Blanchflower. 'The first team had played on the Saturday and there was another game on the Monday,' Beal explains. 'Bill felt that Danny was getting to a certain age where he couldn't play Saturday-Monday, so he put me in. I suppose that was just the beginning of the team gradually breaking up, getting a little bit too old.'

The 10th game of the season had seen Greaves scoring his third hat-trick in a 6-1 win against Birmingham City. After an earlier treble against Nottingham Forest, Pat Collins had written in *The People*, 'Only he, with his uncanny goal flair, could so dramatically change Tottenham's pedestrian performance. And only he could have scored such a cheeky hat-trick.' His repeat performance in a 6-1 win against Blackpool had found *The Times* reporting, 'He scored three goals of unquestionable quality, set up two more and always was in his most devilish mood.'

A total of 15 goals in the first 12 matches was not bad for someone who, on the eve of the season, had confessed to concerns about his well-being. 'I feel finished,' he'd said. 'I haven't been doing anything right in practice. I feel as if I haven't got anything left. I've been playing like a Third Division forward. I just don't know what's wrong with me.' Not much, as it transpired.

Yet a 7-2 defeat at Blackburn Rovers that had punctuated that early sequence of results – and the 3-3 and 4-4 draws against Sheffield United and Arsenal that followed it – hinted at an inconsistency in this Spurs team that would have felt familiar from his Chelsea days. It would not sustain a title challenge, even though Tottenham still found themselves on top of the League in February 1964. March saw them suffer consecutive defeats against Everton, Manchester United and Liverpool, who finished third, second and first respectively, and the final three months of the season produced only three wins.

Greaves observed what he acknowledged as a necessary break-up of a great side and felt it was a tribute to Nicholson that they maintained a presence in the title race for as long as they did. He was again the division's top scorer, with 35 goals in 41 games. And with productivity came expectation. It remained a characteristic of reportage of his career that any off day was quickly remarked upon. 'Greaves made no impact on the game,' was the verdict after a home defeat against West Bromwich Albion over Christmas; typical of any report of a game in which he didn't find the net.

In the early months of the season he'd stood poised for his 200th goal in six years of First Division football. 'The only one that counts is the next one,' he said when asked how many of his haul he could clearly recollect. After four goalless games, the milestone remained unattained and questions were raised about whether Greaves was feeling the pressure. He had, after all, scored four for England against Northern Ireland in the meantime. Even he was forced into admitting that the situation was 'a bit worrying'.

Perhaps not as much, however, as the stories arriving from Italy that he faced the possibility of eight months in jail if he ever returned to the country to face charges of libelling AC Milan. He had accused them in print of treating him 'as a prisoner' during his time there and had considered that they'd 'purchased my body and soul, and not only mine but my wife and children's'.

'Why can't they let everybody forget it all?' he asked in exasperation. 'I was criticising the discipline the Milan club imposed on its players. It will be very annoying if the sentence is passed. I might want to go back for a holiday. And what happens if I am chosen to play [there]?' Asked if he would consider defending the case, Greaves scoffed, 'Not likely. I don't fancy eight months in an Italian jail.'

Four days later he was freed from the shackles of impending football history when he finally scored his 200th League goal in a victory at the Bolton Wanderers ground that held such bad memories for him.

Meanwhile, Tottenham's defence of the Cup Winners' Cup lasted as long as it took for the draw to throw them together with FA Cup holders Manchester United in the first round. By the end of the first leg at White Hart Lane, hopes of advancement were high after a 2-0 win. Yet the return match at Old Trafford brought a 4-1 defeat and left them facing life without Mackay after his leg was broken in a challenge with Noel Cantwell. 'I did not feel any immediate pain,' Mackay recalled, 'but felt immediate panic when I looked down and my foot had twisted round by 90 degrees.' He never forgave his opponent's recklessness, accusing him of being nowhere near the ball in his challenge. 'He may not have set out to break a bone, but that was the end result.'

Spurs could not help but miss the man described by Greaves as 'the greatest player ever to have worn a Tottenham shirt' and rated by Nicholson as his best signing for the club, citing his 'enormous contribution on the field', his 'dynamic character' and noting that 'his effect on other players was remarkable'.

Mackay's absence was particularly apparent during the slog of a title battle in the deep mid-winter and when they drew Chelsea in the third round of the FA Cup, a tie for which Greaves was appointed captain and which was lost in a replay. 'He tore into opponents and he tore them apart,' was Greaves's assessment of Mackay's effectiveness in such situations.

The loss of Mackay as a footballer, however, was nothing to the human tragedy that was to devastate the club in the summer of 1964. John White finished training on the morning of 21 July, asked if any of his colleagues fancied a round of golf and, with the skies becoming darker, set off for Crews Hill Golf Club in Enfield without any takers. No more daunted by the weather than he ever was by muscle-bound defenders, White embarked on his solo round. When the rain became a tumult, he sheltered under a tree, where lightning struck him, killing him instantly. He was only 27, and left a wife and two infant children.

Nicholson was one of the first people to be informed after the discovery of White's body. He exploded in fury at the policeman on the end of the telephone. He'd received two hoax calls relating the death of Greaves in recent weeks; why should he believe this story? Once the awful truth had been confirmed, White's team-mates were given the news. 'I don't mind admitting I cried,' Greaves would recall. 'We'd lost a wonderful, humorous, mischievous, lovable human being. It was a senseless death, beyond a tragedy.'

A late-season eclipse and a traumatic summer meant that no one knew quite what to expect from Tottenham when they kicked off the 1964-65 campaign. The team was continuing to evolve, Nicholson having spent £70,000 on Fulham wing-half Alan Mullery, seen as Blanchflower's successor, and £35,000 on St Mirren winger Jimmy Robertson before the spring transfer deadline.

Robertson was given unexpected status by his new manager. 'I roomed with Jimmy for four or five years,' he explains. 'I think Bill felt that it would be good for me. I was only 19 and he thought

Greavsie would look after me. We got on well, even if it was always me who had to make the tea in the morning. Jim was a great character, very quick-witted, and loved a drink with the lads.' Unsurprisingly, Robertson struggles to remember Greaves suffering a single sleepless night before a game. 'He just took everything in his stride.'

As the new season played out, Tottenham were never able to string more than two wins together. Their home form was formidable – 18 wins, three draws and no defeats – yet away from White Hart Lane they won only a single match and lost 16 times. Greaves's output of 29 League goals was enough to make him the top flight's leading scorer for the fifth time in his career and for his fourth successive full season in Division One.[14] For good measure he bagged a couple of hat-tricks in FA Cup wins over Torquay United and Ipswich Town, before Spurs went out once again to Chelsea in the fifth round.

There were signs early in the season that the absence of White was impacting on his productivity. Not only had he been denied the supplier of many of his goals, but he found himself taking up the role of provider for others to a greater degree than he had previously known. 'This wasn't planned,' he said. 'Before, all I had to do was get goals. Now I have to find myself retreating more than ever to get the ball. People have often criticised my ability to pass the ball accurately and I am developing this. With Cliff Jones, who likes to run with the ball, at inside-left, we have to change our tactics. But I must say I enjoy playing this way and I hope other people do. I'm still after the goals, but they will be harder than ever to come by.'

Things changed once more for Greaves in December 1964 with the arrival of a man with whom he would strike up one of his most productive partnerships. Nicholson was already aware of the ability of Dundee striker Alan Gilzean before getting a closer look

---

14 Level with Andy McEvoy of Blackburn Rovers.

at him in November when he scored the first goal for a Scotland XI in their 6-2 win against Spurs in John White's memorial game at White Hart Lane.[15]

Gilzean could have joined Sunderland, or even gone to Italy to play for Torino, yet the prospect of partnering Greaves, whom he had admired for years, played a large part in his decision to move to London. 'Before I even signed for Dundee, when I was maybe 17, Chelsea were on television against some foreign team and Jimmy was playing,' he remembered only a few weeks before his death in the summer of 2018. 'I watched the game and Greavsie was unbelievable. For a guy so young to have so much ability was amazing; his ball control, his speed, his awareness and his calmness. Then whenever I saw him I thought, "Christ, that guy is very, very special." He never used to hit rocket shots into the net, he used to roll them in. He got better and better.

'When that chance came to leave Dundee to go to England I got better offers from Sunderland and Torino, but Greavsie was a big influence, as John White had been. When I played for Scotland I roomed with John and he told me all the ins and outs of Tottenham and the pay scale. Spurs had won the Double and my boyhood ambition – and why I wanted to go to England – was to play at Wembley. I was fascinated with that. Bill Nicholson came up to sign me twice. I never signed the first time, but I was more determined the second time because I wanted to play with Greavsie. I would have loved to play with John White, too.'

After signing for £72,500, Gilzean's thoughtful, unselfish play, particularly his ability in the air, would mesh profitably with Greaves's predatory instincts. Greaves scored both goals in a 2-2 draw against Everton on Gilzean's debut, prompting the *Tottenham Herald* to predict in a headline, 'Perfect partner for Greaves has arrived'.

---

15 Greaves set up the opening Spurs goal for White's brother, Tom, who was granted a one-day transfer from Hearts so that he could skipper the home team.

Mullery recalls, 'Those two as a pair were fantastic to have in your side. You knew they would score goals at any time and you knew they would give you 100 per cent. It came naturally to them, but I think you have got to give Bill Nicholson credit. Bobby Smith had gone off to Brighton and we just didn't have that centre-forward. I arrived just before Gilly and I think Bill watched him about nine times to make sure he would fit in with Jim.'

In their first nine games together, Greaves and Gilzean shared 17 goals, enabling headline writers to revel in references to Tottenham's 'G-Men'. 'We could be better than the partnership I had with Bobby Smith,' Greaves suggested. 'Since Gilly joined us I have been much happier. As soon as we started playing I felt he had the ability and it didn't take long for the understanding to develop. He has helped me in many ways. I can't speak for him, but it helps that I like the fella.'

Gilzean, meanwhile, had quickly realised that he would not be disappointed by the player with whom he had been smitten from afar. 'I was struck by his dedication to scoring goals,' he recalled. 'Once you put him on the pitch with a ball at his feet, or in the gymnasium where we had these little ice hockey goals for five-a-sides, the skill he displayed was just unbelievable. People like him come along once in 50 or 60 years.'

Walter Winterbottom had ended his reign as England manager with a 4-0 win against Wales in November 1962 – Greaves scoring a late final goal – and the reign of Alf Ramsey could not have made a worse start, a 5-2 defeat in France in February to end their hopes of progress in the European Championship. Things looked even bleaker five weeks later when England lost 2-1 at Wembley against a Scotland side inspired by Jim Baxter, who scored both goals.

May brought a home daw against world champions Brazil, before Greaves finally scored his first two goals for Ramsey's England in a 4-2 win in Czechoslovakia. He added another couple in an 8-1 victory in Switzerland and was on target once more in a 4-0 win in Wales in the first game of the 1963-64 season.

The FA's celebration of its 100th anniversary brought a FIFA Rest of the World XI to Wembley for what was classified as a full international for England players. Greaves was denied twice early in the game by Lev Yashin, including a left-footed shot on the run that had the great Soviet Union keeper diving to his left to push away. After a goalless first half, he appeared to have opened the scoring after taking a return pass from Bobby Smith, beating two defenders, going wide of Yashin and steering the ball in from a narrow angle. It was, said *The Times*, 'a breathtaking stroke of magic'. Yet Scottish referee Bobby Davidson had already blown for a foul committed against Greaves outside the box, an act for which he quickly apologised. Terry Paine eventually put England ahead, only for Denis Law to equalise for the World team. Greaves saw his cross from the left graze the woodwork before being on the spot with three minutes remaining to score the winner after substitute goalkeeper Milutin Soskic fumbled Bobby Charlton's shot.

'It was really a dream finale,' Greaves would recall, emphasising that the importance of the game to the England team went way beyond what might have been expected of a commemorative match. 'The whole side became absorbed in the drama of the situation for there was a wonderful sense of urgency about the lads that drove us to victory.'

Desmond Hackett decided that Greaves 'has written his own history into the Wembley arena', while *Charles Buchan's Football Monthly* said, 'Greaves removed any doubt about being world-class. He was the greatest forward on view.' According to the *Daily Mail's* Brian James, 'This, above all, was Jimmy Greaves's greatest match. The quick wit and quicker aim of the deft, little Londoner have never before been spurred by such zeal for combat.' And *The Times* argued that Greaves had 'shown himself to be a thoroughbred worthy of the highest company'.[16]

---

16 Further endorsement of that opinion was furnished at the end of the year, when Greaves finished third in the European Footballer of the Year voting, behind Yashin and Italy's Gianni Rivera.

A month later, Greaves scored four goals in an 8-3 hammering of Northern Ireland. The world truly did appear to be at his feet. John Lennon would even interrupt a Beatles concert to acknowledge Greaves in the audience. And then he was dropped by his country. In the nearly four months between the Wembley victory over the Irish and the scheduled April trip to Hampden Park to face Scotland, Greaves had gone from world-beater to, according to one newspaper report, 'the problem soccer man of 1964'. *The Times* argued that 'until he recovers his zest, sharp finishing power and maximum fitness a rest will be the best thing for him and England.'

At this distance, and studying the bare facts of the record book, it is hard to know what the problem was. A return of 10 goals in 15 League and Cup appearances since the turn of the year would create little concern for mere mortals. Goalscoring deities such as Greaves clearly operated to a different standard of expectation. Spurs' failure to win any of their games against fellow title challengers in March seemed to indicate to some a collapse of his confidence and mechanics. 'It would be doing him a favour to permit him a well-needed rest,' said the *Daily Express*. Ramsey was concerned enough to replace Greaves and Spurs colleague Smith, offering West Ham's Johnny Byrne and Liverpool's Roger Hunt their third caps.

'I'm disappointed,' Greaves responded. 'Who wouldn't be? But I'm not going to worry about this. I am not going to cry or panic. I think I have showed in the past I can do it. It doesn't seem to be very long ago that I was being talked about as the so-called star of the England team against the Rest of the World. If I remember correctly I scored four in England's last game. I feel that my last England games were top grade, but I have obviously been dropped because of my club form. My recent games for England don't seem to count.'

Acknowledging that it was Tottenham who paid his wages, he concluded, 'If I'm never picked for England again, then at least I have had a good run.' He need not have worried. After England lost 1-0 to a Gilzean goal, Greaves was recalled for the home game against Uruguay the following month, partnering Byrne, who scored twice in a 2-1 win. Making his debut was Fulham right-back George Cohen. 'Jimmy was good in the dressing room, a jocular guy,' he remembers. 'I am sure he was suffering from nerves like everyone, but he didn't show it and he was a great character to have around. He kept the guys' minds off the game.'

Greaves was said in this contest to have displayed 'the old urgency, if not the split-second timing'. In the meantime, fears about a return to Italy meant he had been omitted from the Football League team to face the Italian League in Milan. His next assignment would be a trip to Lisbon to face a formidable Portugal side.

On the day before the squad departed, they trained as usual at the Bank of England sports ground in Roehampton, just south of the Thames, before heading back to their base at the Whites Hotel, close to the FA headquarters in Lancaster Gate. After dinner, a group of seven players set off for a walk along Bayswater Road, Greaves among them. After a long, hard season, Greaves recalled, 'some of us were desperate for a few hours' leisure time' rather than spending the evening stuck in the hotel playing cards or watching television. 'Jimmy convinced us that there'd be no harm in going out for just a couple of pints,' Gordon Banks recalled. 'He knew a quiet pub along the road and that's where we headed.'

Greaves and Banks had been joined by skipper Bobby Moore, Byrne, George Eastham, Bobby Charlton and Ray Wilson. With the game still four days away, they allowed themselves to venture into the West End for a couple of drinks, Greaves making them stay a little longer than they originally intended as he had not had the chance to buy a round. At 11.30pm, Ramsey sent his trainer, Harold Shepherdson, to check on his players' rooms, at which point their breaking of curfew was discovered. Shepherdson was sent back to each room to place the passport of the missing players on their pillows. 'As soon as we saw the passports we knew we'd been rumbled,' Moore recalled, while Charlton said that 'the implication was huge and dark'.

The players were allowed to fly to Portugal and Ramsey said nothing. Eventually, three days after the incident, he ended a training session by announcing, 'There are seven players who I think would like to stay and see me.' The remainder having departed, Ramsey addressed the miscreants. 'If I had enough players in the squad, not one of you would be in the side,' he told them. 'In fact, I don't think you would be here at all. But I haven't enough players. And I don't think you will do it again. Because I think you now realise it would not be worth the risk.'

Moore would tell biographer Jeff Powell, 'It would have been ridiculous if some of those great players had not gone on to the 1966 World Cup just because we had a few drinks four days before a match.' All seven men played in a thrilling 4-3 win, Byrne scoring a hat-trick. Ramsey ended the night by telling his squad they were free to enjoy a beer and added to Greaves and Moore, 'I'll have a gin and tonic, if you'll be so kind.'

After two goals for the Rest of Europe against Scandinavia in Copenhagen – 'he was magnificent', said his team manager, the West German boss Helmut Schoen – Greaves found the net again in a 3-1 England win against the Republic of Ireland in Dublin. On the way to Brazil for an international tournament to celebrate the 50th anniversary of that country's football association, Greaves watched his colleagues stick 10 goals past the United States in New York. He was being saved for more serious matters, the game against the world champions. Greaves equalised Brazil's opening goal but the hosts romped to a 5-1 win with four second-half strikes. A draw against Portugal and defeat against Argentina made it a fruitless tournament for Ramsey's men.

Victory in Belfast to open the 1964-65 campaign was hardly cause for celebration. Four goals down at half-time, Northern Ireland gave England a scare by clawing back to 4-3, exposing some concerning frailties in the process. Greaves helped himself to a hat-trick – 'because he seldom misses the kind of chances the Irish defence seemed determined to give him', wrote Ken Jones in the *Daily Mirror*. Draws against Belgium and Holland and a win against Wales before the turn of the year prompted little optimism with a World Cup on home soil getting ever closer. The fact that 21 players had appeared in the early-season games, including a handful of debutants, gave little indication that Ramsey knew his best line-up.

Early in September, Desmond Hackett had watched Greaves play against Burnley and declared in the *Daily Express*, 'I have seldom seen him play with such skill, such industry and such admirable effect. What an England captain Greaves would make in this wondrous mood.' Far from bestowing such an honour upon him, the Football Association instead warned him shortly before Christmas that he might be charged with bringing the game into disrepute after he and Arsenal's Ian Ure admitted in a newspaper article that – shock horror – fully grown professional footballers, including themselves, swore during matches. FA secretary Denis Follows said the players had been 'asked to reply to us. What action we take will depend on the answers we get.' Such action could conceivably have threatened Greaves's England place under more bureaucratic regimes. Ramsey, known for his loyalty to his players and – despite his infamous elocution lessons – his propensity to drop his own occasional expletive into conversation, was never likely to have gone along with such a course.

England emerged from winter with the traditional April game against Scotland. Greaves's goal gave them a 2-0 lead, only for Denis Law and Ian St John to snatch a Wembley draw for the Scots. The game was notable for the debut of Leeds United centre-half Jack Charlton and the first time Ramsey had used the combination of Banks, Cohen, Wilson, Stiles, Charlton and Moore in the first six jerseys. Back at Wembley a few weeks later, Greaves scored the only goal against Hungary and, said the *Daily Mirror*, was 'back to his dominating, battling best'. His final England game of the season was the first of their three-game European tour, a 1-1 draw in Yugoslavia in which young Blackpool midfielder Alan Ball made his debut.

Gradually the final pieces of Ramsey's World Cup team were taking their places. Greaves, the kind of goalscorer who would grace any international team, was surely among the most valuable of all.

8

LEAVING THE SHADOWS STANDING

'Putting it in the simplest form, I earn my living by giving goalkeepers backache. Nobody is fussy how I do it – with my head, chest, stomach, or if I bounce them in off my left ear – as long as I get them. And I don't know how I do get them.'

T HE inside-forward slips the ball beyond the full-back to the right winger. 'Great pass,' comes from deep within the packed terrace. As the No.7 shapes to deliver a cross into the penalty area another voice pipes up, 'Roy is running into the box. He's unmarked.' The cross is duly delivered and the No.9 connects with a thumping volley from near the penalty spot, almost ripping the net from its moorings. Melchester Rovers have scored again, Roy Race the hero once more.

Such scenes were portrayed on a weekly basis once Roy of the Rovers kicked his first ball in the pages of *Tiger* in 1954, a symbol of the enduring place that the English centre-forward occupied in the national consciousness. Wingers such as Stanley Matthews and Tom Finney might have been blessed with their own particular genius, but the No.9 was the goalscorer, the alpha male. Alongside him, the inside-forwards played clearly defined supporting roles. Melchester's Blackie Gray was never going to get his own comic strip. The inside-forward was responsible for prompting and setting up; the dutiful sidekick asking the plain best friend to team up in the dance hall so that the princess was free to be swept off her feet by our hero. Roy Race could never have been anything but a No.9, a fictional continuation of the line of Dixie Dean, Tommy Lawton, Jackie Milburn and Nat Lofthouse – the players boys longed to be when they kicked balls around streets, backyards and playgrounds.

Jimmy Greaves played an important part in changing all that. If Roy of the Rovers had been dreamt up 10 years later, he might well have been a poacher in the manner of Greaves; just as his creation in the 21st century would likely have seen him born as a modern-day Messi-style 'No.10'.

In the years immediately before Greaves's first season as top scorer in the First Division – in the midst of which was the creation of Race – centre-forwards dominated that particular honour: Ronnie Allen, Lofthouse, John Charles, Bobby Smith. Stan Mortensen had led the way earlier in the decade, along with Jimmy Glazzard of Huddersfield Town, smaller but brilliant in the air, and Preston North End's Charlie Wayman, who at 5ft 6in was overlooked by England because the consensus was that a genuine international No.9 had to be taller than that. The only notable exception was 1952 chart-topper George Robledo, the Chilean forward who accompanied Milburn in Newcastle's attack.

Yet in the years that interspersed and followed Greaves's six seasons in pole position, the likes of Dennis Viollet, Tony Brown, Francis Lee, Mick Channon, even George Best, were to be found leading the charts as often as traditional centre-forwards such as Jeff Astle, Andy Gray and Bob Latchford. The mould had been broken. No longer would the No.9 dominate; for every Alan Shearer in the Premier League era there would be an Ian Wright.

It may be fanciful to claim that Greaves changed the game, or at least the nature of the goalscorer. Football was evolving anyway. Finally, as the Hungarians had shown a disbelieving nation in 1953, there was more to the game than sending the winger to the byline to pull the ball back on to the target man's head. The increasing use of a four-man defence meant that a little more guile was needed; someone who could run on to a through ball or wrong-foot an opponent around the box. But, undoubtedly, Greaves's phenomenal ability to fulfil that role helped to show what was possible; to illuminate the match-winning potential of the man at inside-forward. It changed the perception of goalscoring being the domain of the No.9 – although perhaps not immediately.

Even in John Moynihan's acclaimed book, *The Soccer Syndrome*, published in 1966, the author was comparing Greaves to Wilf Mannion – one of the finest creative inside-forwards of the post-war era but never a pure goalscorer – and describing him as 'an enigma'. 'His goalscoring abilities amazed us from the start,' he wrote. 'But while Greaves has scored bucketfuls of these goals during his subsequent transition from Chelsea to Milan, and finally to Tottenham, he has not always compensated for his lack of work in midfield, especially for England.' The fact that goals were required as 'compensation' for something else suggests a prevailing lack of understanding and appreciation for the new kind of player in his position that Greaves represented. Later that year, it would appear that perhaps Alf Ramsey had been reading Moynihan's work.

Clive Toye, writing in the *Daily Express* in 1962, predicted that 'several million words will be written in the years to come on how James Peter Greaves, a 22-year-old Cockney, scores goals'. The relevance of the geography might be questionable, but the statement proved to be undeniably true. There are a few thousand more coming up here. One reason for the volume is that Greaves himself was unable to offer the definitive guide to his genius. 'I never think about scoring goals,' he once said. 'I can never remember how they happened or what went right at the time.'

One might expect to find some clues in his 1966 instructional book, *Soccer Techniques and Tactics*, which contains chapters on various skills, such as passing, heading and tackling, and a breakdown of the positions on the field. Yet when he points out the need for inside-forwards to possess positional sense, he immediately apologises for introducing 'a touch of the Einsteins' into his text and says that 'good positioning is 60 per cent instinctive flair' in any case. The required ability to read the play is, he writes, 'a gift', while the poaching of goals comes with 'no hard and fast rules'. In other words, if you don't possess the in-born ability of a goalscorer you are unlikely to discover it within the binding of Greaves's book.

A further attempt to get Greaves to illuminate his ability in book form never got off the ground, as journalist Martin Samuel, his future ghostwriter at *The Sun*, explains. 'One of my first projects at Hayters Sports Agency was to ghost a book called *How to Score Goals*, by Malcolm Macdonald,' he says. 'I was told at the time that the project was originally intended for Jimmy, but when they had a meeting to discuss it and asked him for a rough outline of how he scored goals he said, "I don't know. I turned up and the ball turned up. I don't know why I was there and I don't know why the ball was there, but I knew where the ball was going to be." Right, so that was one paragraph and they needed another 75,000 words.

'It was decided that Jimmy couldn't possible encapsulate how he scored goals; whereas Malcolm, who wasn't an instinctive goalscorer, worked and worked at his career and his art. He kept notes on all the defenders and goalkeepers he played against, to the extent where he discovered on an England trip that Phil Thompson of Liverpool didn't like garlic. So he used to eat cloves of garlic before he played Liverpool, just to give himself a yard of space. He realised that Alan Stevenson, the Burnley goalkeeper, stood on his heels, so if you hit the ball near to him he couldn't get down to it. If you tried to find the corner, he could spring there, but he couldn't get down close to him. Jimmy never analysed things in that way.'

Moynihan at least elicited from Greaves some consideration of how his craft – or was it an art? – had changed over the years since his debut. 'When I first came into the game there wasn't much thought behind it. In the old days it was all the long ball through the middle.' The 'revolution' of defensive football that he said was arriving in the game was forcing him to refine the way he went about his business. 'You can't get a ball through like you used to be able to. Therefore you have got to look for a wall-passing type of game, running on to a ball laid sideways.'

Which still doesn't offer too much insight into why Greaves was so good at scoring goals, regardless of the nature of the defence confronting him. It is left, then, to his colleagues and opponents to attempt to give form to his essence.

Four recurring abilities shaped his genius: the instinct for being in the right place; defence-defying speed over short distances; a temperament that allowed him to retain composure in front of goal; and the basic skills that meant he could direct the ball wherever he wanted it to go. Many have had the majority; few have had all those qualities in such abundance and been able to combine them to such devastating effect.

Around the box, Greaves had the instincts of a pure predator, a hungry polar bear sniffing out a penguin through three feet of ice. It was what led Peter Dobereiner of *The Observer* to describe him 'suddenly popping up through a trap door in the penalty box to score, having a quick snog with his mates and disappearing again'.

Spurs winger Terry Dyson had the pleasure of lining up outside Greaves for several years, concluding that 'he's the best goalscorer I've ever seen; he could just knock them in from anywhere'. He suggested, 'It was all about anticipation and making those runs. Jim would make a run 12 times and always be in a position to score if the ball came to him.'

Long-time opponent and future television colleague Ian St John, no mean operator around the penalty area for Liverpool, explains, 'Jimmy could sniff out where the ball would be dropping in the six-yard box and put it in the net. Thank you very much. That awareness is a talent; to know exactly where the ball is going to arrive at a certain time and get in position to make use of it.'

Bill Nicholson, who wanted to sign Greaves as a schoolboy and was determined that he would one day wear the lilywhite shirt of Spurs after seeing him score against them on his Football League debut through a combination of 'innovation and genius', recalled, 'Sometimes the ball would come towards him and you thought the defender who was marking him would get it before he did, but he would stick out a foot and knock it away. Even when he was late, he seemed capable of winning a rebound off his shins and the ball would fall conveniently for him to shoot ... Jim's anticipation was first-class. It was as though he was willing the ball to come to him.'

Cliff Jones was prompted to ask Greaves one day why he insisted on chasing what appeared to be lost causes. 'You could usually see when the ball went into area and the goalkeeper was always going to collect it, but Jim would always close him down,' he remembers. 'I said to him, "What did you do that for, Jim? You know the keeper is going to save it." Jim replied, "Yes, he will collect it nine times out of 10, but the one time he doesn't I will be there." That was his way of thinking.'

Ron Flowers, a team-mate for England and opponent at Wolverhampton Wanderers, felt that it was his 'ability to combine swiftness of thought and movement' that created his heightened awareness of a goalscoring opportunity and left defenders and, often, the match officials trailing in his wake. 'It has made linesmen flag him offside when in reality he has been onside at the time the pass was made,' he observed. It was the same quality that prompted Toye to write that he was 'a man who takes delight in missing mayhem by a fraction'.

The single attribute that made Greaves so difficult for opponents to deal with, it is universally agreed, was his quickness off the mark. Whether it was getting away from a marker in order to take up a position to receive a pass, or eluding tackles once he had the ball at his feet, his dynamism over short distances could be unstoppable. 'I am by no means slow on my feet,' he said with understatement in *My World of Soccer*. 'Admittedly, I wouldn't run 100 yards in much less than 11 seconds, but it is not overall pace that makes a good inside-forward. Speed over the first 10 or 20 yards is what counts.'

'He was the Lionel Messi of his day,' says Alan Mullery, who cites the Barcelona and Argentina phenomenon multiple times in conversation of Greaves's qualities – and is not alone in doing so. 'A genius. It's an easy word to spell with Jim. He had similar build, similar quality to Messi: pace over 10 or 15 yards; very quick, very good foot movement.'

As Joe Mercer, title-winning manager at Manchester City, put it, 'All of a sudden, when the chance arises, Jimmy is gone. He had left his shadow standing.'

'He was lightning off the mark and with the ball at his feet,' remembered Alan Gilzean, who had several years of watching him up close. 'To be that fast with the ball at your feet is difficult. It was like it was on string on the end of his feet. His balance and awareness of all that was around him, especially in the penalty box, was unbelievable. And remember that the Tottenham pitch was diabolical. It was a mud heap. For him to show the skill he did on the pitch as it was then, well, just imagine if we had a pitch like they have now. Bowling greens now, aren't they? Some of the goals he scored – against Manchester United, Newcastle – he gets the ball, goes past two or three guys on the way to goal as if they were not there.'

Team-mate Phil Beal observes, 'He was so successful because he kept the ball very close to his feet – no more than a yard away – so you never had any chance of trying to tackle him. If you tried, he was so quick he would go straight past you. When I came up against him in five-a-sides, you daren't dive in. He would walk past you; he was so quick on the ball and had such great control. George Best was little bit like Jimmy.'

Former Arsenal defender Bob McNab suggests, 'Jimmy was quick, and what highlights the difference between him and, say, Ian Wright or Denis Law, was that he could score goals from the halfway line. He could beat two or three people. Denis didn't beat people. Players such as Harry Kane and Jamie Vardy are great timers of runs, but you don't see them beating men like Jimmy did.'

Jones echoes that assessment. 'He was one of those players who had that something extra. There have been a lot of great goalscorers, like Lineker and Shearer and Harry Kane, but Jim was the best of the lot. He was a scorer of simple goals and he was a scorer of great goals. They couldn't do what Jim could do. I have seen him pick a ball up and go past three or four players, dummy the goalkeeper and roll it into the back of the net.'

At the height of his career, Flowers nominated Greaves as 'among the speediest men with the ball the game has known since World War II'. Writing in 1962, Johnny Haynes, one of his England captains, had already seen enough to predict that Greaves 'may well prove to be the greatest goalscorer football has ever known. No player has such a facility for being in the right place at the right time in the penalty area, no player has ever had such cold finishing power.' Once again, it was that speed that Haynes felt set him apart. 'Greaves is tremendously fast, but deceptively fast. When he is moving with the ball defenders often look like reaching him, but in fact they never get close, so smoothly does he accelerate. And when he is in shooting position all this hectic speed seems to vanish and everything stops and he has all the time in the world to score.'

As Haynes suggests, acceleration counts for little if, once speed has created the opportunity, nerves and anxiety take it away again. Such a thing never happened to Greaves. There have been professional hitmen with less ice in their veins. 'He was so calm; he never panicked,' says Beal.

'He was so cool coming into the penalty area,' agrees former England colleague Tony Waiters, one of the many First Division goalkeepers who had sleepless nights knowing they would be up against him the next day. 'It was definitely cat and mouse,' the former Blackpool man continues. 'You couldn't afford to anticipate where he might put the ball because he was so calm and assured that, if you did, he would put it the other way. He was so under control. He came in and he would be watching you. If you made one false move that was it.'

Former Leeds midfielder Johnny Giles, a renowned commentator on the game since his retirement, has his own theory about the origins of Greaves's calmness. 'He didn't seem to care if he missed a chance,' he says in his 2012 book *The Great and The Good*. 'It was as if he really didn't give a damn' – not because he did not care about the outcome, but that he was convinced he would score next time. Greaves was never one to worry about losing his touch. Had he been a professional golfer, he would have been the least likely ever to suffer from the 'yips'. 'He was always in that laid-back state of mind,' Giles continues, adding that 'he sort of played for fun'.

Both Waiters and Jimmy Armfield remembered the enjoyment Greaves derived from playing in goal during games of five-a-side in training. Yet they suggested that part of his enthusiasm came from the opportunity to achieve a greater understanding of the choices facing a keeper; all the better to outsmart him. 'On the training ground he would always be working around the goal and if he wasn't practising his finishing, he would be between the posts with the gloves on making saves,' Armfield explained. 'He didn't really bother with what went on in the middle of the pitch; he was a penalty area animal. When he reached the danger zone he was so cool. Even in the tightest situation he had the ability to slip past defenders, go round the keeper and plant the ball in the net.'

McNab observes that Greaves was, literally, one step ahead of the goalkeepers confronting him. 'Goalkeepers have changed,' he says. 'If you watch them now, they come out earlier and plant. In the old days, goalies used to come running out late and you can't dive when you are running forward with one foot in front of the other. You can only fall down. What Jimmy did, he hit it one stride before anyone else would. He had the calmness to do that. Later, Charlie George could do it as well; he gave a brilliant example of that when we beat Manchester City in the FA Cup in 1971.'

Rodney Marsh, who was making his way in the game with Fulham before his transfer to Queens Park Rangers, was another who took note of Greaves's early execution. 'The most fascinating thing about him was his composure. Jimmy's finishing was natural and unique. I tried to copy the way he shot the ball so early, but you couldn't learn it – it was instinct. The ball was often past the goalkeeper before he had even seen it. Jimmy had very little backlift, which goalkeepers hate.'

According to Frank McLintock, 'He got a kick out of tantalising goalkeepers, putting them in a position from which they could not make a quick enough adjustment, then poking the ball just out of reach.'

Flowers described Greaves in 1962 as 'one of the most balanced young chaps I have ever met' and said that he 'refuses to be overawed by anything on the field'. He added, 'He does not lose his poise, confidence or determination. On the contrary he seems to be encouraged by a reverse.'

Nicholson, meanwhile, felt it was a 'natural gift of timing' that made him so lethal. 'When confronted by the goalkeeper he seemed to be able to whip the ball into the net almost every time, while other forwards in a similar position would often find the keeper making a fine save. Greaves gave the keeper no chance.'

Which brings us to the precision with which Greaves, nerveless and detached from the emotion of the moment, executed his craft. Team-mate Jimmy Robertson explains, 'When he put the ball in the net it always found the corners and he very rarely blasted anything. He just popped it in the corner out of the way.'

Greaves, writing in 1962, said that he never consciously worked out how he would deliver the ball into the net once it arrived at his feet. 'I just get in as close as I can and let rip,' was one of his descriptions, which fails to do justice to that knack of being able to shoot, thanks to his two-footedness, before goalkeepers were expecting it. He even argued that such an aptitude for goalscoring sometimes came as a surprise – 'a warm sort of shock'.

He did attribute much of his success to focusing on accuracy rather than strength. Rare was the time when the 5ft 8in figure of Greaves belted in a screamer from outside the box. 'With little power to call upon, I have to work at close range, rather like a boxer with a short reach,' was how he described it.

Flowers concluded, 'Although he possesses a fine shot in both feet, he prefers to take the ball as near as he can to the goalkeeper before gliding it past him. Jimmy, in fact, places his shots with the accuracy of a big-time golfer putting on the green.'

There was another factor in the accomplishments of Greaves. He was not without strength, an asset that Bobby Moore felt was underrated. 'What some people didn't appreciate was that it wasn't just speed and skill, it had a lot to do with determination,' he said. 'Men like him and Law and Pelé, they doubled their strength when going in on goal, and you couldn't get them off the ball.'

Gilzean explained, 'Greavsie could ride tackles. Some players have a natural ability to see what is coming and he would just glide past it and keep the ball at his feet. That is what made him so special. You could closely mark him in the box and he would go around two guys and roll it into the net.'

Mullery continues, 'The amount of goals he scored playing football at the time he played was remarkable. There were people trying to hurt him, trying to snap bits off him, and he used to get through it. He wasn't the bravest man in the world, but he didn't have to be. He didn't have to tackle. He was there to score goals and he did it marvellously. He wasn't scared of being tackled. He would just stare at the people. But that was basically the only way to stop him. You couldn't mark him for the whole game. When we played Manchester United, Nobby Stiles would follow him all over the park and still get beat.'

The longer Greaves's career continued and the more success he achieved, the greater his need for every ounce of whatever strength and bravery he possessed. A hardened cynicism was coming into the game as the 1960s advanced, typified for many by Don Revie's Leeds United, who combined great skill with uncompromising pragmatism to rise from Division Two to the top of the English game. 'Some forwards didn't like the physical stuff,' said Norman Hunter, the player who, for many, personified their approach. 'Jimmy Greaves was a great goalscorer, one of the very best, but he didn't relish the rough stuff.' Hunter recalled Revie telling his players to ignore Greaves if he was outside the penalty area because 'he wasn't the bravest of players or the hardest of workers' and 'he didn't like it when the tackles are flying in'. Near to goal, of course, it was a different matter. 'He was capable of brilliance.'

So, was it possible for opponents to combat the Greaves threat? Mullery, who had plenty of years in opposition to Greaves before teaming up with him at Spurs, suggests, 'The only thing you could do was kick him; that was the only way to stop him. He would beat four or five people and score, so you had to foul him to stop him.'

Cohen, Mullery's Fulham team-mate, adds, 'He was razor sharp in the box. Over the five or six yards he needed to make the final touch, he was there. You couldn't concentrate on where everyone was in the area, but you tried to make sure he was surrounded. You needed guys who were good at marking man to man because you just couldn't take your eye off him. You didn't know where he was on the pitch. Many clubs designated a certain player who was good at marking and was very quick. But the forward thinks first, so you needed someone who understands the play and reads the game well.

'You could mark him out of the game for 89.99 minutes and in that one bit you have left he could be devastating. There was great difficulty in keeping him out of the scoreline. He would always slip you and do something against you. If he didn't score he would help someone else.'

Marsh claimed that 'his best trick was to disappear from a game, leaving you wondering if he'd ever been on the pitch in the first place, then bang. You'd be two goals down thanks to Jim's only two touches in 90 minutes.'

Law, the man against whom Greaves's brilliance was often measured, voiced an identical opinion. 'You might not know he was there for 88 minutes, and he still might finish up on the scoresheet with a couple of goals to his name. Greaves was a different player compared to me and other forwards. He was the best pure striker, best goalscorer, I have ever seen. When he had the ball in front of goal there was always absolute panic among the opposing defence.'

Mike England, who played against Greaves several times before teaming up with him at Tottenham, continues, 'Sometimes someone would be given a specific job to mark him; told to just stay with him and try to keep him quiet because he was the main danger. It was a difficult task, but you did it because he was going to be the most likely one to score. You would think you had him where you wanted him, but then he popped up when you least expected it.'

Robertson remembers, 'When we played Chelsea, Greavsie would be marked by Ron Harris. Jim would say, "I am wasting my time here, I will just stay out on the wing." But that left space for other people to play in, and after you hadn't seen him for 80 minutes he would go on a little run and stick it in the net. Courage was never a problem with him and it was very difficult to tackle him because he was naturally very fit, had a solid build and he would skip out of the way.'

England colleague Armfield admitted that it took him a while to understand why opponents made such a poor job of negating the threat of Greaves. 'Defences seemed to open up in front of him,' he observed. 'Playing at right-back for England and with Jim at inside-right, I had a perfect view and I used to ask myself why international defenders didn't close in on him. Instead, they seemed to veer away in the wrong direction, leaving Jim free to home in on goal. I came to realise it was Jim's skill, pace and positional sense that created this impression.'

The question of whether goalscoring is an art or a science – and is therefore a natural-born instinct or a skill to be learned and refined – would seem to be redundant in the case of Greaves. There are few who saw him play up close who do not subscribe to the artistic school of thought. 'His ability to score goals was magical,' says Mullery. 'You could watch it over and over again on television and on the pitch and how he did it, God only knows. You can't explain it. It was a natural thing.'

Typical views of Greaves's genius were expressed in a *Daily Mirror* report of a 3-0 Tottenham victory against Birmingham City in 1962. Not only was opposing centre-half Trevor Smith quoted as saying 'don't ask me how he does it', but reporter Harry Langton concluded, 'Six hundred FA coaches studying Greaves for six months could never copy what he did.'

In a *FourFourTwo* article on goalscoring, Thierry Henry recalled becoming more proficient in front of goal by working against mannequins, although Kevin Phillips, a prolific Premier League scorer at various clubs, now working as a forwards' coach, suggested that it was possible to drill players on timing their runs, but added, 'I often found myself in positions and didn't really know how I got there. I think that's something you're born with.'

In the same piece, Southampton legend Matthew Le Tissier proposed that 'natural goalscorers are born. They've got an instinct which I think comes very naturally to them. It's very difficult to pass on the skill of scoring goals to someone who just doesn't get it.' Those who witnessed or know the story of Le Tissier's languid brilliance would hardly be surprised to see him supporting the theory of goalscoring as an unteachable gift. If he was hardly renowned for his dedicated hours on the training field, then the same could be said of Greaves.

'He did not like training,' Nicholson wrote, 'but, like many geniuses, he realised that his gift had to be worked at and he would practise like a golfer practises his swing.' Future Spurs team-mate Joe Kinnear argued that 'Jimmy Greaves never had to work at his game – he was just so talented. In training all he mainly did was practise goalscoring. It was amazing to watch him.' Yet one senses that even his willingness to bang the ball into the net during training stemmed less from a need to refine his craft than it did from his desire to avoid any other kind of endeavour. 'He didn't like training and hated stuff like running or cross-country,' Kinnear added. 'He would beg lifts on milk floats or hide a bike and ride it home. If he was forced to do a whole run because Eddie Baily or someone was watching his every step, he'd come in half an hour after most of us had gone home.'

According to Dave Mackay, 'During pre-season, Jimmy wouldn't come in from a road run until I'd be back and showered. He just couldn't do it.' Gilzean concurred, adding, 'Jim wasn't a great trainer. He didn't like the body work and all that stamina work. We used to run 10 laps around the park and him and Pat Jennings would always be at the back.'

Such quirks were easily tolerated by his colleagues. For, as much as a nightmare as he was for opponents – and sergeant-major trainers such as Baily – so he was a dream for those team-mates. 'I had never really played centre-forward before going to Spurs,' said Gilzean. 'I played there for Scotland, but for Dundee I was the dual striker. Jimmy made it so easy. If we had a corner against us we would leave him on the halfway line because he wasn't good in the air and he couldn't tackle. We could hit a long ball up to him and he would go past a couple of guys they had left back to mark him and put the ball in the back of the net. He could turn a defensive position into an attacking position instantly.'

An ever-present element of the career of Jimmy Greaves was the question of how much there was to his game beyond the most difficult skill of all; that of scoring goals. The impression of him as a one-dimensional performer was something that he railed against at times, conscious of the impact it had on managers such as Alf Ramsey who valued multi-tooled players. On other occasions, he appeared content to accept that 'I am what I am' and if the amount of goals he scored was not good enough for some, well, there was not much he could do about it.

In his 1966 book, *My World of Soccer*, he conceded that his role at Chelsea had been 'to score goals, without having to contribute much else. I played a waiting game in the hope of poking one in.' He also suggested that such an outlook was all well and good when he was 'at the kindergarten stage' of his career, but as he matured he needed to be capable of more if he was to be considered an accomplished all-round player. But, he noted, 'It appears at the moment I am stuck with the tag of goalscorer.'

There are enough clips of old games to show him delivering the ball from wide areas to prove there was more to his game than standing on the six-yard line waiting for tap-ins. He was even frequently deployed as a taker of corner-kicks, something Roy Hodgson might have pointed out when criticised for using Harry Kane in the same role during the 2016 European Championship finals.

And when he was in his most socialist mood he pointed out the injustice of the scorer taking all the glory. 'Making goals is a far greater art than scoring,' he'd argued in his first autobiography. 'Only I know full well that all I did was tap the ball into the net and the chap who made the goal will be looking through the paper in vain for a mention of his name and wondering what the hell was the point in playing.'

Early in his Tottenham career he said, 'In my heart I have always wanted to be known as a footballer rather than just a scorer.' Yet, he could never shake the reality that it was his weight of goals that were the true measure of his worth. And, when he was being honest, it was what mattered most to him.

He wrestled with the conundrum in his conversation for *The Soccer Syndrome*. 'It worries me if I don't score during a game,' he stated. 'This, unfortunately, is what people expect me to do. It's a bit unfortunate I have got this role, so I hope to score every game I play. I get a lot of satisfaction by playing well, but I prefer to score because it keeps the spectators happy.'

In other words, why worry about being seen as an all-round contributor when you could be remembered in history as the greatest goalscorer who ever lived?

9

WHAT'S IT ALL ABOUT, ALFIE?

*'I danced around the pitch with everybody else,
but even in this moment of triumph and great
happiness, deep down I felt my sadness ... I had
missed out on the match of a lifetime and it hurt.'*

JIMMY Greaves had travelled home from the 1962 World Cup
in Chile somewhat sceptical about what the tournament had
to offer. Early in 1966, in the same publication that he would
use to apologise for the tone of some his subsequent comments
about international football, he addressed the event once more.
Introducing a chapter entitled 'The World Cup' in his book, *My
World of Soccer*, he wrote, '[It] is supposed to be a sporting occasion,
but unfortunately, with so much at stake in politics and prestige,
the competition seems slightly off-keel. Give me the FA Cup or
European Cup any day.'

Knowing the fate that befell Greaves that summer you might
assume those words had been written in the wake of events that
would, regrettably for him, come to define his England career. The
fact that the book came out before the tournament is indicative

of a couple of things. Firstly, it reflects England's ambivalent relationship with the tournament, and indeed any kind of football that did not involve playing in three inches of mud on a wet February evening. It was somewhat foreign and, therefore, should not be taken too seriously. Secondly, it demonstrates the reality that it was only once the games had begun and England started to look like they might really be able to win that the country fell victim to the kind of all-consuming World Cup preoccupation that would never again loosen its grip.

Even his assurance that 'if I am called upon for World Cup duty, I will be out there plugging away with all the determination I can muster' does not exactly convey someone anticipating what might be the crowning moment of his career; the opportunity to go down in the history of his nation; and the possibility of changing his own life forever. Ironically, it was only after Greaves had missed out on English football's greatest moment that he came to understand its significance. And would have to live with it forever.

England's traditional October games in the 1965-66 season had brought little to encourage Greaves to dream of glory. A 0-0 draw against Wales in Cardiff was followed two weeks later by a 3-2 home loss to Austria. 'If we are defeated in this game it will be a disaster,' Alf Ramsey had said before kick-off. After seeing his team concede three second-half goals and hearing the jeers of the Wembley crowd, he emerged from the dressing room to admit that England had made mistakes in defence, but added pointedly, 'We failed in the 18-yard area. I thought there was only one team in it in the main and the chances we created were numerous.'

Ramsey's comment that 'there is no thought of discarding and starting again' might have been a relief for a goalless Greaves, but it would nevertheless be some time before he wore the England shirt once more.

Greaves had helped Tottenham get off to a fast start to the season, his late winner against Leeds United giving him six goals in five games and putting his team on top of the table. With time running out and Greaves having been held to one goal, Leeds were hopeful of securing a 2-2 draw. 'Jimmy Greaves was the one I really hated playing against,' recalled Leeds defender Norman Hunter. 'I was right on top of my game and hadn't given him a kick all afternoon.' Hunter recalled Gilzean, Sprake and himself all colliding as the Spurs man chased a loose ball. 'We all went sprawling and the ball went up in the air and who should be there? ... Greavsie just tapped the ball into the back of the net.'

Two goals in a victory over West Bromwich Albion on the last Saturday of October took his tally for the season into double figures. His goals were achieved, said the *Daily Mirror*, with the 'easy grace that marks the world-class player'. The same report highlighted the criticism frequently directed at him for an apparent lack of desire in some games, and asked – not for the first time – why he could not find the net as easily for England. 'Anyone would think I intentionally go out in some games with the intention of not trying,' Greaves said with obvious exasperation. Equally maddening was the inconsistency that was becoming a part of this Spurs team's DNA, despite the recent introduction of the dark-haired Northern Irish goalkeeper, Pat Jennings, signed from Watford for £27,000.

Now, personal frustration was about to befall Greaves. Untroubled throughout his career by serious injury, he was reported to have had an attack of flu when he missed a defeat at Nottingham Forest. 'He has been in bed all over the weekend,' wife Irene reported. 'It is very doubtful he will play for England on Wednesday.'

He was to miss a lot more football than an international against Northern Ireland. By the end of the month he had spent time in hospital and been diagnosed with hepatitis. 'I have to cut out all fatty food for about six months,' he explained. 'No chips, roast potatoes or beer. In fact, all the things I like. It looks like being a grim Christmas, but I must follow the hospital instructions. If anything goes wrong between now and February and I end up in hospital again there must be a doubt about my fitness for the World Cup.' Club doctors, and his own GP, arranged for Greaves to be assessed further by Sheila Sherlock, a liver disease specialist, who advised on a plan to get him back in training.

Given the events of his later life, Greaves was keen to point out in future years that, although hepatitis is an inflammation of the liver, his condition was not caused by excessive intake of alcohol. It was more likely to have been contracted by way of a virus.

In what might be seen as a portent, England produced their best performance for some time while Greaves was on the sidelines counting his calories. A functional victory over Northern Ireland was followed by an eye-catching 2-0 win against Spain in Madrid in early December, with goals by Roger Hunt and Joe Baker. As well as creating optimism about the following summer, the game had seen England take the field without a recognised winger. Alan Ball, playing in a wide midfield position, was the star performer, dragging opponents all over the place with his limitless energy. Although Ramsey would persevere with wingers right up to the latter stages of the World Cup, he had seen enough to file away this formation for future use.

'It is difficult to see how Ramsey can disturb this team,' suggested Desmond Hackett in the *Daily Express*. 'The only chance for Greaves is to take over the outside-right spot, currently held by Alan Ball, and do the roving job which Ball did so capably. But Greaves will first have to emphasise that he shares Ball's appetite for action.' If Greaves's hopes of an England future truly did depend on giving the impression that he could match the dynamic Ball for expenditure of effort, then he really was in trouble.

Having missed 12 League games, only four of which Tottenham had won, Greaves was back in his team's colours – wearing an unfamiliar No.11 shirt – for a 4-0 home victory against Blackburn Rovers, during which he was on target with a penalty. However, he found the net only once in the next eight games before being left out for a game at Sheffield Wednesday.

The truth was that, having got through his first couple of games back on adrenalin, he found that his energy levels were not as they had been before his illness. Only hard work would get him to the required physical condition for Ramsey to consider him for a leading role in the World Cup, a harsh realisation for someone famed for his dislike of training. 'I have never worked harder in my life to recapture optimum fitness,' he recalled of weightlifting sessions and drills intended to restore his acceleration off the mark. 'I hardly touched alcohol during this period,' he added. 'My desire to regain full fitness and my place in the England team far outweighed any desire I had for a beer.'

His absence from the Spurs team lasted only one game, being reinstated the following week to score a penalty in a 1-1 draw at Northampton Town. 'Greaves is not back to his best,' Nicholson explained. 'But he needs the matches to help him to return to top form.' He scored again from the spot in the next game, but only one goal from open play in his run of seven matches to end the season suggested that all was not as it should be. Greaves knew his body well enough to recognise that he had lost half a yard of pace, a diminution of his most vital asset. Ironically, Greaves's face was appearing across pages in national newspapers around this time, with wife Irene looking on proudly, as he gulped back a glass of Robinsons Lemon Barley Water. The drink was, Irene revealed in the ad, responsible for 'his stupendous energy'. Given the concern over that very aspect of his game in the wake of his illness, the advertising agency must have felt cursed by the fates of timing.

Yet Greaves remained confident that he was 'good enough and sharp enough' to outperform any other striker Ramsey might have considered. He was given the opportunity to prove his point in early May, when he finally lined up again for his country against Yugoslavia. In their previous two games, England had beaten West Germany 1-0 at Wembley and won 4-3 in Scotland, increasing Greaves's sense of urgency to re-establish himself in the team. He took only nine minutes to score the first goal in his team's

2-0 victory, heading home a Terry Paine cross, and felt that he was 'beginning to motor with some of my old enthusiasm and sharpness'. Yet Ken Jones of the *Daily Mirror* had his doubts, pointing out England's 'eternal problems in front of goal'. He added, 'Greaves took one chance, made half a dozen others, but ended up as guilty as the rest.'

Having returned to the fold with a goal, there was never any real likelihood that Greaves would not make Ramsey's World Cup squad. He was duly named among the 22 players selected from the 27 who took part in England's pre-tournament camp in the Shropshire countryside at Lilleshall. Any fears he had over the lingering effects of hepatitis were being kept to himself. 'It robbed me of that vital extra bit of speed,' he would record. 'But I was not ready to admit that to myself when I was called up for the World Cup. I had worked ruddy hard for the chance and felt I deserved my place in the squad.'

Ramsey's selection plans for the tournament, the last World Cup to be played without substitutes, remained closely guarded. Yet his squad, however much they might have speculated over who would play, were united in their confidence in a man who had played 32 games for England as a right-back and then led Ipswich Town to their remarkable League Championship in 1962. 'When you looked at Ipswich's title, you had to ask how it could possibly happen,' said George Cohen. 'It had to be down to the manager.'

Ramsey lacked public charisma and was often teased for the elocution lessons that had given him a clipped delivery; a long way from the Dagenham he and Greaves had grown up in. He could be terse with reporters, even though he had given them a confident prediction that 'England will win the World Cup' during his first summer in charge of the team three years earlier. Yet the kind of strategic pragmatism through which he had masterminded Ipswich's triumph and the fierce loyalty he demonstrated towards his players meant he never had to worry that the dressing room was not fully behind him.

Greaves acknowledged some of the players even 'loved' their manager, although he would not include himself in that category. 'But I certainly respected the man, held him in the highest esteem and believed him to be a great manager, even before England won the World Cup.'

Ramsey had maintained throughout his time with England that not too much should be read into individual team selections; that no one should become too comfortable or depressed over every selection or exclusion. That was more relevant than ever in England's last four warm-up games in the weeks leading up to the start of the World Cup. All 22 players had the opportunity to play and no discernible first XI appeared to be emerging, although the final match – a 1-0 win in Poland – was the first in which the four-man midfield unit of Stiles-Ball-Charlton-Peters was employed and the line-up was only one player away from being the team that would make history. Greaves played in the final three of those contests, scoring four times in a 6-1 victory in Norway and winning his 50th cap in Denmark.

The Times had stressed the importance of his performance in Oslo by noting that 'for two seasons Greaves has never been sure of his place for England in a regime that demands results and scorns reputations. He must show that he can score the goals that others in recent months have found strangely beyond them.' He responded by equalising Norway's surprise opening goal with a header, before racing away from defenders to poke the ball low past the goalkeeper with his left foot a minute later. Seizing on a loose ball, he completed his hat-trick before half-time and then struck a right-foot volley on the run across goal for his fourth. It was, according to one report, 'a warning to the world'.

Yet there was a view being aired more frequently that Ramsey's insistence on a 4-3-3 system that used only one orthodox wide man, or the wingless 4-1-3-2 he'd deployed in Poland, made it more difficult for someone such as Greaves to be sure of his place. Bobby Charlton sensed that Ramsey was searching for 'what made a team rather than individuals' and that perhaps a Hunt-Hurst front two might better serve the needs of the collective. 'The problem for Jimmy, it was becoming apparent enough, was that in Alf Ramsey's mind it was not so much all about how one player could from time to time hit sublime notes, but perhaps how another, or maybe a pair of them, could strike a more consistent rhythm of effort and integration with his team-mates.'

Greaves could easily be viewed by those who chose to do so as a 'one-dimensional' player. Never mind that his single dimension happened to encompass the essence of the game: sticking the ball in the net. He would have to hope that Ramsey did not desire more than that. 'Greaves has often looked an ordinary player in the English team, which of course he isn't,' suggested John Moynihan in *The Soccer Syndrome*, published before the World Cup. 'While his style does not fit into Mr Ramsey's plans, his use as a danger man is still considerable, his talents compensating for those long, loping disappearances from the scene.' It is easy to imagine that, had substitutes been around in 1966, Ramsey might have used Greaves as the ideal late goalscoring option from the bench.

When Moynihan asked Greaves about how he saw himself fitting into Ramsey's plans, his answer was typically dismissive of anything relating to tactics. 'From what I see, systems like these go by the board at Wembley. The pitch isn't designed for any systems. It is a big pitch, a true pitch. It boils down to how well England play.'

At least if the allocation of jersey numbers were any gauge, then Greaves remained a first choice. Hurst recalls, 'Prior to the tournament, due to the numbers we were given, it looked like being me and Jimmy. We had our club numbers – 8 and 10 – and Roger Hunt, the other great forward I was competing with, was given 21. As it turned out, a loss of form from me meant he started with Roger and Jimmy. But at that stage I was just happy to be there and included in the best 22 players in the country.'

England were to face Uruguay, Mexico and France in the group stages, with all the games in the familiar setting of Wembley Stadium. Once a dog called Pickles had found the stolen Jules Rimet Trophy, and the Queen had performed the pre-game ceremonials in front of a crowd of 87,148,[17] the nation settled in front of its television sets for a Monday evening spent watching Ramsey's team putting the first of those opponents to the sword. Uruguay, however, had no intention of allowing England's forwards to entertain their audience in the manner of the London Palladium stars who filled television screens on the previous night of the week.[18] Their cynical demonstration of massed defence, which earned a 0-0 draw, prompted boos rather than curtain calls and left journalists already sceptical about England's chances in the tournament with little reason to change their minds.

For the first time in 52 Wembley internationals since the war, England failed to score, despite 15 corners to Uruguay's one. Greaves, who had been captured by the Pathé News cameras sitting calmly in the tunnel as the teams waited to enter, shot high and wide from the left edge of the box after being freed by Moore, and saw Jack Charlton head his flighted cross from the right narrowly wide in the dying minutes. 'It was a frustrating start,' he would recall, 'but I still knew in my heart that England were going to win the World Cup.'

Bobby Charlton rained down a barrage of long-range efforts and the final whistle found the Uruguayans celebrating as though they had won the cup. 'If I had to watch Uruguay in action every week,' wrote Donald Saunders in the *Daily Telegraph*, 'I should soon be looking for a more interesting job.'

Ramsey, who loved taking his players to the cinema on the night before a big game, decided that movies offered a way out

---

17 There were still tickets available to buy on the gate, an indication of the slow-developing nature of the World Cup fever that would take its grip a couple of weeks later.

18 *Sunday Night at the London Palladium* originally ran from 1955 to 1969 on ITV, hosted by the likes of Tommy Trinder, Bruce Forsyth and Jimmy Tarbuck, and has been resurrected on various occasions since.

of the gloom that threatened to find its way from the pages of the daily papers to the team's headquarters at the Hendon Hall Hotel.

The squad made a visit to Pinewood Studios, where Sean Connery was filming the new James Bond movie. Greaves was one of those photographed as the actors took a break from one of the first days of shooting *You Only Live Twice*, although the look on his face in one picture as Moore shook hands with Connery suggested he was still more concerned about the previous night's 0-0 than meeting 007. When comedian Norman Wisdom turned up to offer an impression of Greaves in action and asking, 'Is it too late to get in the team?' it seemed like time to return to the serious business of preparing to face Mexico four days later.

For more than half an hour in that game, England again seemed in danger of being stifled. That was until Charlton picked up the ball inside his own half, watched the Mexican defenders back off as he approached the penalty area, and belted the ball beyond the keeper's right arm from more than 25 yards. Greaves, meanwhile, was forced to go looking for space in deeper positions, his usual workplace inside the box being occupied by Mexico's plum-coloured jerseys. Instead, he turned provider for England's second goal after 75 minutes, his low shot from wide on the left being pushed out by keeper Ignacio Calderón for Hunt to knock in the rebound. England had won and Greaves felt he had made a valuable contribution, but what he needed was a goal to feel as though he was really part of the tournament.

Charlton would recall that 'behind his breezy manner, his tendency to play the joker in the company of his closest companion in the squad, Bobby Moore, Jimmy became an increasingly brooding figure'. Observing that Greaves was 'required now to operate in a system which could hardly have been less sympathetic to the special needs of a supreme individualist who offered one specific contribution', he saw him becoming 'the most vulnerable' member of the team if he did not get that all-important goal.

What Greaves got instead was an injury that might be said to have changed his life.

Facing France in their final group match, he had more attempts at goal than in the previous two games, beginning with a 10th-minute effort that he scuffed to keeper Marcel Aubour after England had broken quickly from defence. Four minutes later, he was bursting through the French defence again when Yves Herbet slid with foot raised to bring him down and catch him on the shin with his boot.[19] Under his sock, Greaves's skin opened in a gash that would eventually need stitches.[20] For now, without fuss, Greaves played on apparently unencumbered. The only obvious sign of injury was the spreading dark patch on the lower part of his white left sock. By the end of the game he thought his boot must be split, letting in the evening moisture, only to find when he returned to the dressing room that his foot was now soaked in blood.

After 28 minutes, Greaves had the ball in the net, although he was rightly ruled to have been offside when converting from a Martin Peters header. Four minutes before the break, he accelerated towards the left of the penalty area and, single-mindedly ignoring the option of squaring to Bobby Charlton, shot across goal and beyond the far post. It was the kind of outcome that prompted Eric Cooper to comment in the *Daily Mirror*, 'Greaves was always looking for goals all right, but he failed to see many of his better-placed colleagues. For a long time I thought there must be a boycott on Bobby Charlton.'

---

19 History appears to have unfairly recorded Joseph Bonnel as the man who inflicted the injury. Greaves's various accounts over the years, repeated by others, identify the French midfielder as the guilty man. Yet on the television coverage of the match it is clearly Herbet, in the No.15 shirt, who takes Greaves out by stabbing his boot into the England man's left shin on the exact point of his injury. There are no other tackles that one can observe later in the game likely to have caused such damage.

20 Quite how many stitches were required is another historical guessing game. In his 1972 autobiography, Greaves recalled that it was 'a couple'. In 1979, he wrote that it was four and in 1986 he told *The Boys of '66* author David Miller it was five. By the time of his 2003 memoirs that number had grown to 14. Other reports – both contemporaneous and in subsequent publications – have listed three, four, five, six and 10! It remained the only visible scar on his body into his old age.

Once again, he had to be content with having played a part in one of England's two goals, crossing from the left for Jack Charlton to head against the post. Hunt was on hand to score his second tap-in of the tournament and the Liverpool striker sealed a 2-0 win with a second-half header.

The following day's newspapers showed Greaves lying in the bath with his bandaged left shin propped up out of the water. 'I've got a hole big enough to smuggle diamonds in,' he remarked, 'but I have played with worse.' Yet that shin would now create a week or so of conjecture that would echo in future World Cups in the condition of Kevin Keegan's back, Bryan Robson's shoulder and David Beckham's metatarsal.

Hurst recalls his acceptance of being left on the sidelines during the group stages. 'It wasn't an issue for me. I was just happy to be sitting on the bench. There was no whingeing; we were a very professional outfit. We all had enormous respect for Alf and his decision was final.'

But there is a theory that Ramsey welcomed the opportunity to get Hurst into his line-up for the quarter-final against Argentina. It was not voiced by the manager at the time, but years later he stated, 'Jimmy Greaves had not shown his true form to substantiate his position in the team and would not have been selected for the Argentina match even if he had avoided injury in the French game.' Of course, it is easy to say that after the fact when history has proven it to be the right decision. Perhaps Ramsey preferred that instinct, rather than fate, received the credit for guiding his selection.

The stand-in immediately became the star. It was Hurst's header 12 minutes from time that beat Argentina, who had been runners-up in their group behind West Germany. It was also the first time in the tournament that Ramsey played without an orthodox winger and returned to the option of Peters and Ball operating on the left and right of Charlton in midfield. 'To be honest, he winged it,' was the ironic phrase Greaves used about

Ramsey's team selection in a BBC documentary to celebrate the 50th anniversary of 1966.

The game was guaranteed its place in World Cup infamy by the first-half dismissal of Argentina skipper Antonio Rattin, for what BBC analyst Jimmy Hill termed 'violence of the tongue'. Sent off for his constant haranguing of German referee Rudolf Kreitlein, it took eight minutes for Rattin to depart, during which time Argentina threatened to take no further part in the game.

Meanwhile, Portugal striker Eusebio had assumed the mantle that Greaves must have dreamt of at the start of the tournament. His seven goals, including four in a remarkable 5-3 comeback against underdogs North Korea in the quarter-finals, had propelled his country into the last four, where they would face the host nation. The game had originally been scheduled for Everton's Goodison Park, but pragmatism – some claimed home-team preferential treatment – saw the game switched to Wembley, where 96,000 saw an unchanged England team win 2-1 to secure their place in the final.

Charlton scored twice and Eusebio's penalty, the first goal conceded by England in the tournament, was merely a late consolation. The Manchester United man's second goal, 10 minutes from time, had a significance for Greaves. It resulted from Hurst battling to get behind his marker after Cohen's long ball, before laying on a pass for Charlton to score with a rising right-foot shot. Hurst had turned what looked like a harmless punt by Cohen into a goalscoring opportunity. It was the kind of contribution that observers, Ramsey included, would weigh up over the next few days.

Greaves, so it was said, was approaching fitness. If Ramsey wanted to pick him, he would be ready. 'It was apparent to everyone that Jimmy was training again and expecting to play,' said Peters. But which way was Alf leaning? That was the main talking point surrounding the England camp as the final against West Germany approached, although Bobby Charlton was convinced enough that

Ramsey would stick with a winning team to recall that 'it became a phantom debate'.

What many acknowledged as one of Greaves's assets, his ability to float around the margins of a game before making a decisive intervention, Ramsey perceived as unwillingness to put forth the selfless effort of men like Hunt, Ball and Stiles. Skipper Bobby Moore felt that if Greaves, his friend and room-mate, was fit, Ramsey should pick him. 'You wanted him there,' he said. 'The effect on the opposition would have been enormous.' And it was true that the Germans were far more likely to make defensive plans specifically to guard against a fully-effective Greaves than they would against Hurst or Hunt. Yet manager Helmut Schoen expected Ramsey to stick with his winning team. Noting Greaves's anticipation, dribbling skills and ability around the goal, he added that 'he was not a good team player'.

Predicting a closely-contested final, *The Times* suggested, 'It is the snatching of that half chance that Mr Ramsey will have in mind if he decides to recall Greaves. It would be typical of him to impishly squeeze a winner.' Meanwhile, Brian James told *Daily Mail* readers, 'I would play Greaves. His skill is undeniable. Only his application has ever been suspect, and in a World Cup final EVERYBODY works.'

A counter view, voiced by Ray Wilson to his team-mates and later publicly, was that Hurst was the better option in a tight game because of his strength in the air. He would offer the full-back an easy outlet if he found himself needing to clear the ball in a hurry.

Peters felt that England had not missed Greaves and were a steadier unit with Hurst in the side instead of someone who was 'a bit of a lone wolf'. He also felt that Greaves's insistence on playing without shin pads, increasing the risk of being re-injured, might have made Ramsey more reluctant to play him. 'Looking back,' says Hurst, 'and listening to some of the comments of the team, when I got in the side there was slightly better balance with me and Roger than there had been with him and Jimmy. They were both smaller players, whereas I was slightly more physical, better in the air, so the balance then was probably best with me and Jimmy or me and Roger.'

Even Norman Giller, *Daily Express* reporter and close friend of Greaves, could not bring himself to suggest that his pal should be recalled. 'Jimmy knew from the moment he got the gashed shin against France that his World Cup could be over,' he says. 'Of course, he desperately wanted to play in the final, but – by accident rather than design – Alf had found that collective, with Roger and Geoff prepared to sweat buckets for the team. The performances against Argentina and Portugal were exceptional and Alf was from the old school of "never change a winning team".'

Two days before the final, Giller's newspaper asked in its headline, 'Should Ramsey pick Greaves?' and tasked four of its writers with providing the answer. Clive Toye was the only one to respond in the affirmative, although it was hardly a ringing endorsement. He pointed out, 'Greaves has been in the form that made Brazilian manager Aymore Moreira say in 1962: "He will not score goals against good teams in international football."'

That, of course, was the crux of the matter. All the talk that Ramsey would be foolish to change a winning team would likely have been moot if Greaves had been banging in the goals in the group matches. He had not. He had looked off the pace and unthreatening; more like the man who scored only two goals from open play in 15 Spurs games after returning from hepatitis than the one who had led the First Division scorers so frequently during his career.

His shin injury was rarely mentioned in discussion of the merit of selecting him to face West Germany. Trainer Harold Shepherdson described Greaves as 'fit and raring to go', while journalist David Miller remembered watching the England team train and being convinced of his readiness. It was the loss of form since his illness that set many against him. 'Jimmy not being very well took the edge off his game,' says Cohen. 'He wasn't scoring goals as we expected him to in the early rounds. He looked as if he was out of sorts, even though you always had the feeling that he was going to do something. Then he got his nasty injury against the French.'

Jack Charlton would tell Miller for his book, *The Boys of '66*, 'Jimmy wasn't having a great time, he wasn't scoring and he was missing chances. I suspect Alf had wanted to bring in Geoff for some time, but his loyalty was such he'd found it difficult to leave Greaves out.'

It was a suspicion that Greaves had harboured for the previous three years. 'I recognised straight away that he would find it difficult to fit in someone like me. I think he realised I could do a job but I was not his kind of player.'

Bobby Charlton would even express an extreme version of that view in comments he made when he ended his playing career, describing Greaves as a 'bit of a luxury', someone who would 'score five if you won 8-0'. In a tight scrap, Charlton favoured Hurst, adding that 'you never saw Jimmy much in a game'. Miller would point out in his retrospective of the tournament, however, that Charlton's view was perhaps coloured by the fact that he 'stood to profit from the company of Hurst or Hunt'.

At least one person was unconvinced that Ramsey's final selection was a straight choice between Greaves and Hurst. Hunt was taking nothing for granted. He had never felt entirely secure in his England place, having played only 13 games during a four-year international career before the tournament began, despite a return of 12 goals. In addition, he felt that, as a Liverpool player, he had failed to garner the wholehearted support of the Wembley crowd and the influential London-based chief football writers.

John Connelly recalled, 'He'd personally had a good World Cup, scored goals, worked hard; he was popular in the squad. Yet he doubted himself. The London press was begging for Greaves, of course.' The last comment was not entirely true, but Miller did admit, 'Hunt was regarded as an impediment by many casual observers, and especially by the London press.'

Hunt would tell Miller, 'Alf went for reliable people, but you couldn't be sure in that situation. I wasn't a regular before the World Cup and didn't feel a regular till it was all over. So much of the time it had been Jimmy or me. Of the six times I was dropped, five times it was for Jimmy.'

No one appreciated the qualities of Hunt more than his long-time striking partner at Liverpool, Ian St John. 'I played with him for 10 years and he was a great goalscorer,' he recalls. 'Some managers would want to see the players putting effort into the game and doing the chasing, the tackling, the hard work that is required at times. Jimmy, by his own admission, didn't fancy that. But Alf trusted Roger and he would go for the worker rather than the player who was, not lazy, but was a non-worker. That was how Roger got his chance, and he was a smashing player. He was like Jimmy in that he could get into goalscoring positions, but he would do the hard stuff as well. He would run and chase and tackle; a great team player.'

In a 1995 BBC interview, Ramsey said he 'probably spent four or five nights worrying' about this particular selection. 'This is an unconvincing exaggeration,' suggests Ramsey biographer Leo McKinstry. 'Alf had already decided to drop Greaves before the Argentina game.'

Ramsey used a trip to the cinema on the eve of the final to quietly tell 10 of his players, including both Hurst and Hunt, that they had been selected to face a West German team that had beaten the Soviet Union at Goodison Park to reach the final. The only one of the starting eleven who was made to wait was Ball, whose good news was held back until the morning of the game. Ramsey never explained his reticence over that final place, although Hurst recalls Ball speculating that the manager might have been thinking of leaving him out to allow Greaves to return as part of a three-man forward line.

Greaves, meanwhile, had secretly suspected that his tournament was over from the moment of his injury. He'd become even more convinced of that two days before the final when he had remarked to Shepherdson on the coach back from training that 'it is going to be difficult to get back'. Shepherdson, with whom Greaves had formed a close relationship, looked silently out of the window. Yet Greaves could not help but maintain some small grain of hope and had awoken on the day of the final only 99 per cent certain that he would be on the sidelines. He had his one per cent of optimism eradicated by Ramsey in mid-morning. By that time, Moore had already been told by Ramsey, 'Your friend's going to be disappointed. I'm not going to bring him back.'

In the age of substitutes there would have been the consolation of the prospect of coming off the bench; or perhaps his manager might even have gambled with him from the start, knowing he could adjust if things went badly. The regulations existing in 1966 offered no such flexibility. 'Alf didn't say much to me,' Greaves explained. 'He didn't have to. I knew he was doing what he thought was right.' Greaves expected no great show of sympathy. 'He knew I must have felt choked. I felt sorry for myself and sick about the situation. But I was in no way bitter towards Alf.' Accepting Ramsey's decision, the only thing he wished his manager had done differently was put him out of his misery sooner, although he understood a desire not to show his hand to the Germans and his fear that any early confirmation would have leaked out of the England camp. Ramsey would subsequently tell Kenneth Wolstenholme that he 'decided to leave well alone' and did so with 'a clear conscience. I had to make a decision, and a decision that was best for the team and their chances of winning the World Cup.'

While Ball was calling his father with the good news of his inclusion, telling him to put petrol in the car and drive down to London, Greaves was heading to the room he shared with Moore to pack his bags. 'It's all over for me, mate,' he told his pal.

'I don't care what people say about Jimmy, about how he didn't work and didn't care and how his attitude was all wrong,' Moore would recall. 'I know the man and I knew what he was going through. All he wanted was to play in the World Cup final. He believed he could get the goals to win it for England. He believed he was something special and it broke his heart not to have the chance to prove it.'

Cohen continues, 'It was Jimmy's bad luck and Geoff and Alf's good luck. Alf did what he thought was best for the team. Reputations didn't sit with him very well; you had to show what you could do rather than what you had done. We all know what happened. Geoff played very well with Roger Hunt. They were both strong men, which you had to be against Argentina, and they had hit it off very well. Even though Jimmy was fit, Alf didn't think he was the right choice and left him out.'

Ball would remember feeling that Ramsey had made the right call in leaving his front two unchanged. 'With Geoff, I could always bounce the ball off him, build something. He would help to get you into the game. With Jimmy, you had to play for him. Geoff could do more for our team.'

Some players offered Greaves a semblance of sympathy. 'We were all sick for him,' says Peters. 'You would have put all your money on him being part of it.' Jack Charlton felt the irony that he, introduced to the team only a year earlier, would play in the final, while a 'fantastically gifted player' such as Greaves, with a wealth of international experience, would miss out. Banks recalled that he 'couldn't help but feel desperately sorry for Jimmy' but felt that 'Alf's decision was the correct one'.

As Greaves would have expected, there was a limit to the concern his colleagues were able to demonstrate. Bobby Charlton admitted that he 'never gave the matter over Jimmy much thought' and had confidence in Ramsey to make the right decision. And Cohen explains, 'If you are in that competition, in the final, you have to be pretty single-minded about what you are doing and preparing to do your bit for the team. I think Jimmy took it philosophically, but it obviously hurt and you felt for him. But it is professional football. You have to try to win with the best team possible and Alf thought that this team were winners and that is how it turned out. But it wasn't an easy one for Alf. People like to think he was a hard individual that way, but although he did it for the team I am sure he did feel for Jimmy. He was such a great player.'

Another non-playing squad member, Jimmy Armfield, recalled, 'We all knew that Alf would not be making changes for the final, even though Greaves was now fit again.' He remembered that he 'felt for Jim' and sensed that 'it hit him hard'.

After some players killed the final few hours before heading to the stadium by shopping in Golders Green, where they were allowed to stroll unmolested by the public, the entire squad travelled together to Wembley Stadium. All 22 wandered on the pitch and went into the dressing room. For Greaves, it was purgatory; a sense of dislocation sweeping over him as he saw the scarlet jerseys of the chosen 11 hanging on their pegs. With kick-off an hour away, as players began exchanging their street clothes for those precious shirts bearing the three lions, it was time for Greaves and his fellow reserves to make themselves scarce. Ball watched Greaves depart and realised that, if one of their few world-class players was unable to make the team, then England could not be beaten.

Rather than being close to the bench, England's surplus squad members were given seats in the stands. Armfield described the moment that they found themselves mingling with fans as they headed to their places as 'a time of realisation' that this once-in-a-lifetime event was about to go ahead without them. Greaves said, 'It says something for the wonderful team spirit that Alf had built up that all 11 who had been left out swallowed their self-pity and gave every ounce of their support to the 11 players who were going to represent us.'

Greaves found watching the match a 'fidgety and nervous' experience. So did the vast majority of the 96,924 crowd, especially when Ray Wilson's misplaced defensive header fell for Helmut Haller to fire West Germany into the lead after 12 minutes. At least England eased those nerves six minutes later when Hurst drifted into space and headed Moore's quick free-kick past the German keeper. In a second half that began in heavy rain, England enjoyed territorial superiority, but had to wait until only 13 minutes were remaining before taking their first lead of the match. Ball took a corner, Hurst's shot from 20 yards looped into the air via a defender and Peters pounced to find the net.

Win or lose, Ramsey wanted his entire squad together at the end of the match and had instructed Armfield, the unofficial leader of the reserves, to bring them down to the field in time for the final whistle. With time running out and choruses of *Rule Britannia* falling from the stands, Armfield beckoned to Greaves and the others and they made for the lift. Five minutes later they emerged from the tunnel on the halfway line just in time to see Wolfgang Weber stretch out a foot to convert a loose ball into a last-minute German equaliser. England's dream was placed on hold. The street celebrations that had been set to break out at the end of a tournament that had grown and grown in public consciousness would have to wait. BBC's airing of a *Laurel and Hardy* comedy and ITV's planned *Robin Hood* episode were delayed. And Greaves's discomfort would be prolonged for half an hour of extra time.

He and his colleagues stood on the touchline like unfashionably early arrivals at a party as Ramsey delivered his famous pick-me-up to his stunned players. 'You've won the World Cup once,' he told them. 'Now go out and win it again.'

Driven on by the energy of the irrepressible Ball, England never looked like failing to fulfil their manager's instructions. With 10 minutes of extra-time played – and BBC commentator Kenneth Wolstenholme telling viewers about a replay that might have reinstated Greaves's World Cup dreams – Ball pulled the ball back from the right wing. Hurst swivelled and fired a right-foot shot against the underside of the bar. Azerbaijani linesman Tofiq Bahramov ruled that it had crossed the line when it bounced down and England were ahead again.

This time there was no last-minute reprieve for the Germans. Instead, as Wolstenholme uttered the immortal 'some people are on the pitch ... they think it's all over ... it is now!' Hurst smacked in a left-footed shot that made it 4-2. 'Not too many people agreed with Alf on the morning of the match,' Hurst told David Miller. 'I had to astonish half of Britain that afternoon, just to stop them wanting to string Alf up for leaving Jimmy on the bench.'

Greaves watched the man who had taken his place enter the sport's pantheon as the only man to score a hat-trick in a World Cup final. He would not have been human if he hadn't felt torn apart. One of the first men into the centre of the pitch to congratulate his team-mates, he would admit, 'Even in the great moment of triumph I felt a sickness in my stomach. It was the saddest day of my football life. I had secretly nursed the belief for four years that we would win the World Cup and in the end all I could do was stand and watch my dream come true.'

Norman Hunter, the perennial understudy to Moore, recalls, 'We were all thrilled that we won, but it was an anti-climax. Standing around while everyone was celebrating I found a bit embarrassing.'

England's red-shirted heroes shed their tears and collected their medals. As they set off on their lap of honour, Jack Charlton put an arm round Greaves, smartly and conspicuously dressed in a suit and tie. Then Greaves joined his other street-clothed colleagues on their trek back to the dressing room. There he listened to the distant cheers and the singing and waited for the men who had won the World Cup to return. It was, as Armfield remarked, 'awkward, even though we were thrilled the lads had won'.

No less uncomfortable for Greaves were the evening celebrations at Kensington's Royal Garden Hotel. He left early, returning to

Hendon Hall, retrieving his luggage and going home. Ramsey approached Moore at one point with the question, 'Where's your friend?' and there were suggestions later that he felt Greaves was deliberately snubbing him. But Greaves was a bigger man than that. It was the simple pain of watching others achieve what he had believed was his destiny. 'Don't take it wrong, Alf,' Moore responded. 'He's not doing anything malicious. It's not a protest. He's not walking out on you. He's not even angry. Just disappointed. Jimmy's hurt and doesn't think he can take all this.'

'At no point was I bitter or resentful,' Greaves insisted. In *The Boys of '66*, he said, 'People drummed up the Ramsey-Greaves clash but there wasn't one. I never fell out with him, or had a bad word with or about him.' Greaves went home, got drunk, and took his family on holiday to Majorca the following morning. He was the one player to miss a lunchtime appearance on ITV to relive the drama of the previous day.

In 2003, he would look back and write, 'I got to play in three of England's games in that glorious World Cup and count myself fortunate in that respect.' His words did little to mask the enduring regret.

10

WEMBLEY: ONE YEAR LATER

'Winning the World Cup had a profound effect on some people. It changed the lives of Alf Ramsey and Geoff Hurst. But, contrary to popular belief, it didn't change mine.'

IT remains one of the most frequently asked questions about Jimmy Greaves. Just what effect did the disappointment of 1966 have on his career, on his life? Two interconnected theories abound: that it sent his career into freefall; and/or it precipitated his journey towards alcoholism. Yet only through the lens of hindsight are his final years in football examined so gloomily, a case of looking for clues when you know the unfortunate outcome. Maybe he wasn't ever again the phenomenon he had been in the years between 1958 and 1965. Perhaps the simple fact of age – and the tightening of defences in an era of increasing pragmatism – would have made that impossible anyway, even if he had been the hat-trick hero of 1966.

The man who ended up wearing that mantle, Geoff Hurst, once said, 'It haunts me a bit that it was the start of the slide for

Jimmy.' Yet Hurst is probably being too hard on himself. A simple dismissal of Greaves's post-World Cup years does not stand up to close scrutiny. The following season, he would score another 25 League goals and win the FA Cup. Two years later, he finished as the First Division's top scorer for the first time in four years, a remarkable sixth time overall. He was not exactly a spent force. In the 1968-69 season there was a clamour for him to be back in the England team.

None of which is intended to minimise the long-term impact on his life. There are so many complex and intertwined factors relating to his alcoholism that it would be naïve not to factor the disappointment of the World Cup into that conversation. Author David Miller was right to point out that 'no one, not even Jimmy himself, can ever be absolutely sure how much the emotional trauma gnawed at his soul over the next five years and helped to undermine his stability, judgement and self-discipline'.

That he suffered is indisputable. 'That moment began Jimmy's disenchantment with football,' argued his great friend, Bobby Moore. World Cup colleague John Connelly recalled, 'He was sick. It was the most disappointing thing of his [football] life.' In 1991, there was a reunion to commemorate the 25th anniversary of the World Cup victory, with the squad pictured on the balcony of the Kensington Royal Garden Hotel, where they had celebrated their victory all those years earlier. Greaves was the notable absentee. George Cohen admits, 'Jimmy was obviously very upset and I have never ever mentioned it to him to this day, and would never do so.'

Journalist Martin Samuel, who spent many hours talking with Greaves, says, 'I always thought it must have hurt him much more than he would ever let on. What he has done to deal with it is decide that he will say that it didn't bother him. That is the line and we are sticking to it. Jimmy is an intelligent man and he knows that to say anything else sounds bitter. His country had won the World Cup and he knew how it would be received if he made a fuss about it.'

Events in future years caused Bobby Charlton to re-examine his own attitude to Greaves's upset. 'I do wonder if I might have been more understanding, and felt more compassion for someone whose talent I admired so much – and whose problem of alcoholism, many of his closest friends believed, was only deepened by the great crisis, and disappointment, of his professional life,' he would write.

Norman Giller, who knew Greaves's inner thoughts as well as anyone, suggests, 'Jimmy handled the hurt by burying it. Jimmy has never talked voluntarily about the July 30 day. I have always had to force quotes out of him for the various books and TV and video programmes we have made together. I think the feelings of the Greaves family are best illustrated by the scrapbook that Irene kept throughout the 1966 finals. The cuttings suddenly came to a halt after the semi-finals, apart from the handwritten comment in capital letters: "I HATE ALF."'

If Greaves had hoped that he could put the biggest heartbreak of his career behind him as he embarked on a new season only three weeks after the World Cup final, he was to be quickly relieved of such a notion. There would barely be a newspaper report that didn't make mention of him either bouncing back from disappointment and returning to form, or – if the ball didn't run his way – wondering about the effect on his game of Alf Ramsey's team selection.

It was difficult for anyone to look upon Greaves without seeing the image of him walking about the Wembley pitch in his suit while his England colleagues celebrated. Many felt they needed to tiptoe around him as they might someone who had suffered a bereavement. Alan Mullery was one of those Tottenham team-mates waiting for him when he returned to the club after his post-Wembley holiday. 'I think he felt Alf had let him down,' he suggests. 'But Jim and Geoff were entirely different players and Jim had an injury. Geoff wins the game with a hat-trick, so you can't argue with that. Jim was very upset about it for quite some time, but I don't think he ever talked about it, except maybe with his own family. He just put it to the back of his mind, but he was never the same fellow again.'

Alan Gilzean confirmed, 'It must have hurt him so much, but he never talked about it much. He kept it to himself, but it must have been shattering for him.'

There was, however, no attempt by the media to track down Greaves for his reactions in the immediate aftermath of the tournament. They allowed him to get on with his holiday. Similar privacy was afforded to Alan Ball, even though the player generally accepted to be the unofficial man of the match was pushing to leave Blackpool in what would be a British record transfer when he signed for Everton for £110,000.

For all the lasting legacy of the tournament, the sporting narrative moved on quickly in 1966. Ball and Nobby Stiles had sat unnoticed in a motorway service station eating egg and chips on the day after the final. Monday's front page of *The Times* featured no picture or story of the England team – although, bizarrely, it did carry a picture of the West German players receiving a rousing welcome home and an accompanying story headlined 'Ovation for Germany's team'. The lead story of British European Airways cancelling an £80 million order in favour of British planes was clearly enough patriotism for one edition. The following day, the same newspaper was declaring that 'enough was enough' in relation to celebration of England's victory and focusing instead on how the team might be able to defend their world title four years hence.

It required the passage of time to truly elevate the achievement of 1966 to the mythological status it now enjoys; and to ever more brutally remind Greaves of what he had missed. Roger Hunt, who had won at Wembley with Liverpool a year earlier, commented, 'I felt the FA Cup was equally as big at the time, but as the years have gone on, and we haven't won it again, it's made it different.'

Meanwhile, the direct financial windfall of victory was more reflective of *The Times*' somewhat dismissive attitude than of the obvious additional curiosity and attention that would follow Ramsey's heroes wherever they played in the ensuing months. It certainly failed to reflect the explosion of profile that English football was about to experience.

England's success, and the television coverage of the event, meant that the new First Division season would see *Match of the Day* achieving audiences well into the millions in its BBC One slot, compared to the tens of thousands who had first seen the show when introduced to certain regions on BBC Two in 1964. ITV's localised football shows would soon be annexing Sunday afternoons in the broadcast schedules. New glossy magazines such as *Goal* and *Shoot!*, and various short-lived imitators, were on their way, addressing a younger audience in a more picture-led and conversational way than the preachy, educational tones of *Charles Buchan's Football Monthly*. The personalities that would bring those magazines to life and the faces that would adorn new bubble gum cards and sticker collections – the lifeblood of playground swapping sessions – would be slow to reap the benefit of the sport's enhanced image.

The England players' bonus for winning the World Cup had been £22,000, shared equally among the squad members. Only the likes of Moore, Bobby Charlton and Ball saw significant commercial benefit from their exploits – although endorsement of boots and the odd piece of clothing, ghostwritten magazine articles, branded annuals and an occasional advertisement hardly created a financial portfolio recognisable to World Cup winners decades later. Greaves, who had seen an autobiographical volume and an educational book, *Soccer Techniques and Tactics*,[21] published in his name before the tournament could only imagine what he

---

21 At least Greaves had the self-awareness to open the book with, 'There are plenty of people who will think it is a bit of a cheek on my part to write a book that sets out to give advice on how to play football.'

might have reaped had it been he who had netted three goals in the final. An advertising deal for a set of binoculars – following previous endorsements of products such as Bovril and Zephyr football boots – was not exactly in the same bracket as David Beckham's future Adidas endorsements.

On the field, Tottenham began the season by going two goals up inside 15 minutes against Leeds United, one of the favourites for the title, with Greaves and Alan Mullery setting each other up for goals that created the foundation of a 3-1 win. If the emergence of Revie's Leeds side was to be a defining feature of the English game over the next decade, then so was the unruly crowd behaviour that was already beginning to become an increasingly unwelcome presence at many grounds. A taste of it was to be found at White Hart Lane on the day that the television cameras made their first visit of the season, their traditional excursion to Tottenham's match against Manchester United. Greaves fired in a winning goal two minutes from time, prompting a barrage of beer bottles from the United fans. 'The bottles missed us but plenty of them landed in the penalty area,' said Spurs full-back Joe Kinnear. 'Broken glass was thrown as well.'

Spurs' 2-1 win was their fifth success in seven matches. Greaves had scored six times in that run, including two to help halt Arsenal's four-game unbeaten start under new manager Bertie Mee. A draw and three more wins found Tottenham leading the First Division by mid-October and when Greaves scored in a 4-3 win at Fulham it meant he'd found the net in seven successive matches, his best run for five seasons. The thrilling contest at Craven Cottage was exactly the kind of game that would cause Greaves to recall, 'It was a lot like the glory days of the early Sixties again.'

Greaves saw that the players Bill Nicholson had signed to create a new team had 'got over their growing pains', while Dave Mackay, fit again and leading the side, would call 1966-67 'a vintage season and one where we played some of the best football in my time at Spurs'. Historically, no one would ever suggest that

Nicholson's new team was a match for the Double winners, but Mackay believed they were, on their day, just as entertaining and compelling to watch.

Bolstering the defence was Mike England, the Welsh international centre-back signed from Blackburn Rovers during the summer for £95,000, a record fee for a defender. 'I had been going to Manchester United, but it fell through,' he recalls. 'But it turned out to be a nice move. I was absolutely delighted not to have to deal with Jimmy Greaves anymore. He was a defender's nightmare. He was one of those class players, like George Best, who just have something special, a wonderful ability to go past people like they are not there. He used to make scoring goals look easy.'

England realised immediately that Greaves was a law unto himself, indulged to a certain extent by Nicholson because of his unique value to the club. 'Jimmy was his own man. Most of us, when we went training, it was a question of "this is what you do; this is how you do it". We would be training very hard and Jim would do his own little thing, quite different to what most of us were doing. I remember Bill giving us our team talk. He said, "Jimmy, you do realise you have got to work a little bit harder? When you lose the ball you have got to track back and try to retrieve it." And Jim said, "Bill, if I am going to track back and retrieve the ball I am not going to have the energy to score all the goals I am getting at the other end." We all laughed and Bill just said, "All right, Jimmy, good point."'

Steve Perryman would observe the same phenomenon after forcing his way into the team during the final months of Greaves's Spurs career. 'The players told me that Bill's meetings were getting longer and longer. Jim was sort of looking up in the air and Bill would say, "Go on then, Jim, what do you think?" Jim would say, "Bill, you can keep talking to us and at us, but basically, when it comes down to it, you can either play or you can't play." And Bill would say, "Go on then, off you go." Jim was so sharp, so bright, he was probably thinking, "I don't need to hear this again." But it wasn't done in a big-headed way. I have never known Jimmy be anything other than a gentleman.'

Gilzean continued, 'On a Saturday we all used to go into the gym and warm up for the game, but Jimmy would be outside talking to his mates. He would come in about 20 minutes before kick-off, take his clothes off, put on his kit, do a few stretches, have a last few puffs on a cigarette and he would go out and be sensational.'

Greaves felt that the effects of hepatitis were finally receding. 'I didn't feel like a player in "immediate decline",' he would remark. In the *Tottenham Hotspur Football Book* that would be published the following year, editor Dennis Signy claimed that 'the turning point in the season for Tottenham can be traced to the return to peak form and fitness of Jimmy Greaves'.

After a slow start to the season that even Nicholson admitted was concerning, Gilzean recaptured the kind of form that reassured everyone around the club that the partnership with Greaves had grown into everything its early promise foretold. 'We were made for each other,' Greaves would conclude shortly after his retirement. 'We had a telepathic understanding right from the off and I was never happier than when playing with Gilly by my side.'

'It was easy for me,' was Gilzean's memory of the partnership, 'because Jimmy was such an exceptional player. When I occasionally – well, quite often, actually – gave him bad passes, he made them into good passes with his pace.' Little work, it would appear, was needed to create the empathy that defined the way they worked alongside each other. 'We just had an understanding,' Gilzean continued. 'Obviously we always had a practice match each week against the reserves and Bill Nick and Eddie Baily would stop us if they thought we were doing things wrong, but right from my first game I knew it was going to be a good relationship. What I was good at was getting up in the air and heading the ball and laying it off. With Greavsie's exceptional pace and dribbling ability, there was a very good chance it would work.

'When Pat used to kick long balls, I just used to have to get above the centre-half and get a header and put it within 10 yards of Greavsie and he would catch it. It made my life a lot easier, knowing you've got a guy alongside you with that skill and ability to make a bad ball into a good one and score at the end of it.'

Phil Beal adds, 'Greavsie and Gilly seemed to know each other's play inside out; each other's strengths and weakness. If we had a corner, Gilly would usually go to the near post and Jimmy knew exactly what was going to happen. Gilly always got the flick-on and Greavise would be around to finish it off. When Pat took goal-kicks, Greavsie knew where Gilly was going to flick that ball for him to run on to.'

Gilzean's quiet public personality and unathletic appearance – his receding hairline putting years on him – meant that Greaves felt his partner never received as much appreciation from others as he afforded him. 'I would say he is one of the greatest players I have ever seen or played with,' he said at the time. 'He is tremendously talented on the ball, is a master at the flick header and is a lot harder and braver than many critics seem to think.'

Speaking to author James Morgan for his book, *In Search of Alan Gilzean*, Greaves explained, 'We read each other's minds and we knew exactly what the other was going to do. It was a great partnership and it was an unselfish partnership, we were both good for each other. In terms of what he did for me, he was the best. We both felt a great deal for each other as players and as men ... I thought the world of him. It was a privilege to play with him and to know him.'

But even the goals continuing to flow from his rapport with Gilzean were not enough to push him back into the England team. When Ramsey picked his side to face Northern Ireland in Belfast in October, the first international since the triumph of the summer, it was the same eleven men who had beaten West

Germany. After a 2-0 victory, it was another unchanged team that faced Czechoslovakia at Wembley a couple of weeks later. Before that game, Greaves was photographed walking from the training field at Roehampton with reporters trailing in his wake. 'Glum-faced and alone … still waiting for his chance to play for England again,' was how the newspaper caption described him.

Tottenham's loss of form around that time, however, would have prompted glum faces even from Cesar Romero, lighting up screens that year as the grinning Joker in the first season of the *Batman* television series. Beginning with a home defeat against struggling Blackpool, Spurs picked up only one point from a run of six games. When they finished the season in third place, only four points behind champions Manchester United, it didn't need the Caped Crusader to solve the riddle of how the title had slipped away from them. 'Our undoing was a sequence of poor results back in the autumn,' Greaves recalled. The fact that they would not lose a League match after 14 January, when they went down by a single goal at United, said much, he felt, 'for the character and spirit of the players'. Yet he admitted that 'the damage had been done'.

Mullery says, 'The team by now was almost a complete change round of what Bill had in 1962. He had started to make a very good side and you have to give him credit for the players he brought to the club. People were always talking about the Double-winning side, but we could have won the Double, too.'

When Greaves finished 1966 with two goals against Newcastle United in a 4-0 win at White Hart Lane, Norman Giller wrote in the *Daily Express*, 'You don't need a crystal ball to forecast that 1967 will bring Jimmy Greaves better footballing fortune than 1966. Greaves kicked goodbye to a year he will want to forget with two superbly-struck goals.'[22]

---

22 Greaves gives a detailed description of a solo run and clinical finish that gave him one of his goals when writing about the game in *Greavsie*, mentioning that it would be replayed frequently on television. In fact, he was mixing it up with a goal he scored against the same opposition three years later in one of his last *Match of the Day* appearances for Tottenham.

The new year was indeed going to bring Greaves greater fortune, in the shape of the final club honour he would win. He would also get back into the England team, albeit for the last caps of his career.

Three barren years on from Rotterdam, Nicholson had stressed to his players during pre-season the importance of taking another trophy back to White Hart Lane. Terry Venables, a recent signing from Chelsea, observed, 'Tottenham was so different to anything I had previously experienced,' and added, 'Certainly the expectations seemed higher.'

Gilzean admitted, 'We underachieved; we should have done better. We went on to win three cups in the early '70s, but we never won what we wanted – the League. Consistency seemed to be the problem and we had not been lucky with injuries. Greavsie had his illness and when I first came to the club I never played with Dave Mackay for about a season because of his broken legs. We were in a transitional period; a lot of the Double team had left. There was a big transformation and, around that time, the only team that could go through that and keep winning was Liverpool. We never did it. For the players we had, we underachieved.'

The autumn meltdown in Division One meant that Nicholson's demands would have to be met in the FA Cup. A third-round trip to the forbidding environment of Millwall's home at The Den would not make things easy and Spurs were happy to come away with a 0-0 draw, Gilzean scoring the only goal in the replay at White Hart Lane.

The fourth round saw Tottenham overcome another Second Division team, Portsmouth. After a goalless first half, Gilzean scored the first two goals in a 3-1 win and Greaves raced away from two defenders to add the third. Greaves was scorer of both goals in a 2-0 home win against Bristol City to earn Spurs a quarter-final berth. An expert finish after 10 minutes could have been equalised in the 75th minute after England's handball gave the visitors a penalty. Full-back Tony Ford saw his penalty saved at the foot of the post by Jennings, only for a retake to be ordered because of the Spurs players' encroachment. At which point Chris Crowe stepped up and struck the ball wide. Greaves showed how it should be done in the final moments of the game after another handball decision.

By this time, Greaves was seeing a potential pathway back to the England team via selection for the Football League team to face the Scottish League. 'This is a man with an indelible bruise on his heart,' said one preview. 'This is a night when Greaves could prove himself and play his way back into the England team and the approval of manager Ramsey.' As it turned out, Greaves didn't score in his team's 3-0 win, their first success against their Scottish counterparts for 18 years, but the *Daily Mirror*'s Ken Jones observed, 'This was a new Greaves. He may not be eager to concede the point, but responsibility now runs parallel with his genius.'

Back in the FA Cup, Spurs had been drawn at yet another Division Two team in the sixth round. 'We have no intention of developing a Greaves complex,' promised Birmingham City manager Stan Cullis before his team stifled Tottenham in a 0-0 draw that Greaves would recall as a 'very tense, dull game of football'. Yet Spurs quickly demoralised their opponents on their way to a 6-0 win in the replay, Greaves scoring twice in the second half.

Sir Alf Ramsey, as he had been appointed in the New Year's honours list, had already seen enough. On the eve of the Birmingham replay he had named Greaves in his team for the following Saturday's game at Wembley against Scotland, his first change to the World Cup-winning line-up. As it had been so often in the past, the man sacrificed was Roger Hunt, whose season at that point had brought him 12 goals compared to the 25 of Greaves. 'I know just how disappointed Roger must be feeling,' Greaves commented. 'I remember how choked I was when I failed to get into the team for the World Cup final.'

Insisting that the bout of hepatitis was now behind him – and that it had taken his recovery to make him realise how debilitating it had been – he continued, 'I feel as good now as at any time during my career. The next World Cup in 1970? It doesn't pay to look that far ahead in this game.'

Events at Wembley bore out that last comment. Hampered by an early injury to Jack Charlton and further hindered by Greaves suffering a bruised ankle, England struggled to make headway against opponents determined to reward the vast hordes who had journeyed south. Too often Hurst and Greaves were left fruitlessly chasing long balls and it took the insouciance of Scotland midfielder Jim Baxter to insert the odd moment of calm into a frenetic 90 minutes. After Denis Law swept Scotland into a first-half lead, Celtic's Bobby Lennox drilled home a second after the break. A limping Jack Charlton pulled one back at the end of a move in which Greaves had twice been involved, including a cheeky back-heel in the box, but Jim McCalliog scored a well-worked third for the Scots. Hurst's header was only a consolation. Scotland were 3-2 winners, with Law declaring them to be the new world champions.

It was not the return Greaves had imagined. He even had to miss the following week's Division One game against Southampton because of the injury he'd picked up. Spurs could not afford to be without their talisman seven days later when they faced Nottingham Forest, another team chasing the Double, in the semi-final of the FA Cup. Forest, who would finish second in the table, had reached the last eight in one of the great ties of the decade, a pulsating 3-2 win against Everton in which Ian Storey-Moore had scored a brilliant hat-trick.

'It's going to be a man's game,' warned Forest skipper Terry Hennessey, the bruising, balding Welshman. The Tottenham defence could attest to that after half an hour at Hillsborough, during which they had been put under some heavy pressure. But a piece of typically instinctive Greaves finishing – untypically from outside the penalty area – drove Spurs into the lead. He missed a much easier opportunity from inside the six-yard box in the second half, but Frank Saul was quick to seize upon an error by Hennessey to increase the lead after 66 minutes. Hennessey reduced the lead with a header from a corner, but could not prevent Spurs' return to Wembley and was in tears as he left the field. Who said real men don't cry?

Chelsea's controversial semi-final victory over Leeds – Peter Lorimer's apparent equaliser from a powerhouse free-kick having been ruled out – meant that the FA Cup would feature its first all-London final. No pictures of cheerful northern fans cavorting in the Trafalgar Square fountains during their grand day out for the newspaper picture desks to rely on.

Instead, the media labelled it the 'Cockney Cup Final' and the nation lumped the teams together in a kind of sequined celebration of Pearly Kings and jellied eels. Quite apart from the fact that neither club hailed from the East End, the teams could not have been much different in personality and persona. Tottenham, for all the brilliance they were capable of on the field and their hard drinking off it, were as much a public reflection of the conservative, disciplinarian Nicholson as Chelsea were of their flamboyant manager, Tommy Docherty, and the environment in which they existed. Their proximity to the King's Road and the kind of west London addresses desired by pop stars and actors made them the club to which the showbiz crowd attached themselves.

'They may have been mods and probably danced in places called discos to The Who and The Small Faces,' noted Mackay. 'Fashion models, photographers and film stars attended their matches. Over at Spurs, we wore cardigans and slacks, sported short back and sides haircuts and tapped our Hush Puppy shoes to Russ Conway tinkling away on his piano.'

Attracting much of the attention in the build-up was a man who had swapped the discotheques of Chelsea for the snug bar of Tottenham, midfielder Venables, signed for £80,000 just before the end of the previous season. 'Completely stunned' to discover he was available for sale, Venables had heard Docherty announce it was 'in the best interests of the club' to sell him, having complained a couple of days earlier that there were 'too many big-heads in the team'.

Giller, who covered both clubs for the *Daily Express*, observes, 'Tommy would put himself first, the club second and the player third. If he felt there was somebody such as Terry Venables who was doing things to undermine him he would be a very bad enemy.' Docherty insists that Venables had become a 'luxury' and that his interest in coaching was becoming a distraction. He also felt he had signed a better replacement in Charlie Cooke from Dundee. 'I should have sold him earlier,' he says.

Venables took a starring role when the Tottenham players headed to the EMI studios to record 13 well-known songs for a Cup final LP, *Spurs Go Marching On*. A wannabe crooner who would eventually sing live on the *Parkinson* show, he earned praise for his lead vocals on 'Bye, Bye, Blackbird'; Greaves less so for his performance on 'Strolling'. An EMI spokesman noted, 'Jimmy Greaves and the rest had better stick to football.' Meanwhile, Venables's midfield partner, Mullery, was more concerned about recovering from a thigh injury than forging an entertainment career.

Another emerging storyline was the issue of player bonuses and tickets, both areas in which Tottenham's players appeared to have an advantage over their rivals. Rumour reached the Chelsea players that Tottenham were receiving anything up to 10 times the two free and 10 purchased tickets allowed by FA regulations, an amount confirmed by Spurs full-back Joe Kinnear in later years. Standard practice was that anything not needed to fulfil the needs of friends and family was sold at a profit to the touts, one of whom, Kinnear recalled, was such a fan that 'he used to sleep in Jimmy's Spurs shirt'. A 10-shilling (50p) ticket for the game was fetching as much as £10, while 70-shilling seats changed hands for £30. Tottenham warned season ticket holders that they risked the loss of future privileges if they were discovered to have sold the Wembley voucher from their books to touts.

Docherty warned his players of 'serious trouble' if they looked to profit in such a manner, but admits now, 'The players were selling tickets – but that was because the wages then weren't what they are like now. It was a chance to pick up an extra bonus. The players did it and I did it.'

Meanwhile, the Chelsea camp heard stories that their Spurs counterparts had been promised £2,000 each for winning and £1,000 if they lost; many times the amounts written into the Chelsea contracts. Several players warned Docherty that they would refuse to play, forcing a late deal to be struck. The squad would reportedly share between £12,000 and £19,000 if they won, but would have to be content with £50 appearance money each if beaten.

It meant that Chelsea, considered underdogs by the majority, were hardly the most contented set of players to line up for a Wembley final. More significant, the Spurs men felt, was that Chelsea were the new kids on the block, lacking the Double champions, European trophy winners and veterans of internationals that they could boast. Chelsea might have some precocious talent, even in the absence of Peter Osgood – who had broken his leg earlier in the season – but they were not battle-hardened. 'We looked at them and knew that we would win,' says Mullery.

Jimmy Robertson adds, 'Wembley was just part of the process. We seemed to be playing well every week and were on a long run of not losing. We had a nucleus of people from the Double side and experience to fall back on.'

Gilzean recalled, 'When we came out on the pitch at Wembley, Dave Mackay said, "Look at Chelsea. They don't fancy this." He said it out loud so their players could hear it. We were always in control early on against Chelsea and Jimmy Robertson got us off to a flying start.'

In fact, Robertson's strike did not arrive until the final minute of the first half, but Gilzean's recall of his team's early dominance is accurate. With Greaves marked tightly by Ron Harris, as usual, Gilzean and Robertson offered the greatest threat to a Chelsea defence in which Marvin Hinton had surprisingly been assigned to man-mark Gilzean rather than playing his usual roving, sweeping role – against which the Scot was less effective. Saul saw a half-volley blocked and Greaves and Robertson were denied by keeper Peter Bonetti before Spurs went ahead, Mullery breaking from midfield and seeing his low shot ricochet for Robertson to finish.

Midway through the second half, Robertson set up a second for Spurs when he headed on for Saul to shoot past Bonetti. Pat Jennings had been forced to make a couple of first-half saves, but it was not until five minutes remained that Bobby Tambling headed in from John Boyle's curled cross from the left to give Chelsea some late hope. Yet Tottenham had little problem in holding out for victory.

'We learned a hard lesson and got a bit of a chasing,' is the memory of Chelsea's John Hollins, while Cooke concludes, 'The final was shit. I can't tell you how bad we were. I felt physically sick. I was so disappointed for the team. We played crap, abjectly, terrible.'

Nicholson disappointed some of his Spurs players by using his speech at the winners' banquet to express a similar opinion to Cooke, pointing out that it had been a poor game and that his team had not performed at their best. 'I found the manager's pessimism and downbeat approach galling,' said Venables. Gilzean, who would also go on to win two League Cups at the home of English football, understood his manager's stance to a certain extent. 'I played three finals at Wembley and won them all, but I never played in a really good game,' he said. 'When we were 2-0 up we were coasting.'

Greaves was back on the Wembley pitch four days later, for what would be the final time in his career. For the game against

Spain, Ramsey opted to play Greaves, Hunt and Hurst together for the first time. Greaves scored his 44th and final England goal by firing in a low shot on the turn after gathering Hunt's effort in the final quarter of the game. It was his first goal in his past six Wembley appearances. He was also denied by the crossbar and keeper José Ángel Iribar.

The trio of strikers were retained when England lined up against Austria in Vienna three days later. It was Greaves's 57th senior England appearance. Ramsey's team emerged 1-0 winners, although not in the most convincing manner against defensive opponents on a poor surface. When Ramsey praised his team after the game, saying, 'I thought they all did very well under the circumstances,' there was no hint that the international career of England's record goalscorer had reached its conclusion.

11

'JIMMY FOR ENGLAND'

'Everyone got embroiled in the system, even Bill
Nicholson at Tottenham. Individual players like
me became luxuries. Now, it was all systems. It
was the downfall of the game. The people I feel
sorry for are those who came along like Rodney
Marsh and Stan Bowles, great individuals
who were frowned upon. They were rejected in
favour of the automaton.'

CHRISTMAS was only a few days away. The news pages
of the last few weeks of 1968 were filled with stories of
US airliners being hijacked and diverted to Cuba; final
preparations for Apollo 8's mission to send the first men to orbit
the moon; and, closer to home, concerns over a flu epidemic
in Britain. Arriving with the morning newspapers were Sir Alf
Ramsey's usual collection of Christmas cards, posted from all
points across the country by family, friends and fans whose only
acquaintance with him was what they had seen on television.

One particular card could not help but grab his attention.
Rather than a nativity scene or a jovial Father Christmas, the
image adorning the front was Jimmy Greaves. Signed by 25

fans, the card promised a message made up of three words. Opening it up, Ramsey read the missive: 'Greaves for England.' Even in the festive season, there was no escaping from the selection debate that had been following him around since the summer of 1966.

By the time Ramsey's postman came calling on that December day, Greaves had already bagged 25 goals in all competitions, adding to the 29 he'd netted in 1967-68. Nobody had scored more since Greaves had last been selected for the national team. He would finish the season with 27 goals in the First Division alone – the sixth occasion he'd been leading scorer – and 36 overall.

In his 12th season of top-flight football, Greaves might have been considered a veteran, yet it was not age that had led to his absence from the England side. Indeed, only with hindsight can one see 1968-69 as the twilight of a career that would slide towards premature sunset over the next two years. As someone who was only 29 by the end of that season, and was still scoring more goals than any of his contemporaries, he might have been expected to have several years left at the top of his sport. He would be younger heading in the Mexico World Cup in 1970 than Bobby Charlton. Instead, it was a combination of two factors that kept his name off Ramsey's team sheet. Firstly, the manager continued to believe that Greaves's individual style – self-centred as he viewed it – was unsuited to his vision of how an England team should perform. In that, he remained unmoved since the World Cup. Secondly, he believed that Greaves had indicated directly to him an ambivalence towards England selection that granted the manager permission for his continued exclusion. A thread that connected both elements was the uneasy nature of the relationship that had always existed between the two men.

When Greaves had been left out of Ramsey's squad for the first match of the 1967-68 season, a Home International against Wales in Cardiff, it cannot be said to have created major ripples around football. *The Times* said it was a decision that might cause

Tottenham fans to 'wrinkle their noses'. There were no epitaphs being written for his international career.

Greaves at least continued to feature somewhere in Ramsey's thinking. As well as being named as a squad player for subsequent full internationals, he was one of the more experienced men named in a Football League side that thrashed the Irish League 7-2 in Dublin. He scored the first goal and watched his future team-mate, Martin Chivers, grab a hat-trick. Within a few weeks, the Southampton centre-forward had arrived at Tottenham in a £125,000 transfer, a sum that Football League president Len Shipman described as 'too ridiculous for words' before adding, 'I was talking recently to a club director who visualises fees reaching £250,000 within the next six years.'

Chivers joined Greaves on the scoresheet on his Spurs debut, a 2-1 victory at Sheffield Wednesday, and then recalls his new team-mate dropping him in it with manager Bill Nicholson after his first game at White Hart Lane, a 1-0 derby victory over Arsenal in which Greaves scored the only goal. In a post-match aside, as they sat together unpeeling their kit, Chivers remarked, 'I can't play on that pitch, there's six inches of mud out there.' At which point Greaves shouted out to the manager, 'Chiv's just told me he can't play on that pitch.' Chivers squirmed in embarrassment and Greaves grinned mischievously as Nicholson barked back, 'I've got news for you, son. You're playing on it every other week, so you'd better get used to it.'

Greaves had long proved able to glide across whatever surface he was presented with in search of goals. Tottenham's season, however, was proceeding with the kind of sequence of slip-ups and sublime performances that had characterised so many recent campaigns. Having begun by drawing the FA Charity Shield against Manchester United 3-3 at Old Trafford – a game made famous by goalkeeper Pat Jennings scoring with a punt downfield – they were heading for a seventh-place finish in Division One and a fifth-round replay exit against Liverpool in the FA Cup. The club had opted out of the Football League Cup one year after playing in it for the first time.

Hopes of another triumph in the European Cup Winners' Cup had ended in a second-round defeat against Olympique Lyonnais, going out on away goals after winning the second leg 4-3 at White Hart Lane. 'It's just bloody heartbreaking,' said Nicholson. 'I want to be sick.' Chairman Fred Wale even added, 'Some of our players quit.'

As always, the press either slated or feted Greaves from game to game. After that victory over Arsenal in mid-January, Greaves was described by the *Daily Express* as 'dismally undistinguished'. A few days later, when he scored twice in a 3-1 FA Cup win at Preston North End, the same publication likened it to 'the return of an old friend to see Jimmy Greaves back in goal snatching business'.

By the time Ramsey was choosing his squad for the February international in Scotland, Greaves's scoring had been slowed by some absences through injury and he found himself ignored once again. That match, a 1-1 draw, was the final stage of two seasons' worth of Home Internationals that had doubled up as qualifiers for the later stages of the 1968 European Nations Cup, as the European Championship was still being called. Despite the Wembley defeat by Scotland a year earlier, Ramsey's team had earned a two-legged quarter-final against Spain, for which Greaves was once again named in a squad of 22 as the home leg approached.

Ken Jones of the *Daily Mirror* offered Greaves some hope of a recall by noting, 'England's ability to get [goals] has never been more worrying. Missed chances against Scotland might well have cost England a place in the quarter-final.'

But as his team prepared for their most important game since the 1966 final, Ramsey was faced with the same decision with which he had been confronted back then. Why would he do anything different now? Was Greaves any more trustworthy now than he had been two years ago?

England managed only a 1-0 first-leg lead, Bobby Charlton equalling Greaves's record of 44 goals for his country. For the second leg, a month later, Greaves was once again named in the squad. With the emphasis in Madrid likely to be on protecting their advantage rather than hunting for goals, Greaves saw that his chances of making the starting eleven were slim. Another few days of making up the numbers at training was all that he could foresee.

Admitting that he was feeling 'pretty fed up', Greaves spoke to Ramsey and asked him outright, 'Am I likely to get a game this time, Alf?'

'No, not at the moment,' replied Ramsey, whose honesty could always be relied upon. He told Greaves that he valued his presence in the squad and on the sidelines.

It was not enough for a man who felt he was too experienced to be going along for the ride and had no great love of training anyway. He had also sensed moments during the season when he'd struggled to maintain his former enthusiasm for the game – not that his return of goals would have led anyone to suspect such a thing. A total of 23 League goals would be low only by his own standards, with only four men scoring more in the First Division. Making up the numbers for England, meanwhile, was doing nothing to relieve him of the 'depression' he could slip into on occasions.

'If you have no intention of picking me I'd rather not hang around kicking my heels,' was the gist of the message Greaves delivered to Ramsey. He would insist later that he never suggested he did not want to play for England again, even if he was privately resigning himself to that fate and beginning to imagine concentrating purely on club football. He remembered Ramsey giving the impression that he appreciated his frankness. Yet, as Leo McKinstry suggested in his biographical reappraisal of Ramsey, 'Alf found it intolerable that any player should seek to impose a condition on his playing for England.'

Greaves was one of the six players Ramsey subsequently released from the party before travelling to Spain, where England won 2-1 to reach the final four of the tournament in Italy. A few weeks later, he watched on television as England's hopes of adding a European title to their world crown ended in a 1-0 defeat against Yugoslavia in Florence, where Spurs team-mate Alan Mullery became the first player to be sent off while playing for England.

What would prove to be the final great season of the professional career of Jimmy Greaves, 1968-69, began with a goal in each of the first two games. After the second of those, a 2-0 win at Everton, the *Daily Express* called it 'another reminder that his magic is not fading'.

Substituted, to the disgust of the Spurs fans, late in a home draw against West Bromwich Albion four days later, Greaves was about to embark on a goalscoring spree that would eventually bring the clamour for his return to the England team tumbling on to Ramsey's doormat. September brought hat-tricks against Burnley, in a 7-0 win, and Exeter, in a 6-3 League Cup victory, while Bobby Charlton had already observed after Greaves's goal against Manchester United, 'He's still as great as ever; he is still as quick and sharp as he has ever been.'

Having thought long and hard before signing a new contract during the summer of 1968, Greaves attributed the rediscovery of his zest for the game partly to the act of clearing his thoughts of likely international selection, leading to a more relaxed state of mind. 'I reckon the reason I did so well was that I didn't really care … about myself,' he would record. 'I was determined not to lose sleep if things didn't go well for me.'

He began October with another treble, including what is considered one of the finest goals of his career. 'We were playing Leicester City and Pat Jennings smacked the ball up to the half-way line,' Mullery recalls. 'Jim went on a run and beat four or five people. I was just watching, shouting, "Go on, Jim!" Then he just walked around the goalkeeper and stood on the line and back-heeled it into the goal. There was a picture of about four defenders, just lying on the floor, just left there.'

Mullery's memory may have allowed a certain embellishment – the photograph in Monday's newspapers illustrated a more orthodox side-foot finish – but had the television cameras been present it would have become one of the most repeated of Greaves's goals. Instead, only the 36,622 at White Hart Lane got to enjoy that moment of brilliance, the first of the three goals he scored in a 3-2 victory. If Allan Clarke, the striker for whom Leicester had just paid Fulham £150,000, felt he had made a point by giving his team the lead, then Greaves quickly reminded him that he remained the master. Nicholson called it 'the greatest goal I have seen' and Tom Freeman told *The Times* readers that it was 'one of the finest goals ever seen at White Hart Lane, or any other ground for that matter'. The *Daily Mirror* pointed out the potential value of such a finish when England contested the World Cup in Mexico. The Tottenham programme devoted a column to the goal when Spurs entertained Manchester United a week later, relaying that he finished with 'an elegance that defies description' and suggesting that 'it is unlikely we shall see another goal like it on the ground this season'.

To defender Phil Beal, the goal was a perfect endorsement of Greaves's approach to the game. 'He never used to come back over the halfway line,' he says. 'He would say, "I do my work up there in the penalty box. I can't tackle and I can't defend. That is what you defenders are for." If ever he did make a tackle he would come off after the game saying, "Did you see that?" Jimmy would stay up the field because he knew if he got the ball up there, he could go past any defenders that the opposition had kept back.'

In a home win against Queens Park Rangers a few weeks later, Greaves would play the role of provider in one of the most cherished moments of Beal's Tottenham career, his only goal in more than 400 competitive appearances. 'I picked the ball up just outside our penalty area and ran with it,' Beal recalls with the assuredness of someone who has spent half a century recounting this particular tale. 'No one came near me. I don't know why; they must have thought, "Well, he is not going to keep it." In the end I went beyond the halfway line, which for me was a miracle, and I found myself on the edge of the penalty area. I gave it to Jimmy. Nine times out of 10 he would never give the ball back to anybody around the box, but he gave it back to me. I thought, "Bloody hell." Anyway, I scored.'

At training two days later, Beal approached Greaves to ask, 'Why did you give me that ball back on the edge of the box? You don't normally.'

'Well, there were no television cameras there,' Greaves shot back. 'I thought I would try to give you a bit of glory.'

Meanwhile, England were about to begin the new season by being held 0-0 in a friendly against Romania in Bucharest, with Roger Hunt and Geoff Hurst still occupying the striking positions. Speculation before the announcement of the squad was that Hunt and Greaves were once again vying for the same position. The *Daily Express* claimed a private poll of a dozen First Division players had been split down the middle. Spurs manager Nicholson had said of Greaves, 'He seems as sharp this season as he has ever been. Some of his goals have been quite spectacular.'

Timing was always one of Greaves's qualities and he chose a home game against Sunderland 10 days after that England blackout to score four goals. The bandwagon for his return to the national team was in full forward thrust. 'How much longer can England afford to ignore the claims of Britain's top hot-shot?' asked Victor Railton in London's *Evening News*. In *The Times*, Geoffrey Green wondered 'if Sir Alf Ramsey can continue to ignore him for an England attack that has failed to score in three of their last four matches'.

Chants of 'Jimmy for England' could be heard at most Tottenham games. 'It was daubed all over walls and buildings,' remembers Terry Baker, Greaves's future agent and close friend, then just a young fan. 'My exercise books in my last year at school had it all over them, and I got the cane for covering every surface in the school with it.'

'We felt sorry for Jim,' says Tottenham colleague Mike England, 'but Alf Ramsey wasn't going to change anything. He had his own ideas of what his team formation was going to be and you had to respect him for that and the success he'd had. It meant Greavsie missed out. But he was a brilliant player and he could have played in quite a few more games than he did.'

Derby and England defender Roy McFarland remembers asking Ramsey about Greaves in later years and being told that he had been paired with Bobby Smith, Geoff Hurst, Roger Hunt and several others and it had never clicked. In the end, Ramsey had to conclude that the reason was Greaves.

Ramsey was honest enough to admit that, on one level, it was personal – a matter of personal preference. 'Had anybody else been in charge of this England team it is probable that Greaves would have been included,' he told reporters. 'I agree that Greaves is still a considerable player, but I do not consider that he fits into my scheme of things.'

According to critics, Ramsey's 'scheme' appeared to be 'anyone but Greaves'. When England lined up against Bulgaria at Wembley in December, Manchester City's bulldozing and dynamic Francis Lee was given a first cap. One report noted that Greaves had already scored more goals than the entire Arsenal team in 25 matches. After Christmas, when Romania were the visitors, it was the turn of Gunners forward John Radford to be given a debut.

Radford had been propelled into the international picture on the back of Arsenal's solid start to the season, which had included reaching a two-legged semi-final against Tottenham in the League Cup. Beaten 1-0 at Highbury, with Mike England up front in place of the injured Martin Chivers, Spurs were denied a place in the final by the events of a mean-spirited second leg. It was described by Desmond Hackett as 'little short of a disgrace to soccer'. In among a series of ugly fouls and flashpoints, Arsenal extended their aggregate lead and Greaves fired in a 68th-minute shot to put his team back in contention – only for Radford to keep Spurs from Wembley with another goal four minutes from time. 'It was one hell of an anti-climax,' Greaves noted.

Meanwhile, Ramsey's next squad announcement was in March, ahead of the Wembley friendly against France. *Goal* magazine devoted a double-page spread, headlined 'It's Goals ... Or Else', to the issue of England's inability to find the net. Nat Lofthouse, who knew a thing or two about that subject, suggested, 'When you look at Greaves – the way he snaps up goals from all over the place – it makes you wonder whether he wouldn't be the answer.'

Wales manager Dave Bowen argued, 'You can afford a pure finisher up front. Greaves is one of the best.' The publication's own writer, Peter Barnard, weighed in with, 'Not many months ago I was prepared to write off the Greaves for England school of thought as Spurs partisanship and nothing more. But the incredible Jim has scored so many goals this season that Sir Alf Ramsey can no longer ignore the chants.'

Oh yes, he could. Reporters were left to express their continued surprise at Greaves's omission, especially with Hunt retained despite having been substituted by Liverpool a day before the squad announcement and having scored only eight League goals during the season.

In one respect, Greaves and Ramsey were in accord. Both seemed to have had enough of the constant raking over the coals of this selection issue. 'I never expected a recall,' said Greaves, aware that if he was not picked during this purple patch he never would be. 'It seems pretty obvious that it will never come. Seemingly this is Alf's wish, so the sooner the fuss dies down the better. I hope everyone drops it – although I appreciate what people are trying to do.'

Ramsey, meanwhile, was fed up with being painted as the bad guy. In his mind, Greaves had articulated a desire not be chosen and it was time to share that with his critics. 'I am being crucified because I am not selecting Greaves, yet he has told me he does not want to play for England,' he explained. He also added that

Greaves 'did not want time away for training without having a game'.

Greaves was unhappy that Ramsey allowed it to be known that he had effectively voluntarily retired from international football. 'I like and respect Alf and appreciate the loyalty he shows to his players. This, though, was one time when I felt let down,' Greaves said three years later in *Let's Be Honest*, his collaboration with Reg Gutteridge. In his 1979 autobiography, he went even further. 'I was astonished by that statement because deep down I still wanted to play for my country,' he said. 'Alf completely misunderstood me if he really did believe that I had asked him not to select me to play for England anymore.'

Perhaps Ramsey had genuinely felt that Greaves did not wish to be picked again. Or maybe his reluctance to train with the team without a guarantee of playing was further proof to the manager that he was not quite made of the right stuff. Ramsey may, of course, have chosen to be deliberately misleading to get the press off his back.

Besides, Greaves was a thorn that Ramsey must have thought had gone from his side. 'Alf had me marked down in his photographic memory as a ringleader of the drinking squad,' Greaves said of an incident as far back as 1963, when he'd asked if the players could leave the hotel for a drink after their game against Czechoslovakia. Then there had been the night out before the trip to Portugal and an incident in New York, where Greaves and Bobby Moore had ventured out late at night to see Ella Fitzgerald perform in a nightclub.

Ramsey also recalled being picked up by Greaves after the manager had chided his player for not contributing to a team discussion about the merits of club directors. Explaining his reluctance to engage in such a conversation, Greaves said, 'There's small choice in rotten apples, Alf.' Ramsey attempted to mock Greaves for his terse remark, urging him to say more and reminding him that English was the language of Shakespeare.

'That is Shakespeare, Alf,' Greaves deadpanned. Ramsey was no more amused by that than he had been by the occasion when Greaves and Moore delayed the departure of the team bus in West Germany because they were chatting in a hotel lobby. 'Mr Moore and Mr Greaves, we will go when you are ready,' he'd been forced to call out.

Ramsey was relieved to be rid of such disruptions to his ordered world. As George Cohen points out, 'Greavsie was never the most disciplined. He had his own way of doing things and that brought him into conflict with Alf on occasions. Alf accepted individuals, but only on his terms.'

Former Chelsea team-mate Barry Bridges told McKinstry, 'Alf was great if you were doing the business for him, the straightest guy you could ever meet, but you would not want him as an enemy. If you crossed him he would not get you straight away but he would get you in the end. You would get your comeuppance. I sometimes wonder if that is what did for Greavsie.'

John Sillett, who had been a team-mate of Greaves and Ramsey, says, 'Alf would be disciplined and straight down the middle. If you swore in the dressing room he would be at you. And he didn't like a laugh and joke before the game. You had to be deadly serious, whereas Jimmy would like the odd crack. And when he would go into the shower or toilet for a fag, Alf hated all that.'

On the field, even Greaves knew that his qualities were more removed from Ramsey's requirements than ever. And what Ramsey perceived as his deficiencies – work rate, teamwork and so forth – were becoming even more apparent. Greaves was not about to compromise, even though he saw Ramsey's methods and philosophies becoming absorbed more broadly into the game. The increased use of the 'systems' he abhorred was never going to change his own approach.

Ian St John explains, 'He was so funny about his lack of running around in games and so-called lack of effort. He would make jokes about it all the time. He was used to hanging around and, all of a sudden, the ball would come to him. Where other players run around all energy, Jimmy would laugh at that type of thing.'

England continues, 'The game has changed and everyone now has to work their tails off. Jimmy's great delight and love was scoring goals, hanging around the penalty area. That was his game when he was at his best. The idea of trying to run back was not in his mind. All he thought about was scoring goals.'

Mullery adds, 'Jim was not doing what they do now, putting people under pressure if you lose the ball. Everybody attacks the player, but he didn't do that. I don't think I have seen him win a tackle in all the years I played with him.'

Yet journalist Norman Giller, a close friend of Greaves, believes Ramsey struggled with the omission of his country's leading scorer more than might have been apparent. 'He used to lose sleep worrying and wondering if he dared play without Jimmy, the greatest goalscorer of his time, but who could disappear from matches for long spells. Alf believed in the collective, Jimmy was a free spirit. Alf could only see football in team terms, while Jimmy thought everything should be off the cuff. He despised coaching and most coaches. It worked at Tottenham because Bill Nicholson was astute enough to know that Jimmy preferred to play by ear, so he had the rest of the team organised to be support players. Alf only saw Jimmy a dozen times a year and could never convert him to his disciplined way of thinking about the game.'

In the end, a 5-0 win against France and an impressive Home Internationals series – the first time the tournament had been condensed into one week at the end of the season – meant that the 'Jimmy for England' campaign was forgotten. A new strike force of Hurst and Lee was becoming established and Ramsey's team were rated as having a reasonable chance of defending their world crown in Mexico, especially after they were unlucky to go down 2-1 to Brazil in Rio de Janeiro on their summer tour.

'I was always proud, yes, very proud to play for England and I feel I served the team well,' was Greaves's own conclusion. 'It hurt me deeply that people were thinking that I did not care about international football. I was capped 57 times and scored 44 goals. You don't put that sort of service in for England if you are past caring.'

Meanwhile, Spurs, knocked out of the FA Cup in the quarter-finals by eventual winners Manchester City, would finish their season in sixth place in the First Division. Greaves led the goalscorers in all four divisions with his haul of 27. Sir Alf Ramsey might not want him in his team, but Bill Nicholson would be happy to have Greaves's services to himself for a good few years yet. Wouldn't he?

* * * *

Greaves scored the first Spurs goal of the 1969-70 season in a 3-1 defeat at new champions Leeds United, a typically brilliant thrust into the home team's penalty area before cutting back to his left and side-footing the ball into the corner. The result was a portent of the season the club would endure, a disappointing plod towards a finishing position of 11th and early exits in both cup competitions. For Greaves, it was a less valuable omen. There was to be no goal-a-game romp in this campaign.

He did score again in the second match, a 4-0 win against Burnley, but missed a penalty against the same opposition a week later as he found the net only once in seven League games. Even allowing for the fact that he often found himself operating in slightly deeper positions since the return of Martin Chivers from a serious knee injury, it was a concerning output.

Into the club's problematic start to the season came teenaged midfielder Steve Perryman. 'By the time September comes around results hadn't been that great,' he remembers. 'They played Jimmy in midfield because they were short of players and Roger Morgan, who was a winger, played a couple of games. So, for whatever reason, they brought me in.'

Perryman will always be indebted to Greaves for the welcome he offered his nervous new team-mate. 'Can you imagine how I felt stood in the tunnel before my first game against Sunderland

and I am alongside Greaves, Gilzean, England, Jennings, Mullery. That is quite daunting, isn't it? You ain't even worked out who you are yet, or your game. You have been good enough for someone to believe that you are good enough for that day and you don't know if it is going any further than that. Jim was approachable; he would talk to you and calm you down. For a youngster coming into the team, that was gold dust.'

Perryman has good reason to remember the game played on 18 October, when *Match of the Day* captured Greaves scoring twice in a 2-1 win against Newcastle United. His brace included another of his most replayed goals. Picking up the ball just beyond halfway, towards the left touchline, he sprinted away from defenders as he ran diagonally into the box, rounded goalkeeper Iam McFaul and rolled the ball into an empty goal from the six-yard line.

'Jimmy at home, you couldn't touch him,' says Perryman. 'I don't know why Bobby Moncur was running at the edge of our box, but I ended up reading what he was going to do. As I tackled him I smashed the ball upfield. It goes to Jimmy on the halfway line; he turns, runs, beats two or three, rounds the goalkeeper and puts it in the net. The papers said I made the goal. No, I fucking tackled it. I didn't know where it was going. Jimmy was shit off a shovel; a professional goalscorer.'

BBC viewers would not see Greaves score at White Hart Lane again and either side of Christmas he endured two miserable matches that took him to six games without a goal. After a 2-0 home defeat to West Ham, broadcaster and journalist Brian Moore noted that 'for him to miss so many chances ... was unbelievable. With his head tucked forlornly on his chest, it was he more than anyone who denied Spurs at least a draw.' On Boxing Day, Spurs beat Crystal Palace 2-0, but, according to Gerry Harrison in *The Times*, Greaves was 'at the right end of a fistful of chances, but on the wrong side of luck, accuracy and urgency'.

At the end of 1969, managers who had led teams in the First Division in the 1960s were asked to vote for their leading striker of the decade. Unsurprisingly, Greaves came out on top, ahead of Hurst, Lee and Denis Law. The events of January 1970, however, made the vote seem like a taunt; labelling him as a man out of time, a relic of the past.

He did score three goals across the two games it took for Spurs to dispose of Third Division Bradford City in the third round of the FA Cup. Perryman recalls, 'We have been drawn away at Bradford and it is on ice. Here is naïve Steve running about in midfield trying to make tackles, which is impossible. I have tried to put this ball through someone's legs and it has got cut out and they have broken on us and scored, so we are now in the dressing room 1-0 down. Bill Nick is talking tactics and every now and again he throws in, "Jim, make an angle. Keep making angles." Then he throws in, "You must have been stood behind that fellow for Steve to attempt to put it through the legs." Jim had had about five mentions in the team talk and at the end he stood up and said, "Steve, don't try any more fucking flash stuff because I get a bollocking for it."'

There was nothing flash about Greaves and his colleagues being shut out in two fourth-round matches against Crystal Palace, a goalless draw at White Hart Lane followed by a 1-0 defeat at Selhurst Park. On the Friday morning before their next League game, against Southampton, Nicholson made his response to those results known to his players. Four experienced men – Greaves, Gilzean, Joe Kinnear and Cyril Knowles – were told they were being dropped and asked to leave the remainder of the team meeting. 'This was something that had to be done,' said Nicholson. 'There was no alternative. We must rebuild from the ashes. I could have made changes for the Palace replay, but say I had left out Jimmy Greaves? You press guys would have crucified me.'

Beal argues, 'I think Bill probably went a little bit too far in dropping those players, but the Cup was important in those days and he thought the players weren't pulling their weight. Usually,

Bill would give you three games, though. If you were bad in three games then he would leave you out. That is how he worked.'

Gilzean would be reinstated within a couple of weeks; Kinnear and Knowles were back in their full-back positions for the final few games of the season. All would be mainstays of the trophy-winning seasons that were around the corner. For Greaves, there was no coming back. Suggestions arose immediately that he would be meeting Nicholson to discuss his future. Ken Jones wrote in the *Daily Mirror* that 'his stature as one of the game's great stars has steadily diminished since his exclusion from the World Cup final', which might have been somewhat revisionist and overlooked his form of only 12 months earlier. But it did indicate that Spurs without Greaves was no longer impossible to contemplate, especially with his two-year contract due to expire at the end of the season.

Given the form he had been in throughout the previous year, Greaves's fortunes were going downhill at a rapid rate, although Nicholson recorded, 'I cannot say when I first noticed a decline in Jimmy Greaves as a player.' Noting that 'his reactions had slowed' he pointed out, 'Reflexes are the first thing to go with a footballer and he relied heavily on them.'

Quite how much Greaves was eroding that aspect of his game with his off-field activities is difficult to gauge, but he did admit that his social drinking, always considerable, was moving towards more dangerous territory by this time. 'Knocking back the booze became more than just a habit,' is how he recalled this period. 'It started to become a necessity, like water to a plant.'

'Bill had probably seen something we hadn't seen in Jimmy at the time,' Mullery suggests, 'with the drinking and things like that.' Nicholson had been given cause to warn Greaves about his behaviour after Tottenham's European Cup Winners' Cup victory at Hajduk Split in Yugoslavia in the autumn of 1967. Following a 2-0 victory, the Spurs players had celebrated in a men's club. Just as he was deciding to return to the hotel, Greaves was collared by a group of Russian businessmen, who persuaded him to drink numerous toasts to all manner of global figures. Eventually, he had to be carried to bed by his team-mates, one of whom Greaves managed to push into the hotel's indoor swimming pool. Nicholson sought him out during the flight home, reminding him that he was 'old enough to know better' and warning him to restrict his drinking.

Meanwhile, Greaves had developed other, healthier, distractions from football. Shortly after his return from Milan, he had gone into business with his brother-in-law, Tom Barden. He was now chairman of a parent company with an annual turnover of £1 million, its businesses expanding from boxes and packaging into country-club management, sports shops, insurance, travel and clothing. 'Jimmy was not the player he had been and I knew he was concentrating more on his business career,' recalled Nicholson, who had allowed him to return home during a summer tour of Canada in order to attend to important business matters. In addition, Greaves was planning to drive for the Ford team in the London to Mexico World Cup Rally at the end of the season.

While he continued to turn out for Spurs reserves, reports emerged of interest from Ipswich Town manager Bobby Robson and Manchester City's Joe Mercer. West Ham United, geographically still Greaves's local club, was cited as another possible destination if he and Nicholson concluded that he had no future at a club where he had scored 266 goals in 380 competitive matches. Greaves would also claim that he was told by a third party that Brian Clough would like to take him to Derby County, newly promoted to the First Division under the captaincy of his old pal Dave Mackay. Yet such a development was never pursued by either party.

Dialogue between Nicholson and his unhappy striker produced no plan of action. 'There will no quick decision on his future,' Nicholson announced. He also voiced his increasing frustration at the media's preoccupation with the story. 'I am sick to death of all this fuss about Greaves. I know now just how Sir Alf Ramsey must have felt when everybody was on his back. Greaves has been a wonderful player for Spurs, but that doesn't mean I have to bow to pressure to make a decision before I am ready.'

On 16 March, transfer deadline day, Nicholson was ready.

While newspapers were speculating that West Ham could eventually be a destination for Greaves, either now or perhaps during the summer, there was no suggestion that his former England team-mate, Martin Peters, might be heading in the other direction. Hammers manager Ron Greenwood knew, however, that one of his World Cup winners was keen to escape what he saw as the shadow of the other two, Bobby Moore and Geoff Hurst. 'He felt he was the "third man". He believed the other two were getting all the credit and limelight,' Greenwood would reveal.

Greenwood and Nicholson agreed to meet outside Chingford Greyhound Stadium. 'Martin wants away,' Greenwood offered. 'What do you think? What about a straight swap for Greavsie?' Nicholson quickly agreed in principle, although the relative ages of the two men – Peters was almost four years younger – meant that any deal would necessitate a cash adjustment. In the end, an agreement was reached that would make Peters the first £200,000 player in British football – with the value of Greaves within the deal estimated by reporters at anything from £54,000 to £80,000. Now Nicholson had to sell the idea to Greaves.

Doing some chores at his new home in Upminster – on the same road as one of his previous houses – Greaves assumed that the transfer deadline would be passing without any developments. Then the telephone rang. It was Nicholson informing him of his agreement with Greenwood, who was now waiting to talk to him at West Ham. Shocked, but aware that an immediate decision was required, Greaves travelled to Upton Park and agreed to the transfer.

Greenwood would recall Greaves telling him, 'Give me a blank contract and I'll sign it.' But while the West Ham manager took such a response as genuine enthusiasm, it might equally have been a reflection of a 'couldn't care less' attitude.

'I wish to God I had told Bill I was not interested,' Greaves would later say, but he was swayed by the prospect of playing alongside his great friend, Moore, and having to travel only 15 minutes to the Chadwell Heath training ground. Publicly, he was full of enthusiasm. Returning home to pose for photographs – hammering a nail into a wall, of course – he said, 'It's tough leaving a club like Spurs, but the time is right for the break.'

Norman Giller suggests, 'At the time, he took it in his stride and a shrug of the shoulders. It was only when he dwelt on it in later years that he got angry at the way Bill Nicholson handled it. Bill was desperate to get Martin Peters – and he had wanted Bobby Moore even more. You have to remember that Jimmy had lost his appetite for the game at the time. Bill Nick was convinced he was more interested in rallying because of the concentration he gave to preparing for the drive to Mexico. The move suited Jimmy because he lived locally to West Ham and he was starting a wide range of business interests in Essex. In brief, he was not deeply hurt at the time, but it dawned on him much later that he should have stayed at Tottenham, where his heart was. The West Ham club he joined was a viper's nest of unrest.'

Three years later Greaves would tell literary collaborator Gutteridge, 'I found it very hard to leave White Hart Lane. I enjoyed almost every moment of my career there. I shall always remember with pride that while I was with Tottenham I played for what I maintain was the greatest British side of all time.'

The speed with which the transfer moved to conclusion meant there was no chance for any formal farewell between Tottenham and the man who'd scored more goals for them than anyone in the club's history. 'It rankles with him forever,' says Terry Baker. 'No one said goodbye. No directors or management. He just went in, cleared his locker and left with no fanfare or consideration of his achievements at the club.'

Despite the newspaper conjecture, the reaction to the swap from within the Spurs dressing room was one of surprise. 'I was amazed Bill let Jim go,' remembered Gilzean. 'I went in to train and Martin Peters was there. I couldn't believe it. It was great to have Martin because he was a fabulous player, but it would have been great to have them both. That would have been special. Jim had more in him, as long as his legs kept going.'

Beal adds, 'It was a surprise to us and certainly to him. He was hurt by it. I never saw a decline in Jimmy. There were times when things didn't work out for him and he would say, "We will have to make up for it next game." He always thought he could go out and score four goals next game, which he could.'

As a newcomer to the team and therefore less steeped in the Greaves legend, Perryman was perhaps more able to see the logic in Nicholson's strategy. 'The coaches were probably planning it for half a season or whatever,' he suggests. 'Gilly was still going, Chivers was coming off injury. Nobody wanted to see a character like Jimmy leave the club, but in the end you sort of thought it might be best for him as well.'

Perryman could also see that Greaves was a player of a different time, even though still only 30. 'It was the era of work rate. It was work rate and organisation that helped Tottenham win two League Cups and a UEFA Cup. Jimmy was not that type of player; he was the one who put the cream on top. Teams couldn't afford to be outworked and therefore the special talents suffered and Jimmy's goalscoring talent suffered in relation to Bill Nick's team. I started off as a schoolboy inside-forward and was known as a passer, but by the time I have played 50 games in the first team I am an "umper and dumper". I am work rate and winning tackles. After two or three years my brother said to me, "Steve, I am not watching you play anymore. All you do is run about. You don't pass it; you don't play. The manager is never going to leave you out because you run more than anyone in the team but it ain't doing your personal game any good." He never started watching me again until I was in my late 20s and I had moved to the back and was bringing the ball out and playing.'

Half a century later, Perryman feels blessed that the beginning of his Tottenham career overlapped the final months of Greaves's contribution to the club's history. 'I was lucky in future years to be a special guest at some of his shows. I used to love the hour or so before you went on; just talking to him. You got a check on what he thought about football. I feel totally privileged to have had one foot in the '60s, because when you play with the likes of Greaves and Gilzean, fucking hell, you have a different perspective on the game and how it should be played. The game became systemised and Jimmy wasn't a system player. But he was a class act and everyone is so respectful of his ability even now.'

A team with a reputation for playing the game more gracefully, and generously, than many of their method-reliant rivals, West Ham looked like a natural home for Greaves. That did not mean that his move had been any more anticipated in the Upton Park dressing room than at White Hart Lane. 'You could never imagine Martin leaving West Ham,' says winger Harry Redknapp. 'He had come through the youth team and gone on to play in England's World Cup team.'

'It was a surprise,' says Geoff Hurst, who had never had much opportunity to develop a partnership with his new clubmate at international level. 'I was looking forward to playing with Jimmy. I didn't have to adjust my game, you just knew he was going to do something. I was expecting it to be enjoyable.'

And for one match, at least, it was. Admitting to feeling nerves and the weight of expectation upon him to perform his usual party piece of a debut goal, he took the field at a mud-caked Maine Road to face Manchester City. After only 10 minutes, he took a low delivery from Peter Eustace on the right, paused to control the ball and slotted a neat left-foot finish beyond Joe Corrigan's right hand.

It was the kind of finish that prompts generous praise from Redknapp. 'Jimmy could run with the ball like it was tied to his laces,' he says. 'And then everything stopped. When he got in front of goal, Jimmy would go to shoot, a defender would come sliding across to block it and Jimmy would pull it back on the other foot. Then another defender might come in and he would go to shoot, come back the other way, the goalie would dive, and Jimmy would roll it in the other corner. And walk away as if to say, "Well, that is what I am supposed to do."'

Another simple tap-in from just outside the six-yard box meant West Ham were well on their way to a 5-1 victory. Greaves took the goals in his stride, with only the most modest of celebrations. He appeared more animated on behalf of Ronnie Boyce when the midfelder volleyed Corrigan's clearance back past him from 40 yards in the second half.

The general goodwill surrounding his successful return to League football was reflected by City coach Malcolm Allison, who said it was possible to take a beating and 'still feel a great warmth for the man who inflicted it'. He continued, 'There can be no over-stating the greatness of Greaves's achievement. He makes his colleagues believe in his special powers. This is why I wanted him so badly.'

Greaves told reporters he had been reluctant to get out of his kit and called it 'a perfect afternoon'. Addressing comments that Nicholson had made on television about him possibly being past his best, he was honest enough to admit, 'I have thought so myself recently ... but then you get a game like Saturday's and it makes you wonder.'

Peters, meanwhile, had scored on his Tottenham debut, a home defeat against Coventry City, and had recognised the shadow from which he would have to fight to emerge. 'I could sense some resentment from the terraces,' he said. 'They'd loved Greaves. It did not take long to realise that, with the best will in the world, I was unlikely to replace Jimmy in their affections. My biggest problem in adapting to life at Tottenham was not going to be me, but Jimmy Greaves.' That Peters went on to become one of the club's finest and most popular players was a testament to his ability and Nicholson's judgement.

Greaves scored two more goals in West Ham's remaining five games as his team finished 17th, having at one point been in severe danger of relegation. Redknapp recalls, 'Everybody at the club idolised Jimmy. Everyone loved him because he was such a fantastic bloke and had been such a great player. But, if we are honest about it, he was past his incredible best when he came to West Ham. He showed glimpses of that greatness, but only in bits and pieces. His problems were starting and once he was drinking he lost that edge, that sharpness, that fleet of foot. It was difficult to maintain that when he as living the life he was.'

It took no time for Redknapp to become aware of his new team-mate's lifestyle. 'His first day at the club, we all went over to the Slater's Arms with Jimmy because we all wanted to be with him. We were still in there at seven or eight at night after getting in there at half-past one. It was too much to keep that pace up, but Jimmy kept going.'

Buoyed by the publicity around their new signing, the club reported increased season ticket sales for 1970-71. But while the Upton Park fans anticipated a full season of Greaves, he had another sporting engagement to fulfil. He was going back to the World Cup. And this time he was driving.

12

YOU CAN DRIVE MY CAR

'If I'd realised just how hard the race was going to be, I doubt if I could have faced the thought of it. The drivers have to be in love with the game to do it. There were times when I felt absolutely sick.'

JIMMY Greaves had not exactly given his final weeks at Tottenham and his early period at West Ham his single-minded attention. He had other things to worry about; notably, how to survive six weeks of speeding around Europe and South America in a Ford Escort. And not just surviving; competing with the world's top performers in their sport. What his former England team-mates would face in the heat and altitude of Mexico as they defended the World Cup seemed like a holiday in comparison.

It was the sporting link between 1966 and 1970 that had prompted rally driver Paddy Hopkirk and promotional mastermind Wylton Dixon to dream up, during a cocktail party in Chelsea in 1968, a race that would begin at Wembley and end at the Azteca Stadium in Mexico City, just as the World Cup finals were about to kick off. Dixon, an abrasive Australian who'd devised the World

Cup Willie mascot in 1966, barely knew that rallying existed as a sport until his chance meeting with Hopkirk, a Monte Carlo Rally winner who was due to participate in the London to Sydney Marathon later that year. But he saw the forthcoming World Cup as the ideal opportunity to create a similar long-distance event, the scope of which ended up being mind-boggling. Drivers would be asked to cover more than 16,000 miles over the course of 27 competition days spread across six weeks. They would race in Europe, South America and Central America – sometimes for 11 hours at a time – and ships would be required to carry the cars across the Atlantic and later the Gulf of Panama.

By the time the blueprint was in place, it would make the London-Sydney event look like a gentle Sunday excursion – and Hopkirk could vouch for how tough that one had been. He had ended up missing out on victory when he and Tony Nash, lying in second place, stopped to rescue the race leaders, who on the penultimate stage had collided head-on with an oncoming car on a stretch of road supposedly closed to traffic. Having pulled the occupants from burning vehicles, they then drove back to warn police and get the road closed, preventing further accidents.

Now Dixon needed to find someone prepared to pay for his grand scheme. Hopkirk had seen the *Daily Express* and *Sydney Telegraph* offer a modest sponsorship for the London-Sydney race, so he and Dixon approached the *Daily Mirror*, the giant of Fleet Street, with its daily circulation of five million. The newspaper loved the idea so much that they stumped up £250,000 – a phenomenal amount for the time – to launch the *Daily Mirror* World Cup Rally.[23]

'It is still considered to be the best ever,' according to Ted Taylor, organiser of the Historic Marathon Rally Show. 'It covered tough terrain, some of the stages were at high altitude and at times they

---

23 Former *Mirror* journalist Anthony Howard, one of those assigned to coordinate coverage of the rally, reckoned the event ended up costing the newspaper almost £1 million, calling it 'maybe the last of Fleet Street's serious such extravagances'.

were going for a long distance at 100mph. It was continuous, hard, very fast driving.'

The route was designed at the request of the RAC by John Sprinzel, a legendary figure in the rallying world, and included deserts, rivers, jungle tracks and stomach-churning mountain trails. 'There will never be one like it again,' he recalls. 'It was hard and high. When I was doing the recce for the course with [rally driver] John Brown and a reporter from the *Mirror*, it took us an hour to change a wheel up in the mountains; we were just so exhausted. We were either laughing about it or just sitting down exhausted. Crossing the Andes at 15,000 feet, we realised the crew might need oxygen tanks.

'We were supposed to just see if the route was possible, but we did the whole thing, picking the stages and the controllers; interviewing all the auto clubs. When we got back they said I couldn't drive the event because I had been over the route. They said I had to run it. I said, "OK, my fee for running it will be a new Porsche." They agreed and I got a new Targa 911.'

The *Daily Mirror*, meanwhile, was planning to assign a vast team of 20 reporters and 12 photographers – 'equipped with oxygen for high altitudes and emergency medical kits' – to the creation of stories worthy of keeping the event on the front page. It would be no easy task. The days leading up to the rally's launch saw newspapers dominated by the gripping drama of Apollo 13's attempt to return safely to Earth after an on-board explosion aborted its moon mission. Then, while the rally was in full swing, Labour's prime minister, Harold Wilson, buoyed by optimistic opinion polls, announced that he would take on Ted Heath's Conservative Party in an early general election in June.[24] There was even a threat that newspaper production might be halted during the rally by an industrial dispute with its printers,

---

24 Wilson, and other observers, would believe that Labour's surprise election defeat on 18 June was down in large part to the downbeat and disaffected mood that settled on the population of England after they lost their World Cup quarter-final against West Germany four days earlier.

members of the National Graphical Association – a potentially disastrous piece of timing.

Aiming to mix some stardust with the petrol fumes, the *Mirror* and the event organisers went looking for 'celebrity' contestants to race alongside the cream of the rally world. Prince Michael of Kent was recruited to lead an entry from the Royal Hussars and 17th/21st Lancers; various all-female driving teams provided another news angle. But it was a footballer who was top of the target list. 'The whole rally was to do with football,' Sprinzel continues. 'The *Mirror* were putting up the money and we were trying to get the football crowd on the terraces and the motorsport enthusiasts. The original idea was to get the two sports combined, which I thought was a good idea. Walter Hayes, who was the boss of Ford publicity at the time and ran the Ford team, told us that Tony Fall was going to be taking a footballer with him.'

Of all the English players who would not be in Sir Alf Ramsey's likely World Cup squad, Greaves was the biggest name. And the decision to end the football season early, in mid-April, to allow the England team maximum preparation time before the tournament, meant that he would be free before the rally began on 19 April. 'I only ever heard Jimmy being mentioned,' explains Stuart Turner, Ford motorsport director at the time. 'He was "the one" – possibly because of all the debate about whether he should or shouldn't be in the England team. There were some media mentions that he should be playing, not messing about on a rally.'

Greaves, frustrated with where he found himself in his football career, was attracted by what he saw as a 'thrilling and unique experience' and Ford agreed that he could team up with Fall, an experienced driver, if he proved himself up to the task. It was Turner who identified Fall as the ideal driving mate for Greaves. 'A key part of a team manager's job can be pairing the crews for rallying and, knowing Tony quite well, I thought he would be a good partner for Jimmy,' he explains. 'It helped that as part of the build-up I sent Tony to Peru with Gunnar Palm to do the Rally of the Incas in an Escort. They won, giving us useful feedback on the car and conditions.'

Greaves arrived for his first day of testing, having half-expected Ford to have had second thoughts. 'I first met Jimmy when he arrived at the Ford competitions department, based at Boreham, near Chelmsford,' Turner continues. 'My main concentration was on winning the rally and Jimmy might have noticed my "what the hell have we let ourselves in for?" expression when I saw the number of journalists with him. When they'd finished taking their pictures with a car, I sat alongside Jimmy as he set off round the test track. The moment we were out of sight of the journalists, he pulled in and said, "If I'm making a prat of myself with this, say so and we'll stop." I said that if that was going to be his healthy attitude then it was not going to be a problem.' Ford confirmed Greaves's place in the event and set about arranging insurance for him, at the cost of £4,500.

Still at Tottenham, but out of the first team when he signed up for the event, Greaves threw himself wholeheartedly into his rally training, working to learn the driving and navigational skills he would need. At one press day, he was filmed taking instruction from Roger Clark, another successful Ford driver. So dedicated was he to this experiment that he suspected that Bill Nicholson took it as a sign of his diminishing appetite for football and his increased focus on life without the game, which probably hastened his departure from Tottenham.

'He was good,' Sprinzel remembers. 'Most professional sportsmen are good at anything they take up. We had a lot of cyclists who took up rallying towards the end of their careers and they were all bloody good rally drivers because they took it seriously.' And, rather than wondering who on earth Greaves thought he was to rock up and attempt to tackle their sport with no previous experience, the other drivers appeared to welcome his unexpected presence in their midst. 'There was certainly no resentment,' Sprinzel continues. 'Tony Fall was a very respected driver and people knew he would not take on somebody who wasn't up to it. Everybody liked Jimmy and he was a lot of fun on the way round. He brought out big crowds wherever we went.'

Turner adds, 'I didn't get any negative feedback about it, although people had enough on their plates preparing for the rally to be over-concerned about what others were doing.'

The rules were that each stage had to be completed within a certain time without the drivers exceeding the designated speed limits, incurring penalty points for slow times. The fewest penalty points would determine the winner of the £10,000 first prize. The majority of the 96 cars, from 22 countries, were modified versions of commercial models, and there were even a couple of Rolls-Royces in the field. Greaves was co-driver in one of the Ford works team's three Escorts, with Clark driving one sponsored by the new football magazine, *Shoot!*

'It was quite big prize money for the time and this was the first time advertising was allowed on cars,' Sprinzel explains. 'Before that, you could have the word Dunlop in about five-inch letters on your overalls and that was it. They finally realised that to pay for an event like this the cars would have to have sponsors.'

Sprinzel had been warned by Dean Delamont, manager of the RAC Competitions Committee, 'This is too tough. We won't get anyone to finish it.' Rally controller Graham Robson, who wrote the definitive account of the rally to celebrate its 40th anniversary, explained, 'The London to Sydney was good, but many people thought it was just too easy, so the World Cup Rally was deliberately tough. Where John Sprinzel was involved, there had to be adventure and there was plenty of that once the cars got halfway up South America.'

Hopkirk would end up describing one of the South American sections like 'driving flat out from Edinburgh to Dover in the fog, on unmade roads strewn with rocks and animals'. There would be times when an exasperated Greaves wondered what he had signed up for.

At least it all began in familiar surroundings. One week after Chelsea and Leeds United had battled to an FA Cup final draw on a Wembley mud heap more appropriate to rallying than football, the entrants congregated in the stadium car park to make their final preparations. The following morning, 25,000 people were on hand to see them move inside, where an uncomfortable-looking Sir Alf Ramsey was waiting to wave the starting flag at 10.30am. Meanwhile, a lump of turf dug up by Bobby Moore was placed among the fleet of cars for delivery to Mexico.

The involvement of Greaves – and others whose presence was intended to keep the team of *Daily Mirror* journalists in stories – meant that the rally was considered the most prestigious of events for auto manufacturers and the buoyant British motor industry. Ford and British Leyland, in particular, saw it as a major marketing opportunity in their battle for the loyalties of the car-buyer. 'It was the first time anyone had given a shit about rallying,' says Sprinzel.

One by one, the cars rolled off a ramp in front of the Wembley stands, proceedings taking a break at the mid-point while renowned drummer Ginger Baker and his band, Air Force, performed. Failing to hear their cue to cease, they had the plug pulled after 20 minutes so that the cars could continue making their way carefully towards the centre of London along roads lined by the public. Inevitably, special cheers were reserved for the No.26 Ford Escort of Greaves and Fall. More crowds awaited as the drivers reached Parliament Square, rolled across Westminster Bridge and made towards Dover to cross the English Channel to Boulogne, before completing the first day with an evening drive into Germany.

Over the next six days, the contestants made their way around Europe. Having journeyed east across the northern part of the continent, they turned back on themselves when they reached the Iron Curtain and headed through the southern European countries to Lisbon. 'Those first seven days across Europe were really just a warm-up,' according to Robson, even though the fifth day saw an Antiguan driver escape without injury after driving his Hillman Hunter head-on into a truck and another racer slam his Morris 1800 into a tree. 'The stages in the Balkans were pretty difficult, weeding out the no-hopers early on.'

Greaves and Fall faced a tough decision in Yugoslavia when they came upon a bridge that had been repaired with some precarious-looking wooden planks. Whereas the Finnish driver Hannu Mikkola revved up his Escort and created enough speed to jump over a small gap in the middle of the temporary crossing, Greaves's experienced partner advised them to turn back and take a longer alternate route.

Sprinzel believes that Fall was the ideal partner for the rookie Greaves. 'He was a great guy with a good sense of humour. He was perfect for the job. You didn't want somebody who was totally dedicated to take Jimmy because a lot of the drivers drove nearly everything. I hardly ever let a co-driver drive because I couldn't relax and I think many others felt pretty much the same. Some would never let anyone into the driver's seat, whereas Tony probably would if Jimmy had shown himself to be competent in practice runs.

'Even though I never saw him in the driver's seat – and I was in all the main control rooms – I am sure that whenever Tony got tired he would let Greaves drive. He would not have let him drive on special stages, but they would be a team and Jimmy would have done a fair share of the easiest bits, for sure, because you couldn't drive those distances on your own. Some stages were nearly 1,000 miles long, so you needed someone else.'

Turner adds, 'My guess would be that Jimmy drove a third of it, but some drivers clung to the wheel longer than others.'

And when he was not steering, Greaves fulfilled the traditional roles of the co-driver, which Sprinzel jokes was to 'feed them drinks, light the cigarettes and read the pace notes'.

'The co-driver on many events is the office manager,' says Turner, 'responsible for the timekeeping, route finding, documentation etc.

But on the long, long distance events the duties probably get more evenly shared.

'A big debate before the event was whether to go with crews of two or three. I put my foot down for two-up.'

The rules meant that the drivers also had to perform more maintenance duties on their cars than in some other rallies. Sprinzel explains, 'At the rest halts, the cars were kept locked in the *parc fermé* so you could not stay up all night working on them. You had to go to bed or eat or whatever. We thought we would get a lot of private entrants and they would not have the back-up of all the service crews. We didn't want the big teams to have an advantage so we didn't let them enter the *parc fermé*. But the driver and co-driver could stay and work for a while, so the team would throw spares over the wall for them to work on. It was quite fun trying to stop them cheating.'

Turner hoped that attention to detail might give his Ford team the edge over their rivals. 'We even changed the rear lights to save a kilo each side,' he says. 'My team instructions said that if they were given change for anything they should throw the coins away to save weight. A forlorn request that was.'

The drivers had already travelled further than in most international rallies by the time they reached Portugal. At least they could now enjoy a break while the cars took two weeks to be shipped from Lisbon to Rio de Janeiro in Brazil, where their journey would become a whole lot tougher.

Fall and Greaves, despite needing repairs to a broken axle, ended the 4,500-mile European section in 10th place. But Greaves's absent-mindedness almost ended their rally on the quayside in Rio. The pair's customs paperwork, pace notes, money and personal documents were all kept in a briefcase, whose care was entrusted to the co-driver. As they pulled away from the dock for the short drive to the start point for the first Brazilian stage, Greaves forgot that he had left the case sitting on the roof of the car. Fortunately, the team behind them saw it fly off into the road and stopped to pick it up. Its safe return ensured the Greaves team's continued participation.

As the rally climbed into Chile, heavy snow slowed the cars on the 121-mile section between Putaendo and Illapel, making the Agua Negra pass almost impenetrable, but the Fall/Greaves team impressed by completing it in the second-fastest time. The next leg, a 510-mile stretch into La Vina in Argentina, was to be fraught with problems. They were one of two Escorts to be afflicted by a series of broken rear wheel studs and were in danger of grinding to a halt in the Andes because it was impossible to get the wheels to stay in place.

For a while, some temporary repairs offered respite but, in the end, the car had to be pushed to the completion of the leg on three wheels and a brake disc. Some further fixes got them back on the road, but they still had to limp through the next couple of days with only three studs on each wheel before reaching La Paz in Bolivia. At that point, they were still occupying a place in the top 10 and were one of only 39 cars still running. They had outlasted Prince Michael, who was now travelling with the rally as part of the organising group. 'He ensured we got great service at the airports,' according to Sprinzel.

But it was in the next stage, an 11-hour journey out of Bolivia into Peru, where the wheels literally came off. Fall had researched the route well and was feeling confident of a good performance, but the car's new studs stretched, which saw them temporarily lose a wheel. Then came a staggering series of 10 punctures, which meant that tyres and inner tubes had to be changed on the side of the road. 'By the time the eighth one happened, we were absolutely shattered,' said Fall. 'We changed the tyre and decided to have a five-minute rest at the side of the road, even though Stuart [Turner] would be mad with us afterwards. As I passed the other rear wheel I kicked the tyre in disgust and the damned thing went down. There was only one thing to do, we lay down and we nearly went hysterical with laughing.'

Greaves was dispatched to flag down a bus and head further along the route to bring back some tyres from a Ford service point. With no sign of his team-mate's return, Fall managed to set off. He eventually came across Greaves sitting despondently by the side of the road. The bus, Greaves explained, had turned off before he could locate the Ford service crew. 'It's been a bloody disaster,' Fall told reporters when they finally arrived in Lima four and a half hours behind schedule.

'They had a traumatic time in Bolivia,' Sprinzel concedes. 'They had to take buses and God knows what. To finish the rally after all that was a fantastic achievement. Normal people would have given up, but they didn't and I thought that was incredible.'

Greaves confessed there had been times, especially in Chile and after a 57-hour stretch without sleep in Bolivia, when the thought of quitting had been an attractive one. Had it been worth allowing his football to suffer during preparation for the event just so that he could risk his life? It required some encouragement in phone calls home to keep him, literally, on the road to Mexico.

Turner, however, expected nothing less. 'You can't do 16,000 miles, including 14,000 feet up in the Andes, and expect a totally uneventful run, so pulling out was never on the cards.' Besides, Greaves had been prepared somewhat by 'team members filling him with OTT tales about rallying before the start. He fitted into the team perfectly. He and Tony were coping so well. And keep in mind that, once the event started, I had one aim for the team – to win. If necessary, and mercifully it wasn't, I'd have pulled the Fall/Greaves car out in order to use bits to keep the potential winner going. Jimmy was keen and enthusiastic about the job. He didn't need anyone to carry him.'

It was around this time, Sprinzel laughs, that the Ford crew warned that 'at the end of it all we are going to have a football match between the teams and Sprinzel's head is going to be the ball'.

By 21 May, with the World Cup less than two weeks away, the rally had arrived in Colombia, with Greaves and Fall up to sixth position. The England football team had just left the country after winning a pre-tournament friendly the previous day by four goals. As Greaves would soon find out, his great friend Bobby Moore had whiled away some spare time during their visit by browsing in a jewellery store at the Hotel Tequendama in Bogota. The shopping excursion was to have global repercussions, but for now Greaves had other concerns.

The cars had been shipped via an Italian liner from Buenaventura in Colombia through the Panama Canal. After that, they would make a supposedly gentle journey of 350 miles along well-appointed roads into Costa Rica. Yet the Citroën DS21 of Frenchman Paul Coltelloni was hit head-on by a local vehicle trying to turn into a petrol station and his co-driver Henri 'Ido' Marang died from head injuries.

Meanwhile, Fall and Greaves continued to suffer bad luck. 'If any other car had suffered more punctures in this event, then it was unknown to the rest of the crews,' wrote Robson, 'and if any other crew had suffered from breakdowns so far from service and support it was not publicised.'

Driving along a supposedly clear road at high speed, they collided with a stampeding horse, which was killed on impact. The roof of their Escort was damaged and the windscreen shattered, while blood from the horse's head sprayed around the two men, along with flying glass. Fall was unable to prevent the car going into a spin and they were fortunate that no other drivers were on the same stretch of road at the time. 'I was trying to fall asleep when I felt the car swerving,' Greaves explained. 'Tony couldn't possibly avoid [the horse]. He tried, but the poor horse was hit so hard its head was taken off and the body somersaulted to crash through the windscreen. Tony and I were splattered in blood and shaking like leaves. We both felt sick for hours afterwards.'

If a runaway horse could not halt Greaves and Fall, then nothing would, and they duly cruised into Mexico City on 27 May as sixth-placed finishers behind winners Hannu Mikkola and Gunnar

Palm, their Ford team-mates. Formula One hero Graham Hill and FIFA president Sir Stanley Rous handed the trophy to the winners, but it was Greaves whom the crowds were more interested in seeing and he who received the loudest cheers as he delivered the symbolic square of Wembley turf to local officials. 'Jimmy Greaves has earned the admiration of the motoring world,' Hill declared. 'It is an outstanding achievement for him to finish so high in a field against some of the greatest rally drivers in the business.'

Once they had made their way to the rally's hotel headquarters, Greaves and Fall threw themselves fully clothed into the swimming pool. Having not had a drink since the rally left Rio, Greaves sat happily in the water for two hours sampling Mexican lager. But then he had a mission to attend to.

While Greaves had been completing his rally, Bobby Moore had been arrested during the England squad's stopover in Bogota as they travelled from Ecuador to Mexico. Accused of stealing a bracelet from one of the hotel stores during the team's earlier visit, Moore had been taken to court and placed under house arrest at the home of the head of the Colombian Football Federation. After four anxious days, he had been released and allowed to fly to Mexico City, where he had arrived – unshaven and wearing the same clothes – just before the rally drivers.

Moore was to spend the night in a British Embassy house before joining his team-mates in Guadalajara. Greaves was determined to see his friend, even though when he arrived at the building he was informed by the BBC's David Coleman that no one was being allowed in. At the rear of the house, Greaves was helped by Fall and Norman Giller to climb over a wall into the garden. Racing across the grounds so as not to be seen by security guards, he entered through some French windows to find Moore sipping a beer and reading a magazine.

'Right, Mooro,' he blurted out to his startled host. 'What have you done with that bracelet?'

It was a suitably strange ending to a surreal few weeks.

Greaves went off to the Caribbean for the two-week holiday that Ford had promised him and barely gave any more thought to his wild adventure and the remarkable feat of finishing so high in what is still regarded as the toughest rally ever staged. It barely merited a passing mention in his autobiographies. 'Jimmy really entered into the spirit of it, but he's never really talked about the rally since,' said Robson. 'I think it was something he did, and that was that.'

The rally world, however, is quicker to remember both the race and Greaves's part in it. 'Everyone was full of praise for the way that Jimmy Greaves and Tony Fall kept going,' Robson would write. And Sprinzel adds, 'Jimmy said he never had to work so hard in his life. He really loved it, though. It was special to him. It was special to many people.'

Turner, who had the satisfaction of having the winning car in his stable, states, 'In my book it was very much the toughest event ever held, what with the distance and the altitude. It certainly got massive publicity and not just in the UK. For once, we didn't measure the media coverage, we weighed it. Just as well really because, being new to Ford and its systems, I didn't find out that I hadn't really got a budget for the rally until afterwards. But I kept my job – just.' The victory by Mikkola and the publicity generated by Greaves saw to that.

'For Jimmy to finish sixth was a very fine achievement,' continues Turner, who saw enough in his celebrity driver to make him wish he could have worked with him again. 'Jimmy was always good company, but totally dedicated to the job in hand. If he hadn't been so immersed in the ball game, I think he could have become a regular rally driver. He certainly had the drive and determination.'

Or, as Robson concluded, 'Making a prat of himself, he might have thought. No way – on this event Jimmy was one of the real heroes.'

13

TAXI FOR MR GREAVES

'I made up my mind to retire after the Blackpool Affair, which was blown up out of all proportion.'

THE Imperial Hotel, looking out onto Blackpool seafront, was still filled mostly by those who had taken advantage of the establishment's special New Year's packages. On this first day of 1971, with petrol set to rise by two old pennies (about 1p) per gallon and Paul McCartney planning to take court action to achieve a legal split from The Beatles, the hotel was temporary home to an additional party who had checked in during the late afternoon; the footballers of West Ham United.

Their visit to the pleasure centre of the north-west, for a third-round FA Cup tie at Bloomfield Road the following afternoon, appeared likely to be rendered futile by freezing weather, leaving the players to find ways of spending a wasted evening away from home before a return to London next morning. Manager Ron Greenwood had placed no restrictions on their activities. Some played cards, some went greyhound racing, others opted for an early night. There wasn't much on television to grab the attention of young, red-blooded males, the centrepiece of BBC One's programming being a Gala Performance of ballet and opera from the London Coliseum, while ITV was pinning its late-evening hopes on a two-decades-old movie. The one scheduled sports programme of the evening, BBC Two's highlights of the second day of the third Ashes Test in Melbourne, had been washed out – as the entire contest would be.

Believing their team were no more likely to see action than Ray Illingworth's England cricketers, Jimmy Greaves and Bobby Moore were settled comfortably in the hotel restaurant, enjoying a few lagers after their meal. At around 11.30pm, they passed through reception on the way to their beds, stopping briefly to chat with members of the BBC television crew assigned to cover their game for *Match of the Day*. 'The pitch is iced over,' one of the cameramen confirmed, having been at the ground earlier. 'It will be a miracle if we play.'

Conversation was interrupted by the hotel doorman calling out to the BBC men, 'Your two taxis have arrived.' He was informed that there must be a mistake, as only one had been ordered.

Greaves barely allowed a pause for thought. 'We'll take the other one,' he piped up. With Moore and three other colleagues, he clambered into the taxi for a journey that would end up hastening him towards the premature end of his Football League career.

* * * *

It had hardly been a happy few months for Greaves since he returned from his rally adventure and reported for pre-season training. He looked jolly enough when captured by the ITV cameras sharing a joke with Alan Gilzean before kick-off on his return to White Hart Lane for West Ham's opening game of the season, a match that attracted more than 53,000. He would have appreciated the buzz of excited approval when he won a midfield tackle against Spurs defender Dennis Bond with his first touch and launched an attack. But even though he scored an inevitable first-half goal, the Hammers ended up drawing the three London derbies with which they had been forced to begin the season – including matches against Arsenal and Chelsea – and were soundly beaten at perennial title favourites Leeds United. By the time they lost 2-0 at home to Newcastle United they had gone five more League games without victory and had slipped to 20th position. Their only success had been a League Cup win against Hull City.

Harry Redknapp remembered being so angry at being substituted in the Newcastle game that he finished a post-match row with Greenwood by throwing a bottle at the dressing room door as the manager departed.

'You're a nice one, Harry,' said Greaves, who had been watching the conflict with a beer in his hand.

'Oh, don't you start,' Redknapp snapped back.

'You could have picked an empty one,' Greaves elaborated. 'That was our last lager, wasn't it, Mooro?'

There was an immediate opportunity for a change of scenery – and a few more drinks – with a trip to New York to face Brazilian club Santos; Pelé and all. No one welcomed it more than Greaves. On the flight, he, Moore and a business associate, Freddie Harrison, were joined at the bar by Greenwood. As the drinks were ordered, Harrison proceeded to slip a Bacardi into every Coke ordered by the Hammers manager. Greenwood would say that he was well aware of what was going on, but was happy to unwind and allow himself a little indulgence. The drinking session turned into a mutual confessional between Greaves and his boss.

Greaves was famously not one to spend too long analysing his game. When Greenwood had invited the Israeli skipper, midfielder Mordechai Spiegler, for a trial after being impressed by him in the 1970 World Cup, Greaves found himself having his ear bent by the eager-to-learn visitor on a bus ride to training. 'Do me a favour, Ron,' said Greaves as he disembarked, his head still buzzing with Spiegler's interrogation. 'Don't ever sit me next to him again.'

Yet, with the Atlantic below him and only one goal to his name all season, Greaves was dissecting the Newcastle defeat. He admitted to Greenwood, 'Do you know what? For the first time in my life, I think I froze in front of goal.' It was the equivalent of

Tommy Cooper saying he couldn't remember any gags. Greenwood responded by admitting that he was seriously considering resignation in the wake of the team's disastrous start to the season. Feeling a similar level of disillusionment that Greenwood was clearly suffering, the thought of battling on through the upheaval of a new manager was not something Greaves wished to contemplate. As Greenwood returned to his seat to sleep off the effects of the rum, Greaves resolved that if the boss followed through on his threat, then he would retire immediately. Yet after Greenwood awoke, the conversation was never mentioned again.

West Ham eventually reached 10 games without victory in Division One before beating Burnley 2-1 at Upton Park. It was not to be any kind of turning point. Having gone out of the League Cup to Coventry City, a home defeat against the same opposition in the League at the end of November saw Greenwood reach the end of his forbearance. With his team lying 19th after only two wins, he made them wait 75 minutes in their muddy kit before allowing them to get into the bath, instructing them to air their grievances freely. 'I really don't know what will come of this,' said Greaves when he emerged from the meeting. 'We were all choked and fed up over this result. Everybody spoke honestly. You have to thrash things like this out from time to time.'

The truth, however, was that Greaves was rapidly losing the motivation to show the leadership and commitment one might expect of one of the club's biggest stars. He was becoming more motivated to get to the bar.

'The booze didn't develop out of the World Cup, it came more out of my move to West Ham,' he would tell author David Miller. 'West Ham were a bad side when I got there. Hurst had lost a bit of his enthusiasm. There was some question of Moore going, and the atmosphere was bad. I wasn't on my way to being an alcoholic [at Spurs].'

Hammers defender John Charles said of the club at that time, 'We were always on the piss. We went from club to pub. Mooro was as good as gold on the field and off the field, but he was a pisshead. He liked a gin and tonic. He liked a lager too. You couldn't get him drunk. He was one of the best drinkers I knew.'

For the most part, Greaves insisted that the reason he drank while at Spurs was 'because I liked it' – although in analysing his behaviour in later years he argued that it also helped to relieve the stress of performing at the highest level in a sport that was increasingly becoming a hostage to the pursuit of victory at all costs.

At West Ham, however, alcohol had become something he could no longer function without. 'I don't know how come he began drinking,' says former Spurs colleague Phil Beal, 'but we know it was at West Ham where he really started. At Tottenham he was never a heavy drinker and if he had meetings to go to he wouldn't even go to the pub. No way would you see Jimmy knocking them back at that stage.'

But now Greaves recognised that he was 'into the early stages of alcoholism'. After training he would often hunker down for the afternoon in the Slater's Arms pub opposite Romford Greyhound Stadium. He would also find his way into a variety of bars closer to his home, saying that it took six or seven lagers before he began to feel relaxed.

Greaves had always intended to step away from football when it ceased to be enjoyable. 'And from the start of the 1970-71 season I was thoroughly miserable about West Ham's game and my contribution to it,' he recorded. He felt the club had too many modestly talented players, including himself in that category by that stage of his career.

Against Derby County at the Baseball Ground, he celebrated his 500th League appearance with only his fourth goal of the season in an impressive 4-2 victory over the team that had finished third in the table the previous season. Once more, it was a false dawn. Two more defeats followed before West Ham boarded the New Year's Day train to Blackpool.

At West Ham, a team he recognised as able to drink the Spurs crew in the Bell and Hare under the table, he was becoming trapped in a vicious, potentially ruinous, circle. The less he enjoyed his football, the more he drank, using alcohol as a 'crutch', something that could support him when worries about his form became too heavy to bear. So, when the spare taxi turned up at the Imperial Hotel, he accepted it like the half-chances he'd become famous for sticking away.

He was joined by Moore, strikers Brian Dear and Clyde Best and team physiotherapist Rob Jenkins. At Moore's suggestion, they instructed the taxi driver to follow the BBC cameramen to the 007 Club, owned by the former British heavyweight boxing champion Brian London.

Best was an unlikely participant. The powerfully-built teenager from Bermuda, one of the few black players in the First Division at the time, didn't drink – but he did enjoy listening to Greaves. Far from being deterred by additional competition for a place in the first team, Best had welcomed Greaves's arrival at Upton Park, even though he recognised that his glory days were far behind him. 'I was always very attentive in his company in terms of learning off him,' he said. 'I just wanted to learn, to improve, to enhance my skills – and who better to learn from than one of England's most famous forwards?' It partly explained his eagerness to join the group in what he thought was going to be 'a short visit to say hello' to Brian London. 'It didn't seem that big a deal,' he added.

Upstairs at the 007, the clientele, dressed to reflect the James Bond motif, gambled at roulette tables or made use of a dance floor that was roped in like a boxing ring. Downstairs, darker and more intimate, was where sports stars and celebrities enjoyed a little more privacy in the Gold Room. The West Ham party arrived shortly before midnight and, according to the various reports, were there until shortly after 1.30. Content with their own company, they left the dancing and gambling to the club's other customers. Greaves's recollection was that he managed to put away several beers, outpacing his colleagues by a distance. Best, meanwhile, downed a couple of glasses of ginger ale and lime. They returned to the hotel, ordered coffee and sandwiches and booked alarm calls for 10am. 'I suppose we all realised at the time we were leaving ourselves vulnerable,' Moore would admit, but added that they all achieved 'a good night's sleep by anyone's standards'.

On waking, they were surprised to hear that the game was going ahead, even though the pitch was still hard and frozen. Both Greaves and Moore, in recounting events in later years, insisted that they felt no ill-effects of their night out. Yet West Ham played as though suffering a collective hangover. A Blackpool team who were heading for relegation and had just fired manager Les Shannon were inspired by their young Scottish midfielder Tony Green, who had been pushed further forward to capitalise upon what the home team saw as Moore's vulnerability against extreme pace. Green scored twice in a 4-0 victory, cutting a swathe through a flimsy defence. 'The surface was at times like ice, but he reminded me of a ballerina,' Best recalled. 'He mastered the elements better than anyone. We just couldn't get near him.'

West Ham's fans, many of whom had taken the opportunity to combine New Year at the seaside with supporting their team, were not happy. Greenwood received a call from club chairman Reg Pratt on Monday, informing him that some supporters had seen the West Ham group out on the town in the early hours before the game. The manager was incandescent. He had trusted his players to act professionally – 'like I would like to have been treated as a player'. A few simple enquiries identified the guilty parties and he summoned them one by one to confess. Greenwood even claimed that 'Greaves came in and cried his eyes out', although Greaves recalled merely being angry that what he saw as a minor discretion was being painted as 'the crime of the century'.

Moore believed that 'the problem was not the drinking, it was the result' and that the two had been unconnected. Yet Greenwood, facing what he called the 'lowest point' of his West Ham career, felt that the four players, plus an important member of his staff, had 'let me down badly'.

'It was a bad day for the club,' Harry Redknapp recalls. 'Bad publicity all round. When you are a manager, that kind of situation is very hurtful. But we thought the game would be off for sure. No one would have thought about going out if they had thought the game would be on.'

Greenwood informed his chairman that he was requesting the board's permission to get rid of all five offenders. The directors concurred only in the case of Dear, a former European winner for the club who had recently been given a second chance after ending up on the dole following his release by Millwall. He would be allowed to leave on a free transfer. Greenwood's argument that all five should be treated equally was rejected and a series of fines and suspensions was agreed. In the players' case that meant a two-week ban for Greaves, Moore and Dear, plus one week's lost wages. Best was let off with a smaller fine.

Greenwood chose to remain silent publicly until after Moore had been the subject of ITV's *This Is Your Life* programme on the Wednesday evening, but then told reporters that the four players had been fined an undisclosed amount. 'Ron Greenwood was always a man of principle,' said Best, 'and expected his players to behave the same way – on and off the pitch.'

Yet Moore told Greenwood he should have denied the story to the press, while Greaves accepted the need for punishment but thought it should have been kept private. Greenwood felt that the guilty men needed to be named to protect the innocent from speculation. 'Greavsie and I were sickened by the way Blackpool was blown up out of all proportion,' Moore told biographer Jeff Powell. 'Whether people like it or not, whether they care to admit it, footballers are always doing what we did in Blackpool.' As recent proof he could point to the incident in 1965, when eight of Chelsea's title-chasing team had been caught out after curfew and were all subsequently dropped by manager Tommy Docherty from the vital game at Burnley for which they were supposed to be preparing.

Newspapers set about tracking down 'eye witnesses' to the events in the 007 Club, with one onlooker claiming, 'I could not believe my eyes when Bobby Moore walked into the club at almost midnight. He shook hands with Brian London and seemed to introduce him to the other players with him.' Meanwhile, London was quoted – bless him for his loyalty – as saying that the players had all been drinking orange squash.

An anonymous West Ham player was said to have told the *Daily Express* that team-mates were aware of the late-night session as early as the next morning, but thought nothing of it until after their heavy defeat. 'This was the most crucial match we had played at the club for years and the feeling was that we had been badly let down by a group of players,' went the quote, which read a lot like Greenwood's own words. There were, however, those in the dressing room who shared that opinion. Trevor Brooking, at the time a relative newcomer to the first team, would look back at the incident as 'probably the most spectacular betrayal of the boss'.

Redknapp and midfielder Billy Bonds had been watching television at the hotel before going to bed and, according to Bonds, 'we imagined everyone was too'. They had only learned what had transpired when they heard the news stories, although Bonds's observation on the game was that 'it was pretty clear to me right from the start that one or two of us didn't fancy it'.

Bonds remembered the players opting to keep 'heads down and mouths firmly shut' rather than speaking to the press, but recognised the extent of the hurt Greenwood felt. 'He trusted players to behave responsibly and was not the type of manager to go around knocking on doors.' Yet Bonds, a future Hammers manager, added that 'the whole eleven of us let down Ron and our supporters'.

Greenwood subsequently confirmed that Moore, Greaves and Dear were being dropped from the first team to play at Arsenal

– ironically on the same day that an exasperated Sir Matt Busby was excluding George Best from his Manchester United team to play at Chelsea after he had once again been absent from training and then missed the train to London. And with Arsenal on their way to winning both the League and FA Cup, manager Bertie Mee used the example of Greaves and his pals to remind his players of their responsibilities. 'He told us that fines would not be the Arsenal way,' says goalkeeper Bob Wilson. 'He didn't need to spell anything out. If any player was caught letting down the club in this way I don't think he would expect to play for Arsenal again.'

Greaves ended up spending five weeks on the sidelines – during which he missed three League games – before returning to score the only goal at Coventry, pouncing on a rebound after Hurst's shot had been saved. The result broke West Ham's run of six consecutive defeats, although it could not lift them above 20th position in the table. That was where they would end the season, albeit with a seven-point cushion between them and relegated Burnley and Blackpool.

Towards the end of March, with the end of the season still several weeks away, questions were being raised in the media about the likelihood of Greaves returning in 1971-72. 'I could not tell you what I am doing next week, let alone next season,' he told reporters after he'd scored both goals in a 2-2 draw against Ipswich Town. 'My only thinking is helping West Ham out of relegation trouble.' He might have accused people of 'putting two and two together and making five', but those calculations were far more accurate than he chose to admit. He would look back in later years and say that 'I felt an old man at 31'.

It was a Greaves winner four minutes from time that secured a 2-1 victory at West Bromwich Albion on Good Friday to effectively safeguard West Ham's First Division status, leaving reporters covering the club with little other than his future to focus on over the last three weeks of the season. By the time the Hammers faced Huddersfield Town in the final game, Greaves, having scored only eight goals in 31 League appearances, was widely assumed to be playing his farewell match. *Daily Express* reporter Norman Giller admits, 'I knew it was going to be his last game, but Jimmy had sworn me to secrecy on pain of death. So I hinted at it as best I could. Perhaps this reveals why our friendship lasted. He knew I could be trusted, but the journalist in me was busting to write the true story.'

Giller had to content himself with writing, 'I am making a special trip to Upton Park today just in case it proves to be his final match.' There was to be no big finish, however. After 357 League goals, a record for England's top flight,[25] he was kept off the scoresheet as the visitors went away with a 1-0 win.

'I recall nagging at him,' Giller adds, 'for not going for Arthur Rowley's League goalscoring record [434 goals]. But records did not mean a thing to Jimmy. "You do the counting, Norm. I'll do the scoring," he used to say – jokingly, not arrogantly. His next boast would have been his first. I think the goals he scored in non-League football after his retirement should be added to his overall total. Pelé's 1,000-plus goals include every goal that he scored, from youth football days and in meaningless friendlies.'

Three weeks later, Greaves gave reporters the news they'd expected. 'I have decided to get out while I am still a First Division player,' he said. 'The old legs were beginning to feel the pace.' And he revealed that his outward uncertainty of the final weeks of the season was just for show. 'I made my decision to pack up some time ago. I might play the odd Sunday match, but that will be my only association with football.'

His former manager, Bill Nicholson, declared that 'football cannot afford to lose players of his calibre', while Spurs striking partner Alan Gilzean believed 'he could have played until 35 and beyond because his fitness level was quite high and he had a knack of scoring goals'. He recognised, though, that Greaves was

---

25 Greaves's nine goals in Italy meant that he also held the record for most goals – 366 – in Europe's top five leagues until Cristiano Ronaldo surpassed his total in May 2017.

not happy in his new surroundings. 'He never wanted to leave Tottenham. I think he could have played on for longer had he still been at Spurs.'

Meanwhile, Hurst admits that his colleague's decision came as no great shock to him. 'I think you can tell with strikers,' he argues. 'You only have to lose that little bit of momentum and it can affect your form and your goalscoring. You have only got to look at any striker's record and you can clearly see the demise – me included. You start off scoring quite a few goals, scoring goals for fun for several years and then, at the back end of your career, aged 30 plus, you are scoring less and less often. That was the case with Jimmy. He had been at the top for a long time, playing since he was 17. No matter how great you are, old Father Time takes his toll.

'So it wasn't a surprise when he retired. I think he was grateful to have been at the top long enough to be able to choose to retire. Most people who didn't have his genius might have tried to hang on as long as possible. The heights he hit for Chelsea and Spurs were astonishing and it was probably the right thing for him to do. He felt that enough was enough and he had done a lot more than other people in their careers.'

Former Spurs colleague Steve Perryman suggests, 'Not that I want to be clever, but his retirement suggests it was not that bad a decision by Bill Nick to sell him. I don't want to guess whether there was anything else that played into Bill's decision – and in terms of what was going on off the field, I never saw any hint of problems. But I wonder if Bill knew about that and it played a part in him being allowed to go, and then his retirement.'

Brooking was another who had sensed the end looming. 'When I played with him at West Ham, he was coming to the end of his career and I suspect that the problems that would engulf his private life were already gnawing at him.'

John Lyall, describing Greaves as a 'delightful, infectious character,' recognised that 'we didn't see the best of him at West Ham'. Yet, according to Bonds, 'Some of us thought he had plenty of football left in him ... I am sure he could have gone on getting goals for much longer had he chosen to. But maybe he felt his legs were not what they used to be, and decided it was time to retire and try something else.'

But it was not so much Greaves's legs that had gone. It was his desire, partly eroded by an unquenchable thirst for alcohol. And without football to occupy him, that craving would become the element that governed his life. He was not quite done with the sport yet, but for the next seven years his most significant contest would not be one played out on the field or highlighted in the fixture list. It would be a private battle that took him from the goalmouth to the gutter.

14

THE ROAD TO HELL

'The drink? There was no alternative to that. It was probably inevitable, but I don't know why.'

JIMMY Greaves was a free man – released from the bonds of routine and the obligation of public examination in front of tens of thousands. So what if he put on a couple of stones? He had once described joining Tottenham Hotspur as 'paradise'. He would use the same word to describe the first two years after he departed football. He would soon find himself descending into a private hell.

The seven years between Greaves's retirement and the realisation that to continue drinking might kill him can be split into three distinct phases. First, there were those two years of perceived liberation, during which his increased intake was mostly centred around public houses and bars. For the next two years, he took more of his drinking home with him, hiding bottles of vodka around the house in places where he thought his wife, Irene, would never find them.

And then, after some level of acceptance of his plight, came three years that saw a series of desperate – but never fully committed – attempts to get his life back into some sort of order. There were appointments with psychiatrists, multiple short-lived stays in rehabilitation units and even a return to football. None were able to loosen the grip of alcoholism that was tightening around him, choking the meaning, the goodness and the purpose out of his life, strangling the resolve and resilience of those around him.

While football carried on without the man whose goals had illuminated so many Saturday afternoons, Greaves spent his early carefree days of retirement establishing a routine that began with a token couple of hours attending to his businesses. He was doing little more, however, than killing time until the pub opened and he could down a few beers and vodkas. After a light lunch it would be back home for a sleep and then out into the pubs of Upminster.

His specialist subject became the ability to navigate anywhere from east London into rural Essex via a sequence of pub locations. It was hardly a party piece in which to take much pride. Meanwhile, the weight gain and the growth of a droopy Zapata-style moustache made him almost unrecognisable from the slender and clean-cut on-field figure in baggy shorts. But he was still in the period of denying how serious his problem was and clinging to the belief that he could change his ways any time he chose.

Nominating a definitive cause of Greaves's escalation from social drinker to addict is as futile as trying to decipher the code behind his genius around goal. It is easy to suggest triggers and acknowledge accelerators, but it is generally accepted that no two alcoholics will have followed identical paths. It is a disease as individual as a fingerprint.

'I can pinpoint the day, the hour, the minute, the second that I doomed myself to a life as an alcoholic,' Greaves would write in *This One's on Me* in 1979. 'It was the moment I signed my name to a contract that tied me head and foot to AC Milan. From the day that deal was clinched, I was on the downhill run.' He looked back and recognised himself as being 'frightened, frustrated, bored, aggravated, depressed. All the classic ingredients that drive a man to drink.'

Yet he was to contradict himself. He wrote in his 2003 autobiography, 'My four months at Milan took their toll on me, both financially and psychologically. It was a depressing time in my life but it did not, as some have maintained, act as a catalyst to my later addiction to alcohol.' He seemed to have forgotten that it was he himself who had planted the seed of that theory.

This was no simple case, however, of Greaves choosing to rewrite history. In the first flush of his admission of alcoholism, and in a rush to identify its roots, it was entirely conceivable that he might have drawn a conclusion that would not stand the test of time and the greater understanding that years of sobriety offered him. Nick Charles, a reformed alcoholic who would play a role in the early stages of Greaves's rehabilitation and go on to earn an MBE for his work in the field, suggests, 'You stop drinking and immediately you look back and think, "I reckon I must have been an alcoholic by the time I was, say, 25." Then, by the time you reach five years sober, you see things differently. You realise that the truth is that you never really drank alcohol normally. Not ever.

'I am an absolute believer in genetic predisposition. Alcohol does different things to different people. To some it is a pleasant experience, but it doesn't do that much for them. Genetic predisposition is best defined as someone having a weaker tolerance than somebody else, and a drink gives them a massive lift.'

Greaves's older son, Danny, adds, 'Whether it is drugs or alcohol or gambling, all these are very much connected to the same thing. It is a flaw somewhere in someone's make-up. People talk about flawed genius and maybe, like George Best, my dad's flaw was alcohol.'

None of which is to say that Greaves was destined to be an alcoholic. But given all the events of his life that could conceivably have contributed to his progression into alcoholism, it would have taken someone totally lacking in Charles's 'genetic predisposition' to have resisted. As Greaves himself commented, 'If you delve deeply into the life and times of Jimmy Greaves you will find the answers to why I turned to the bottle for comfort and escape.'

The death of a child has led to the emotional disintegration of many parents. Team-mate John Sillett's view that the loss of his first-born son in 1960 was the initial step on Greaves's path of ultimate self-destruction was supported by Brian Mears, a Chelsea board member at the time. 'The compulsive drinking which was to blight his life in later years was in my view triggered by the dislocation caused by the tragedy,' he would suggest. 'The alcohol addiction ... was a substitute for a real sense of identity, in my opinion.' Greaves would remember the 'anger, frustration and sheer inner pain' of the period and the 'deep, lasting scar on both Irene and me' that was its legacy.

Then came the much-discussed isolation of his months in Italy, a period in which Greaves increased his drinking to 'blot out the nightmare' that he was living. 'The traps had been set,' he concluded.

His transfer to Tottenham placed him back inside the drinking circle of English football, an environment where it was easy for the boundaries of tolerance and the warning signs of over-indulgence to become confused. According to Steve Perryman, 'When we got relegated in later years one of the papers went back to the Double team to pass comment on the current team situation and I will never forget Maurice Norman saying, "I hear they don't even drink together." That sort of comment showed the way things had been.'

Apart from the social element, Greaves would also describe players with 'adrenalin pumped so high that a lot of us needed the calming influence of an after-match drink to bring us back down to earth'. And England colleague Bobby Moore recalled Greaves drinking 'a couple of pints the day before the big game', noting that 'Greavsie didn't think anything of it and in fact it was what he needed'.

It was a time when players socialised not only with each other, but with the fans. Spurs team-mate Tony Marchi explained, 'If you went up to Manchester they'd be there. You get in a hotel and they were booked there too. You'd have a beer with them at night.'

London clubs, of course, were far from unique in their attitude towards players' social lives. At Liverpool, the members of the Boot Room who guided the team's fortunes would much rather their players were sitting in a dingy bar getting sloshed than out in the fresh air playing golf and risking tiring their legs. Alan Gilzean recalled, 'At any club at that time there was a drink culture. You couldn't do that nowadays, not with iPhones and things like that. If you went to Manchester or Liverpool everyone went out and had a drink. That was just part and parcel of football. It couldn't have been that bad because England won the World Cup.'

Of course, Greaves's exclusion from the 1966 final was a blow whose impact has been debated for half a century. Sillett contends, 'I think it was a big nail in his coffin. He never forgave Alf Ramsey for that.' Yet Greaves always downplayed the long-term significance of that disappointment and we have seen how post-World Cup performance tends to bear out his belief that it was not a catalyst for disintegration.

His friend, Norman Giller, goes as far as saying, 'There is so much nonsense written and said on this topic. Yes, Jimmy was disappointed, but not to the devastating extent that people who don't know him make out. They give the impression he went and lost himself in a lake of booze all because Alf had left him out of the 1966 final. Rubbish! Jimbo was on a path to alcoholism regardless of what happened in 1966.

'Those of us who drank with him regularly will confirm that many could outdrink him. He had some sort of chemical imbalance that meant he was affected more than most by what is the poison of alcohol. Bobby Moore, Alan Gilzean, Dave Mackay – I could reel off a dozen names of footballers in our drinking school who supped more than James. The fact that he became addicted to drink had nothing whatsoever to do with the World

Cup. Jimmy never ever brought up the subject of the World Cup when discussing his problem at AA meetings.'

Another close confidant, Terry Baker, who would guide Greaves's later career in one-man shows, concurs. 'He often used to be asked on stage whether he became an alcoholic because he was left out of the World Cup. He never said this on stage, but privately he said to me in one of our rare sombre moments, "Of course it was devastating because I wanted to play, but do people really think that missing a game of football turned me to drink when I'd lost a son at six months old?" Missing a game of football meant nothing in the bigger scheme of things.'

But it can't have helped.

There is some consensus that the single event that created the greatest acceleration of Greaves's drinking was premature retirement from League football. By the time he returned to White Hart Lane to play in front of 45,799 in his testimonial match against Dutch side Feyenoord in October 1972 – scoring the first goal in a 2-1 win – he was beginning to realise the extent of what he called his 'biggest mistake of all'. He would recall, 'I turned to the bottle. In no time at all the bottle had turned on me. I was a slave to drink.'

The terrace hero who has difficulty in adjusting to life after the cheering stops is a story as old as organised sport itself. The archives are full of tales of depression, alcoholism, all kinds of mental health issues afflicting ex-athletes. Greaves differs to many of those in that retirement did not trigger his drinking by becoming his method of coping; it merely allowed him the opportunity to hasten along a course to which he was already committed.

Giller adds, 'He had been drinking too much throughout his career, when booze was part and parcel of the football culture. He had good teachers at Chelsea in the days when the club was known as Butlin's. And I remember being in Mexico with him at the end of the World Cup Rally and he was hammered every day. He spent three hours sitting on a chair in the hotel swimming pool with a waiter bringing him a tray of beers. Then, in that following season with West Ham, he and Mooro were the leaders of the drinking gang. Ron Greenwood gave them several lectures, but they just dismissed him as an old killjoy.

'It only became a problem when he finished his League career. In our drinking days, he would get drunk very quickly while the likes of Moore and Gilzean would be unaffected. He had the benefit of being able to run it off in his playing days; but once he had retired, the drinking sessions became more frequent and without the exercise in between.'

By the time he'd been out of professional football for two years, Greaves was ready to up his game. 'For the next two years I drank heavily, knowing I had become an alcoholic,' he said. It was to be a period when 'the real drinking started'. In another recollection, he said, 'No way I could go a waking hour without a drink.'

Drinking in pubs was no longer enough. They had to close their doors at some point. On top of the 18 or so pints he reckoned he was downing, which meant he often couldn't remember where he had been by the time he got home, he now needed to hide bottles of vodka around the house. He might have one in the cocktail cabinet from which he would occasionally and openly fill his glass. But there were others, from which he trusted that he could take a nip without being detected.

'I can remember times being in my car on the common or somewhere and I wouldn't know how I got there,' he would admit. 'I would wake up and it would be dark, freezing cold and, looking at my watch and seeing that it was about six o'clock, and not really knowing whether it was six o'clock in the morning or evening.' He would, of course, have a bottle to turn to and would 'take a couple of belts at it to try and get things in perspective and if it was six in the evening I would go to the nearest pub. If it was the morning I would drive somewhere and drink my bottle until the pubs opened.'

Between opportunities to imbibe, he was becoming increasingly irritable, depressed and confused. 'You go around a long time saying, "What is happening to me? The nerves are shattered. Am I having a nervous breakdown? Let's have a drink to calm the nerves."'

He would succumb to what he called 'wild displays of uncontrollable anger'. Windows were broken, doors came off hinges – and worse. Irene revealed the state of conflict in which she was forced to exist when interviewed for the 1980 documentary *Just for Today*:

> I had so much aggro that I thought I was beginning to hate him. Obviously, I really hadn't stopped loving him. I was losing the man I once knew, he just wasn't there anymore. This guy could have been anybody.
>
> He was very vindictive [and would] go back continuously into the past. You know Jim, how modest he is, but then it would be how great he was, he was the best and there was nobody like him. We should all be eternally grateful that we live with him and know him. Even if I walked from one room away from him, two minutes later he would come after you and say, 'Listen, I have got to tell you this.' This lovely modest guy turned into this lunatic.
>
> The worst I ever got with him was when I virtually nearly killed him. He'd come home, crashed out as usual, and my boys were left somewhere else and he was supposed to pick them up, and I just went up and started hitting him with everything I could get hold of – glass, anything, until my eldest daughter came out and stopped me. I think I honestly would have killed him. The frustration of trying to get through to this guy; it is like trying to talk to someone who is anaesthetised really. You try and get them the next day when they are a little bit with you, but you have got to be very, very quick before they are at it again.

'Difficult times,' is the somewhat understated summing up of Danny, who was eight years old when his father retired from professional football. 'Anybody who has had parents who've had problems with drugs or alcohol would find it difficult. It is not very nice seeing your parents argue. It was not very nice Mum and Dad splitting up for a period. But ultimately, like anyone will say, they are your parents and you love them and want them to be together and you hope they address things and sort things out. But they weren't pleasant times.'

As much as Irene had become attuned to her husband's moods and aware of when to stay out of his way, sometimes it was simply impossible. To his ultimate and everlasting embarrassment, Greaves admitted, 'I am told there were times when I actually got violent and I found it hard to believe but I couldn't deny it because drink had taken over and memory blanks were commonplace.'

Elder daughter Lynn, speaking in the same television documentary, added, 'On a few occasions he got physically violent, but he is not a violent man. Next morning, once he had sobered up, we would say what he had done and what he had said and he would never believe it. The things he said more than anything were quite revolting.'

Irene had originally attempted to shield her children from the extent of their father's problems. 'I think Mum tried to hide it from us at first,' Lynn recalled. 'I began to see there was something wrong and then when I eventually found out it was a great shock.'

By around 1975 or 1976 – he had difficulty being exact about any dates during this period of his life – Greaves knew deep down what Irene had recognised a long time before: that he was an alcoholic. And barely a functioning one. 'Alcoholics desperately want to stop drinking and can't. I had got to the stage where I had admitted that I was an alcoholic, but I couldn't get off the bloody roundabout. There was no way; whatever I did I went back to the same old booze treadmill. I couldn't see a way out.'

Mercifully, he still had enough money to ensure that he could afford 'good booze'. It was that, rather than any great willpower or resolve, that separated him from the unfortunate souls he had seen on the streets drinking whatever they could lay their hands on. And, even several years into retirement, his natural level of health and fitness shielded him from the severest physical consequences of his actions. Which, of course, allowed him to get back on the drink more quickly and meant that only those closest to him would know how much he had consumed.

Those people included his trusted old photographer friend, Norman Quicke, who recalled spending an entire Sunday out looking for Greaves with Lynn; brother-in-law and increasingly estranged business partner Tom Barden; and old friend Giller. 'But I had a career that was at full sail and seeing Jimmy drunk was almost a matter of amusement rather than concern,' Giller confesses. 'It was poor Irene who was seeing the most and worst of it behind closed doors. We had a mutual mate, Norman 'Speedy' Quicke, a *Daily Express* sports photographer who was their near neighbour. Norman and his wife used to babysit and he started whispering to me that he was worried about Jimmy's drinking and that there was growing tension at home. Suddenly Jimmy cut off from socialising and was going off on his own to drink.'

Greaves gradually sold his interests in everything but a pair of menswear shops and a travel agency. The fact that the travel business required him to do a lot of socialising in order to drum up business was evidence that drink 'impaired my judgement'.

If not ready to take the serious steps he needed to combat his addiction, he was at least self-aware enough to look for things that might mitigate against the way he was steadily poisoning himself. Charity football matches, rounds of golf and games of squash were intended to exercise the body he was abusing and also offer a distraction from the clawing desire for the next drink. When he was caught asleep at the wheel of his parked car by police, it might have been the beginning of a sequence of events that brought his problems into the public domain – as it would have done in the 21st century – but the officer accepted his explanation that he'd stopped because he had been tired and advised him to drive on with his window open.

'How on earth I never wrapped the car up, killed somebody, had a head-on, side-on, you name it – it was quite unbelievable. How I got away with never being nicked for drinking and driving I will never know. If there is a higher power he was certainly looking after me when I was drinking and driving and, more important, he was looking after everybody else.'

Initially relieved to have exited football, Greaves had come to recognise that the gap it left was now filled exclusively, and perilously, by alcohol. Perhaps a handful of games could help to drain some of the drink from his life.

Irene agreed that a return to competitive football might have a positive effect and Greaves signed to play some games for Essex Senior League team Brentwood Town, managed by an old school friend, David Emerick. 'I am sure he can do a fine job for us,' said his new boss.

Four days before Christmas Day 1975, he made his debut – goalless this time – in a 2-0 home defeat against Witham Town. Further appearances would bump up the crowds wherever he played, although Brentwood's unenclosed ground made it impossible for them to take advantage by charging admission. In March 1976, he was back in a League stadium, scoring the first goal for a Great Britain XI that beat a Scottish XI 3-2 in Alan Mullery's testimonial at Fulham.

At the end of the season, Greaves appeared for Brentwood for the last time in the Essex Senior League Cup final, a tournament in which he had helped them advance by scoring a hat-trick in a 5-3 win against Bowers in an earlier round. He signed off on a winning note as his club beat Basildon United 3-0, but even he would admit that it had been a 'half-hearted effort' to get back into football. Waiting for the supermarket to open so that he could go in and buy a couple of bottles of vodka was still of greater importance than the result of any football match.

Irene could see that desire and feared where it was leading her husband. Finally, she persuaded him to seek help from psychiatrist Dr Max Glatt, a pioneer in the recognition and treatment of alcoholism. 'When I first saw him he was pushed along by his wife, which is what usually happens with voluntary patients,' Dr Glatt recalled. 'One part of them wants to get out of the mess drink has got them into and the other half sees no way out of that mess.'

Yet the initial relief Irene felt at her husband's willingness to acquiesce to her wishes did not last. 'When I first met Max Glatt I thought he had been living in my living room,' she explained. 'I thought, "Great, a guy who understands what I have been through." I thought he was going to work miracles, but he tried and didn't.'

'My wife virtually frog-marched me to go and see Dr Glatt,' Greaves recalled. 'He told me I had a drinking problem. This, to me, was impossible to accept because I was still working on and off, I wasn't on the Embankment, I wasn't one of those people who walked around with a meths bottle in his pocket. But he told me in no uncertain terms that if I carried on drinking I could very easily become one of those people.'

Greaves continued to make sporadic attempts to turn his life around. He checked into a private nursing home and came out thinking he had 'conquered the monster in one go' and that he could now drink in moderation. In one month's time, his craving was as destructive as ever. The pattern would be repeated again and again, as many as a dozen times by his own reckoning. He had unproductive sessions with several more psychiatrists.

On occasions, he was admitted, initially at the urging of friends, to the alcoholic ward of Warley Hospital, a mental institution housed in an imposing Victorian building in Brentwood. There, while he was drying out – often for two or three weeks at a time – he was prescribed medication to deal with the withdrawal symptoms, but the shakes and sweats would arrive after a couple

271

of days. And, of course, he would soon be back to do it all over again, joking in later years that he went in so often that people thought he worked there. Doctors advised him to attend Alcoholics Anonymous meetings. He did so, but without any confidence in their effectiveness, an approach which, inevitably, became self-fulfilling.

Existing without drink had become 'something I could never see in my life'. The part of his life that he deemed worthy was, he believed, behind him. 'I had had my life and now I was going into a rapid conclusion of it.'

He tried, a little more seriously this time, to find some meaning and escape in football, agreeing to spend the 1976-77 season playing in the Premier Division of the Southern League for Chelmsford City, whose player-manager was the much-travelled Football League midfielder Bobby Kellard. Greaves made his debut in a draw against Maidstone United at the end of September and, despite missing almost two months from the middle of February, would go on to play 38 games in all competitions, scoring 20 goals. His 13 strikes in 25 Southern League matches were not enough to prevent the Clarets' relegation, failure to win any of their final five games condemning them to 20th position, third from bottom.

Playing a handful of games for Chelmsford that season was locally-born teenaged goalkeeper, Nigel Spink, who within six years would be winning the European Cup with Aston Villa. 'It was a surprise to everyone when Jimmy arrived at the club,' he remembers. 'He was a legend. It was a great thrill, a great experience and an honour for someone like me, who was trying to carve out a professional career. Being around someone like him just made you want to go out and create a career for yourself. You could tell he was just a normal bloke and he fitted in well in the changing room. He was a terrific character and it is fantastic to think he played a small part in my career.'

Peter Coker, a regular in the Chelmsford side as a teenager after being released by Crystal Palace, adds, 'He was so normal.

He came training in the rain and he didn't mind driving for four hours on the coach. He used to sit next to my dad, Fred. He always remembers Jimmy telling him about going to Milan and wondering "what the hell am I doing here?" when they took his passport and he had to climb out of a window for a drink and a fag.

'Although I was in awe of him, he made you feel so welcome that it was very easy to talk to him. Some years later, when I was working in London and he was doing his television stuff, I saw him across the road and said hello. He stopped and chatted for about half an hour.'

In November 1976, Greaves had been able to turn back time by running out at White Hart Lane in front of almost 30,000 people and scoring two goals in Tottenham's 3-2 win against Arsenal in a testimonial for Pat Jennings. With Spurs in the midst of a relegation battle they would ultimately lose, Clive White would suggest in *The Times* that their victory over Stoke City a few days later was down in large part to the galvanising presence of Greaves earlier in the week. Manager Keith Burkinshaw agreed that it had been a key factor and, according to Greaves himself, even floated with him the possibility of a comeback. Knowing what others did not – that his performance against Arsenal had been conjured up only 48 hours after a 'particularly vicious bender' – he dismissed the idea for fear of letting down the club that still meant so much to him.

By now, there were times when he needed half a bottle of vodka before he got out of bed, otherwise his hands would shake. Hallucinations were not uncommon. Guinness became a substitute for food. Amazingly, his performance on the field continued to disguise the full extent of his addiction. 'What I remember about him most in the games I played with him,' says Spink, 'was that he never gave the ball away. He played in midfield and he just controlled the game from the middle of the park.'

Spink continues, 'There were odd times when he went missing and there was some talk locally of him having problems; you could see some of it.' Yet Coker remembers it slightly differently. 'We had no idea because when we went for a drink after the game, he never had one. There was nothing to suggest he was an alcoholic, although probably the manager knew. We never saw him drinking much, never saw him drunk. I remember one game when he didn't turn up and when you look back you realise that was probably the reason. But next week he came training and nothing was said.'

At home, however, there was no disguising the depth of his problems. Eventually, he would move out of the family house and return to his parents as Irene, sadly and inevitably, began divorce proceedings. Her husband had become 'like a stranger walking in' and she would explain, 'Divorcing him was purely selfish. I wanted to get rid of him and I wanted him out the way.'

Daughter Lynn, speaking in 1980, said that her mother 'tried everything she could'. She continued, 'When Dad got particularly bad it was getting a bit much for her ... if Mum and Dad hadn't parted when they did possibly Mum would have had a breakdown herself because things were getting really out of hand and she was taking it very, very badly. Up to then she coped really well and if it hadn't been for her I don't think Dad would be well today.'

Greaves acknowledged that Irene 'took as much as any human being could before finally divorcing me'. Drink was now 'costing me the love of my wife, the respect of my kids and my standing in business'. Irene was given power of attorney and managed to raise the money to maintain a family home. Things at least remained amicable enough for Greaves, who would end up moving into his own flat in Wanstead, to be allowed unlimited access to his family.

The moment he would come to recognise as his 'personal rock bottom' was in the winter of 1977, when he found himself braving the frost to rifle through the dustbin in search of the empty vodka bottles Irene had thrown out. 'He was just drinking all the time; virtually a 24-hour job,' Irene recalled. 'I can't really say what his capacity was because they are crafty. He would drink whatever was in the house and then go out for it, and then God knows what he had during the day before he got in. I would go round throwing all the booze down the sink, I thought, or in the dustbin, but he always managed to have something somewhere.'

On this occasion, however, Irene had found the remains of his stash while he had been sleeping off his latest session. He awoke to the panic of being without anything to drink. He rifled through cupboards, turned drawers upside down and ended up 'kneeling by the side of the dustbin draining the last drops out of the bottles'. He could sink no lower.

15

KICKING BACK

*'It was at Barnet where I really rediscovered my
enthusiasm for the game. The place gave me a
cause, a purpose and a sense of belonging. It was
there where I solved my problems.'*

IN the depths of alcoholism, Jimmy Greaves managed to retain a connection to football, both on a practical and psychological level. It might have been what saved him.

The story of Hughie Gallacher was one with which he was all too familiar. It was a cautionary tale that kept coming back to him in his darkest moments, ensuring that he stayed one step away from complete self-annihilation. Gallacher had been a star of British football throughout the 1920s and 1930s, a diminutive forward who ventured down from Scotland to score prolifically for Newcastle United, Chelsea and other teams, totalling almost 400 goals in senior club football. Greaves had often found himself being compared to him in the manner of their finishing. He knew that the retired Gallacher, having lost his wife to illness and been accused of wounding his son with an ashtray after a drinking session, became increasingly lost and alone. The day before facing trial, he stepped in front of a train in Gateshead and was killed.

He was 54. Greaves was no stranger to suicidal thoughts. In the autumn of 1977 he had attended the funeral of former *Evening News* football reporter Victor Railton with Norman Giller, who recalls, 'We stood together side by side looking down at the coffin and Jimmy said, not joking, "I'll be joining you soon, Vic."'

He'd even held razor blades against his wrist, but somehow his knowledge of football history had held him back from applying significant pressure. 'Was I going to follow in [Gallacher's] path all the way to the graveyard?' was a thought that he described as becoming 'something of an obsession'. Mercifully, there were enough people in football aware of his plight determined to keep him away from the metaphorical platform's edge.

Barnet chairman Dave Underwood, the former Fulham goalkeeper, had come to know Greaves during their playing careers and had been a team-mate in the occasional charity game. Underwood, described by former team-mate Bobby Robson as having 'this Bela Lugosi[26] look and ready Cockney wit', was one of the few people aware of the extent of Greaves's personal problems. He also recognised that he was in a position to help by keeping him involved in the game. 'He knew that if I broke completely with football that was [me] finished,' Greaves would admit. He came to recognise that Underwood 'helped me though my self-inflicted pain barrier'.

After his semi-comeback for Brentwood Town, Greaves's spell at Chelmsford City had coincided with some of the most desperate hours of his personal life. He still never regarded himself as fully committed to the sport. His biggest victory, he considered, was the fact that he could still get away with his drinking while being exposed to the public. 'People would see me competing at sport and never believe they were watching somebody who within the past 48 hours had knocked back two bottles of vodka and a couple of gallons of beer.'

---

26 Hungarian-born Hollywood star best known for his title role in *Dracula* in 1931.

Having lost their Southern League top-flight status in 1974-75, Barnet had won promotion by heading the First Division South two seasons later. Under chairman Underwood and manager Billy Meadows, a centre-forward who had broken off from his long Barnet career to play in Hereford United's famous FA Cup upset of Newcastle in 1972, the club had based its renaissance on a cast of players with a wealth of Football League experience.

Former Chelsea centre-back Marvin Hinton was paired with ex-Watford man Walter Lees, while Arsenal and England full-back Bob McNab had featured on the left side of midfield. Journeyman lower division forwards Dennis Brown and John Fairbrother led the attack, with Les Eason, Meadows's long-time strike partner at Underhill, returning for a second spell at the club. 'We felt those experienced players were the ones who gave us the best chance of promotion,' Meadows explains. 'I signed Marvin on the West Bank terracing before he saw the dreadful facilities in the main stand,' he told a Barnet fan website. Young and talented players making their way in the game, such as midfielders Gary Borthwick and Russell Townsend, were in a clear minority.

'Big Dave obviously knew those experienced players and had been involved with them,' says Eason. 'It was a very enjoyable time. We were always known as a good team to watch because of the players we had, even though we probably didn't have a good enough side to win the league.'

To push them a step closer to that ambition in their first season back in the Southern League Premier Division, Underwood and Meadows approached Greaves to sign for the 1977-78 season, although the chairman initially gave him no indication of what he had in mind. 'We sat there and we talked and all of a sudden I popped him the question,' Underwood recalled.

'Would you like to come and play for Barnet?'

'You don't want me, Dave.'

'We do, Jim.'

'Let me think about it.'

'Don't think about it. We want you. Do you want to name a price?'

Greaves paused and shrugged. 'No, go on then. I will come and play for you.'

Meadows adds, 'He wanted to keep playing and Barnet offered a higher level than he'd had at Chelmsford. We paid him the same as everyone else and he was as good as gold. He wasn't doing it for the money.'

There was more to Underwood's motives than a desire to play the Good Samaritan. He knew that the move would energise his newly-promoted club. Eason remembers, 'I was born in Edmonton and my whole family were Spurs supporters so Jimmy was the person I used to go and watch growing up. Anybody who scores goals is worth watching, but he was more than just a goalscorer. He was brought up as an inside-forward who could play up front and in midfield, as I would discover. I remember going home from training and thinking, "I am going to play with Jimmy Greaves." It was a lovely situation. The best way to explain it is this: I was lucky enough to play for England amateurs and play at Wembley, but people are always more interested that I played with Greavsie for a year, especially the Spurs supporters. They envy me more for playing with him than for anything else. That was the stature of the man.'

Steve Ragan, a powerful centre-forward who was to play a leading role in the legend of Greaves in non-League football, remembers, 'Gary Borthwick, Jimmy and I all signed on the same day. Nobody knew whether Jimmy was coming to training on that first day, but he turned up in a really nice car, and then I drove up in a 3.3 Turbo Ford. Jimmy looked and said, "Fucking hell, is that what you got as a signing-on fee?"'

Greaves's arrival at Underhill had almost been derailed by his old Chelsea colleague John Sillett, who was manager at Hereford United. He invited Greaves to play in a pre-season friendly against Dutch team Blauw-Wit Amsterdam, announcing, 'I have been negotiating with Jimmy for two or three weeks and am hopeful he will sign for us on a permanent basis soon.' Yet Greaves confirmed after the match, 'It was just a one-off. I have signed for Barnet.'

Two days later, Meadows greeted his new signing in the Barnet programme for a friendly against Watford. 'I am delighted that this world-class player has signed for us,' he wrote. 'We now have a player at Underhill who ranks alongside Pelé as one of the all-time greats. I am sure Jimmy will do a great job for us and he is looking forward to the coming season.'

Greaves would play 30 of Barnet's 42 league games in that campaign, plus another 16 in various cup competitions, but team-mates were given an early warning that, for reasons initially unknown to them, he would sometimes be absent at short notice. There were, quite simply, days when alcohol made it impossible for him to play. Even though he was fighting the urge to drink every single day, he admitted that there were times when 'I did actually go on benders'. He recalled that 'the club were magnificent; they covered up and said I was injured'.

According to Ragan, 'Billy would say, "Right, the team today is bla, bla, bla, bla, bla. And this is what it is if Jim doesn't turn up..."'

'I remember a pre-season friendly,' says Eason, 'and we were sitting around waiting for him and he never showed. About quarter past seven, Billy came in and said, "It doesn't look as though Jim is going to be here. We might have to get used to that." That comment was made when none of us knew anything about his drink problem. From then on, he missed a couple of games. He turned up once on the coach to an away game and they said he had the flu and he didn't play. There was no reason not to believe that. Probably there were a few people at the club who knew about his drinking, but most of the players were not aware until it came out later.

'His daughter used to drive him to the club and he was usually there at quarter to two, prompt, for a three o'clock kick-off. Nobody ever saw him have a drink. He never came in the bar after the game; he might have had an orange juice and that was it. He was a good lad, one of the boys in the dressing room, but he never really stayed around. I remember once I went out to the loo before the game and he was out there drinking this stuff from a bottle. It wasn't alcohol. It was some sort of medicine, so I didn't think anything of it. You realise later it was maybe something to settle his stomach or whatever. You never thought the worst of him. It was Jim and if he didn't turn up once or twice you just accepted it.'

Inadvertently, Ragan was one of the few people beyond the club management to have been given an inkling of Greaves's problems. 'I lived in Hadley Wood and Mike Smith of the Dave Clark Five[27] was one of my neighbours and a very close friend. He'd had a drink problem as well and when I told him I was playing with Jimmy Greaves he said, "Oh, Jim is in my rehab group." None of us knew. He never came drinking after a game, he only ever had an orange juice and went home. I would never have gone up to Jim and said, "I hear you have a drink problem," but, quietly, I mentioned it to one of the other players.'

Endorsing Eason's pre-game observation, Ragan adds, 'Jim would drink a whole bottle of kaolin and morphine. Incredible. A whole bottle. That is what he did to get ready for the match.'

Given the level that his drinking had reached, it is quite a testimony to his inherent fitness that Greaves was able to play in as many games as he did. And never gave the appearance that he was struggling physically on the field. 'You never watched him play and thought that he had been on the piss the night before,' says Keith Pike, who was covering the team for the *Barnet Press*. 'I was completely unaware he was having problems.'

That was until Greaves was unexpectedly absent once more. 'It was about the third or fourth time he had not been in the side, an away game on a Tuesday night I think it was,' Pike recalls. 'There had been a few other games where you wondered why he wasn't

---

27 One of the leading British pop groups of the 1960s. Smith, the lead singer, died in 2008.

playing, but this time Dave Underwood took me to one side. He said, "This is the problem," and he told me about his alcoholism. He said to me – and this is where my lack of journalistic nous came in – "He is trying to recover from alcoholism and the last thing he needs is publicity about it. I am telling you, hoping that you will do him and the club a favour and keep it to yourself." And I did.'

Pike, in his early 20s and in his first season of covering the team – and aware of the importance to a local newspaper of maintaining good relations with its neighbourhood football club – admits, 'It was an impossible position. What I should have done is said, "Thanks for telling me, but that is news." It was probably wrong, but I did sit on it.'

Greaves had made his competitive debut for Barnet in a Southern League Cup tie at Wealdstone, losing his footing when presented with the chance of a late goal that would have given his team a draw in the first leg. Barnet lost the second leg before kicking off their league campaign with a 3-2 win against Atherstone Town. Greaves was goalless, as were his team in a defeat at Telford United, before he finally headed a goal in a 2-2 draw at Worcester City. Then he scored a late winner – another header – as his team beat Minehead, the previous season's runners-up, at Underhill.

Wearing No.7 and playing in midfield, Greaves's performances, albeit at a lower level of football, contradicted those who'd argued that goalscoring was the only component of his game. Pike continues, 'Because I was a Spurs supporter of yore I was a bit fearful at first when he joined. Sometimes when players stepped down it was a bit sad to see them. But Greaves was a bloody revelation. He had been the best finisher I have ever seen – as a taker of chances he was as good as Messi in my opinion – but he almost played the quarterback role. He played just in front of the back four and pinged loads of passes. He had put on weight, but even though he was playing in a deeper role he would get forward and score goals. He scored from outside the area, which he never did at Spurs.

'The Barnet fans loved him; he was hugely popular. This was a bloke who, unlike one or two others and being as big a star as he had been, came in and put in a real shift while wearing a Barnet shirt. He didn't mind tackling or being tackled and he worked his socks off. The fact he missed a few games didn't affect his affinity with the fans.'

Pulling the strings from the centre of the pitch, Greaves showed a competitive element that his former Division One opponents and team-mates would not have recognised. Future Barnet manager Barry Fry remembers seeing several of their games around that time. 'He was kicking the ball off his goal line one minute and was popping it in at the other end the next,' he said. 'Jimmy was brilliant for Barnet.'

Ragan explains, 'He worked harder than anybody. He covered every inch of the pitch, as well as scoring a load of goals. And he wasn't afraid to stick his foot in; he would tackle ferociously. In those days you could get away with it and he was a hard player.'

The likes of Norman Hunter, who remembered that 'he couldn't tackle a hot dinner', might scoff, but Southern League football in the 1970s was no place for the faint-hearted. 'It was a very tough league,' Greaves would recall. 'Everybody wanted to beat you. It was real combat and I thoroughly enjoyed it. I played in midfield and had to run, or try to run, the show a bit and it meant getting stuck in. You can't be airy-fairy in the Southern League.'

Former QPR and Arsenal centre-back Terry Mancini would sign for a handful of matches later in the season, with Greaves quick to warn him not to try 'too much fancy stuff'. Yet he explained, 'Within the first few minutes of his debut, Terry chested a ball down, dropped it on to his foot, looked up – and was banjaxed by three opponents at once, seeing stars like something out of a Wile E. Coyote and Road Runner cartoon.'

Roger Jones, who had stepped up from sports editor to deputy editor of the *Barnet Press* and was still going to matches, notes, 'When you saw him play, he had a nasty streak about him. He was going into tackles and he would react if anyone fouled him, whereas the old Greaves wouldn't have. They didn't get close to him anyway.'

Underwood would observe, 'Jimmy came here and became a ball winner. I saw him go into tackles and sometimes do some nasty things which I never thought he would ever do. I think he was doing it to prove to himself and the public that he can do this game of football like everybody else can do. I admired him for it. He went out and competed with the big fellows, he didn't care who they were. And he was trying his hardest even though the night before he might have been in a bit of a mess. He was going out there and absolutely tearing himself in half.'

Used to playing in the latter stages of the FA Cup in April and May, it took some getting used to when Greaves found himself in action in the competition in September, although he had also played, unsuccessfully, in the later qualifying stages for Chelmsford a year earlier. He adjusted well enough, scoring twice in a 4-1 win over Camberley Town in the first qualifying round, including a free-kick that had Meadows claiming, 'It was absolutely superb. Possibly only Jimmy could have got that one.' Erith and Belvedere were beaten in the next round via a pair of Ragan goals, before Greaves scored the fourth in a 4-2 win at St Albans City.

The fourth qualifying round sent Barnet to Hampton, who were less than thrilled to see the return of a group of fans who were establishing something of an undesirable reputation in non-League circles and had done their best to upset the locals in an FA Trophy tie a year earlier. This time, the action on the field was enough of a distraction. Greaves had Barnet leading until a punted clearance by home goalkeeper Alan Cooling bounced over his opposite number, Wilf Woodend, to level the score. With three minutes remaining, Brown scored the winner.

When the draw gave Barnet a home tie against Third Division Peterborough United, Greaves's first appearance in the first round proper of the FA Cup made him the centre of the media's attention. Underhill's press box would be overflowing on 26 November; the householders across the road who allowed visiting national reporters to dial in their reports from their telephones were set for a busy afternoon.

Having disposed of Cheshunt in the Herts Senior Cup seven days before the big game, all that remained before Peterborough came to town was a Monday night engagement against Chelmsford in the somewhat spurious Eastern Floodlight Football Competition, a tournament contested by non-League teams from various divisions, its name varying slightly from year to year and often used to give fringe players a run-out in the first team. In some years, the competition was not even completed. In the Cheshunt programme, Meadows had predicted, 'I shall probably take this opportunity to blood one or two more players from the youth side.' Instead, he rested only a couple of the more senior forwards and included Greaves in a stronger than anticipated line-up.

Yet the manager did – bizarrely and significantly – pick reserve centre-forward Ragan in goal. 'Wilf had a bit of a strain and I used to play in goal for Southern England Schoolboys so Bill asked if I would play in goal. I said, "Of course." When you are 21 you'll play anywhere.'

After 58 minutes, Barnet were leading 3-2 – Greaves having scored the second goal – when Chelmsford were awarded a penalty for handball. 'I dived to my right and stopped it,' Ragan recounts, 'but I looked up and the referee was telling them to take it again.' Match official Terry Lewis ruled that the stand-in goalkeeper had moved too soon. 'All hell broke loose,' Greaves would recall decades later. 'The ref decided to send me off, for no apparent reason, and I refused to walk.' Greaves felt he had been singled out because he was the one recognisable face in the group angrily confronting the referee.

Ragan continues, 'Jim just couldn't believe it, no one could believe it. He wouldn't give the ball back to the referee, so he abandoned the game. We weren't even sure if Jim had been sent off or not. It was absolute mayhem. They turned half the floodlights off, so we were in semi-darkness. None of us knew what was going on. The whole thing was crazy.'

But Lewis argued, 'I ordered off Greaves for using foul and abusive language to me. He refused to go. I asked him four times to leave, but still he would not go. I had no choice but to abandon the game.'

Back in their dressing room, the Barnet players heard irate Chelmsford fans outside the door. 'They had a great big bath in there,' says Ragan, 'and in the bath was this great big hose, like a fireman's hose. Jim took it out of the bath, opened the door and soaked all the Chelmsford supporters. There was like a riot going on; everyone was going mad. It was so funny.'

Knowing the personal battles Greaves was fighting at the time, one can't help but wonder at the mental state of someone being so worked up in a relatively meaningless match that he, first of all, allows himself to get sent off and, secondly, refuses to leave the field, giving the referee no alternative than to abandon the game. There could be no greater act of indiscipline. All this in the knowledge that his actions would mean an immediate one-match suspension and rule him out of the biggest game of the latter phase of his career. It was hardly the product of rational thinking.

'That incident alone tells you that was not the old Jimmy Greaves,' says Jones, 'because he was a very placid character. He had a temper on him, which he never had before, and was probably a symptom of the way he was at the time.'

According to Ragan, 'Jim really took the whole thing very personally. The competition wasn't worth anything, but he comes from the area, had played for Chelmsford and his daughter Lynn's boyfriend, Frank Bishop, was playing for them. There was a lot of history there.'

As Greaves's exploits were being digested by readers of the national newspapers the following morning, Barnet decided they were not prepared to let him miss his big day in the FA Cup, or have the gloss taken off their own moment in the national spotlight. By arranging a match before the weekend, Greaves could serve his suspension and be clear to face Peterborough. It might have not been ethical, but nor at that time was it against regulations. If they could find opposition willing to stage a Southern League game, they had the power to do so without approval of higher authorities.

Hillingdon Borough, managed by former Fulham defender Jim Langley, were approached and originally declined because of injuries. They quickly reconsidered, explaining that their casualty list was not as bad as they'd first thought. Or maybe they saw the probability of a couple of cheap points against distracted opposition. Greaves's former team-mate Geoff Hurst, now managing Telford United, also offered his club's services. On Thursday night, less than two days before their FA Cup tie, Barnet took the field at Hillingdon and lost 2-0. Meadows again fielded a reasonably strong team, although Ragan continued in goal and the remainder played as though their minds were elsewhere. Barnet had apparently sacrificed two points in the title race to ensure Greaves had his big moment. It was an altogether bizarre episode, one which would be prevented from being repeated by a change in regulations forbidding teams to rearrange fixtures to suit themselves without approval from the relevant league.

A crowd of 5,181 squeezed into Underhill for what had now assumed the mantle of a Jimmy Greaves showcase. Meadows's programme notes, obviously written at the very start of the week, noted he would be fielding his usual full-strength team 'providing the players came through Monday evening's game at Chelmsford without mishap'. Meadows was obviously no clairvoyant. The game was never likely to match the drama of the days preceding it, but Barnet did lead through Brown after 10 minutes before Peterborough came back to win 2-1. Greaves, though, was far from done making FA Cup headlines.

Barnet would find themselves top of the league on Boxing Day after Greaves scored twice to beat Wealdstone. 'We had quite a good side, although we were all getting on a bit,' he would recall. 'If we won the toss at Underhill, we'd always elect to kick up the famous slope in the first half.' Yet those ageing legs ran out of steam in the second half of the season, winning only eight of their final 22 games and finishing seventh, having dropped more home points than any other team in the division. With 23 goals to his name in all competitions, Greaves was named Player of the Year by the club's supporters. By the time Barnet's fans were making their end-of-season presentation, their new hero was able to accept the trophy with a clear head and no thought of a celebratory drink.

Jimmy Greaves was sober.

A new star of English football, 18-year-old Jimmy Greaves marries Irene Barden (PA Images)

Greaves, left, scores for Chelsea against Wolves in August 1958, a game which was said to have hastened the retirement of legendary England defender Billy Wright, centre (PA Images)

Chelsea manager Ted Drake gives rare instructions to Frank Blunstone, Peter Brabrook and Greaves, who became frustrated by his boss's inability to make his team more competitive (Empics)

After two days' respite from his Italian nightmare, Greaves is forced to return to AC Milan. Joining him on his flight are wife Irene and PFA chairman Jimmy Hill (PA Images)

Greaves greets England striker Gerry Hitchens before the Milan derby. His clandestine meetings with the Inter forward offered fleeting relief from his isolation in Italy (Empics)

Greaves swivels to fire home the first goal in Tottenham's victory over Burnley in the 1962 FA Cup final (PA Images)

Greaves, second left, celebrates his first winner's honour in the game as he and his Tottenham teammates parade the FA Cup (PA Images)

Greaves beats goalkeeper Milutin Soskic to score England's winner against the Rest of the World, a game that cemented his global reputation (PA Images)

Brazil's Zozimo marks Greaves during the quarter-final of the 1962 World Cup, a tournament in which Greaves was a disappointment (Getty Images)

Never one for tactics or training, Greaves tries to look interested as England manager Alf Ramsey explains his plans during the 1966 World Cup finals (Empics)

Trailed by trainer Les Cocker, Greaves departs the England team hotel for Wembley on World Cup final day, knowing he is to miss out on the biggest occasion in his nation's football history (Central Press)

In his smart suit, Greaves looks, and feels, out of place as the England bench celebrate the final whistle of their 4-2 win against West Germany (PA Images)

Drinking was a big part of football's social fabric in the 1960s. By late in his career, Greaves would have progressed from harmless halves to dangerous levels of consumption (Empics)

Some of Greaves's greatest goals were created by his speed, balance and ability to beat defenders, as he demonstrates against Leicester's David Nish in 1968 (Getty Images)

Greaves is greeted at West Ham's training ground after his shock transfer from Spurs by Geoff Hurst, the man who took his place during the World Cup but remained a great friend (Getty Images)

As he had for Chelsea, AC Milan, Tottenham and England, Greaves scored on his West Ham debut, grabbing two goals against Manchester City at Maine Road (PA Images)

Ford rally driver Tony Fall greets his unlikely co-driver, Jimmy Greaves, before the 1970 World Cup Rally (PA Images)

Pictured during a pre-event practice session, Greaves feared he would 'make a prat of myself', but impressed the motorsport community with the way he handled the testing London to Mexico race, finishing in sixth place (Empics)

Greaves in FA Cup action against Peterborough United during his therapeutic two-year spell at Southern League Barnet (Empics)

The front page of the Sunday People *in January 1978, exposing Greaves's alcoholism to the world and setting him on the road to recovery*

A sign of Greaves's impact as a broadcaster in the 1980s was his immortalisation in puppet form by the makers of Spitting Image *(PA Images)*

Ian St John and Jimmy Greaves are pictured in the build-up to the 1990 World Cup, when the popularity of Saint & Greavsie *was at its height (Empics)*

Old foe Ron 'Chopper' Harris, left, joins Greaves's friend and agent, Terry Baker and his wife, Freda, backstage before one of the theatre shows that created his third career (Terry Baker)

Jimmy Greaves at his 75th birthday celebrations, weeks before he suffered a devastating stroke (Terry Baker)

Greaves and his fellow-reserves in 1966 were finally presented with World Cup winners' medals at England's 2009 game against Andorra. Ron Springett, Jimmy Armfield, Ron Flowers, Norman Hunter, Ian Callaghan, John Connelly and George Eastham are to the left of Greaves on the back row, while Peter Bonetti, Gerry Byrne and Terry Paine are on the right of the front row (Terry Baker)

16

NOT A DROP MORE

'I still consider myself an alcoholic.
Once an alcoholic, always an alcoholic.
But today I am sober.'

T HE beginning of the end of an increasingly desperate
existence was an anonymous phone call to a news agency
in Essex. Within 48 hours, Jimmy Greaves had confessed
in a national newspaper that he was an alcoholic. Four weeks later,
he took his final drink. That he never relapsed represents the
greatest, most important, victory of his life.

Having visited various hospitals and clinics over an extended
period, it was inevitable that Greaves would eventually tempt
someone from one of those establishments to call the press. It is
indicative of the loyalty of his friends, the high esteem in which
he was held and the less opportunistic nature of the time that it
took so long. When the Essex News Agency finally received such
a tip-off they did what any local media outlet would do when they
found themselves sitting on a potential bombshell of an exclusive;
they phoned Fleet Street.

'I was senior investigative reporter at the *Sunday People* and the
call originally came into the sports desk,' recalls Frank Thorne.

'Often sports reporters kept things quiet from the news desk because they didn't want the news guys to get them banned from a football ground, which could be the price they paid for an exposé. But the sports editor, Neville Holtham, told the news editor that they had received a tip that Jimmy Greaves had been checking into the alcohol unit of several hospitals in Colchester. The indication was that he was in trouble.'

It was already late in the afternoon of Friday, 27 January 1978, and Thorne and photographer Brendan Monks were assigned to head to the Greaves family home in Hornchurch. 'Irene opened the door,' Thorne continues, 'and when I told her what it was about she let us in, made us a cup of tea and told us what she had been coping with.' It was clear to Thorne that Irene welcomed the prospect that the private nightmare her family had been living was to become public.

'She had tried everything herself, finding bottles of various spirits hidden about the house and throwing them away or putting them down the sink, but he would find other ways of getting booze and hiding it from her. She was at the end of her tether. She still loved Jimmy, but things were out of hand, so she must have been relieved to see us on the doorstep. It meant that, from the original tip-off and confirmation from his wife, we had the story.'

Yet getting Greaves himself to come clean was obviously Thorne's ambition. Irene told him to return the following day, Saturday morning. Suspended by the FA for bringing the game into disrepute with his antics in the infamous Chelmsford match, he had no engagement to fulfil that weekend and was, once again, back at Warley Hospital. 'Even if we never got back into the house again we had the story that Jimmy Greaves was an alcoholic,' Thorne continues. 'It could only get better from there. But I was quite concerned from an ethical sense that here we were about to confront a very sick man. What were the ethics of this? But an agency had tipped off our sports desk so we couldn't keep it secret. The decision was made by Geoffrey Pinnington, the editor, that

I would go back. I still had some misgivings. Jimmy had been a superstar when I was a kid growing up in Manchester. The big game in those days was when Spurs came to town. So here I am in my mid-20s about to confront an absolute hero. But I had a job to do.'

Thorne and Monk were back in Hornchurch the next morning and no sooner had they been let in by Irene than they saw *News of the World* reporter Peter Moore pull up outside the house. 'So, we have got to secure Jimmy and his story and not let the *News of the World* in the house,' Thorne continues. 'I had a word to Irene not to let them in and she showed us into the lounge, where Jimmy was. He looked very ill. I explained to him, "Look, Jimmy, I am sorry to be here, but we have got this information that you checked into several hospitals' alcohol units and Irene has told us that you went to Warley and had treatment. We would like to sit down and interview you with your agreement, but if you don't agree we will go away and the *News of the World* are outside and it is already on page one as far as I am concerned. We can either make a deal and you can help me write the story your way, or we go away and write it anyway."'

Greaves recalled, 'When Frank Thorne said he was going to blow the story I was just coming out of withdrawal in Warley and I think if I had had enough strength I would have strangled him.' Instead, he slumped back into his armchair and sighed, 'All right. How much are you going to pay me?'

'That was the minute I knew I had the story as an exclusive,' adds Thorne, who recalls the fee being at least £10,000. 'Now we were on a deadline. The contract was drawn up in the London office and couriered by motorbike. It was to include Irene as well so that the *News of the World* couldn't get the story from her. I was really up against the Saturday deadline, so I thought it would be far quicker if they had a typewriter in the house. For me to make notes and then go somewhere and laboriously type it out would take time I didn't have. Jimmy's daughter produced a portable typewriter and I sat with Jimmy. As he was coming out with stuff I was writing it all down. He was an incredible interview.'

As had been the case with Irene, it appeared to Thorne that Greaves was grateful for the opportunity to unburden himself of his terrible secret. 'He didn't resent us putting him in this position; he had no personal angst or vendetta against us. He knew we were doing our jobs. Almost everything he said was like gold bars and he saw everything as it was being written and he trusted me.'

Greaves told Thorne, 'I have to face up to the truth. If I carry on drinking I will kill myself. I am a social drinker who went off the rails without realising it.' Then he detailed the established pattern of his drinking; beer in the pubs, vodka in private. Explaining how his intake had exploded after his retirement from professional football, he confessed, 'I was looking for the roar of a crowd in the bottom of a vodka bottle.'

'It almost made you weep,' Thorne remembers. 'He was very, very emotional. He looked a very sick, wizened old man on that day.'

Admitting to lapses in memory that could cost him days at a time, Greaves explained that he had been in two different hospitals that very week. Now, despite his apparent relief at being found out, he feared the reaction to his revelations. 'This is a serious illness,' he continued. 'My marriage has suffered and so have my kids. They have to face their friends at school and at work. I feel sad that it has come to this. Sad for the fans who still have fond memories of my best days. Sad for my family. I just hope that people will understand my plight and have compassion.'

With his 5pm deadline approaching, Thorne wrapped things up, phoned his newspaper and dictated the story to the copy-takers. 'We just made it,' he says. 'It was an extreme pressure situation, particularly with the *News of the World* there. They did knock on the door, but no one answered so they just sat outside.'

The following morning, the *Sunday People* arrived through letter boxes with a front-page close-up of a dishevelled-looking

Greaves next to the splash headline: 'DRINK IS KILLING ME, SAYS JIMMY GREAVES'. Thorne's story ended with a promise that Greaves would be revealing more the following week. 'What was in the paper that day was only a fraction of what he told us,' Thorne explains, 'so clearly this was going to go over more than one week of the paper. It ran for about three weeks.'

The publicity might just have saved his life. For a start, there was an outpouring of support, understanding and affection that took him by surprise; from messages of hope from recovering alcoholics to offers of practical assistance from the likes of comedian Jimmy Tarbuck, who put his Spanish villa at Greaves's disposal. The *Sunday People* devoted an additional week of coverage to the response to their exclusive.

Around football, the reaction – outside of Greaves's closest circle – was sadness and surprise that a friend and colleague with whom they had shared so many drinks now found himself in such a desperate state. 'I never saw Jim unable to control himself because of drink,' says Alan Mullery. 'Never saw any of that. I read it in the newspaper and said, "That has got to be complete lies. Jimmy is not like that."'

John Sillett, with whom Greaves had been close enough in earlier years to share his grief over his son's death, says, 'I never had a clue how bad it had got. He never showed that side; didn't want anybody to know he had problems.'

His former manager, Bill Nicholson, was well aware of the drinking culture around his team, saying, 'There is a lot of free time in football and a lot of energy expended. It is normal to drink and I let them get on with it if it was done in moderation and didn't affect their performances.' But even he was 'amazed' to hear of Greaves's revelations. 'I must say he never gave me reason to suspect he had a problem,' he added, contrary to suspicions about his motives in moving Greaves out of White Hart Lane.

Alan Gilzean, an established member of the Spurs social club, insisted, 'I had never seen any inclination towards heavy drinking at all. All he ever used to drink was halves of bitter. He must have got on it after he left us because he reckoned he was drinking a lot of vodka – but he never touched any spirits when he was at Tottenham.'

Greaves said it was the departure of Dave Mackay, head boy of the Spurs drinking school, to Derby in 1968 that led him to relocate the bulk of his post-match drinking to the pubs near his home in Essex rather than spend too long with team-mates. 'I wasn't aware of it at all,' says Cliff Jones. 'It came as a great shock, but that is how it is. Sometimes an alcoholic can hide it, which I did to a certain extent.'

Bob McNab adds, 'Jim was quite a secretive character and he didn't mix. A friend of mine who drank with the Spurs players said he would come in the pub right outside the ground after the game and have maybe one or two and then he would disappear. I never heard any rumours about him drinking heavily.' Former England team-mate Jack Charlton said, 'I never had any inkling of it until I read it in the paper. I'd often been out for a drink with Jimmy, and he only ever had a pint, or a couple of pints at most.'

Along with the shock of Greaves's confession came sympathy and goodwill. 'We had an avalanche of mail as a result of Jimmy's honesty,' says Thorne. 'All this affection from all walks of life, including fellow alcoholics. I saw Jimmy a couple of days a week for the next three weeks and he didn't have a drink.'

Fellow-journalist and close friend, Norman Giller, recalls the jolt of seeing what he felt was a 'sensational headline' in the *People*. 'Only in hindsight could we see it as a positive thing,' he says. 'At the time I considered it the worst kind of tabloid journalism.' But he is forced to admit, 'Once it was in the public domain, Jimmy thrived on having the spotlight on him and he set out to prove he could beat the bottle. He was ashamed of himself and it was the rock-bottom moment that all alcoholics need to recognise before they can start the fight back.'

Daughter Lynn said two years later, 'When it came out we were horror-struck and were going to stay in for the rest of our lives and never let anybody see us. But I think from that moment on it has been such a change in his life because, instead of people looking down on him and thinking he is a drunk, they have started to really look up to him and now this illness hasn't got the sort of stigma it had.'

One recovering alcoholic touched by Greaves's story was Nick Charles, a former cabaret singer who had been living on the streets and drinking methanol. Sober for a year and working as a taxi driver early in 1978, he recalls, 'I was coming back from the airport with the actor Patrick Macnee[28], who was reading a story in the *Sunday People* about Jimmy Greaves. He knew all about me because I had driven him several times and he gave it to me and said, "You will be interested in this." When I came off the shift I took it back home. I felt sorry for Jimmy because when you are famous and have been in the national press like that, you know you have got to stop drinking forever. I wrote him this long, rambling letter – which he always said he kept – telling him he did the right thing by coming clean. I warned him, "If ever you have a drink now, you will feel as self-conscious as a practising nudist in Piccadilly Circus."'

Such messages sent Greaves back to Alcoholics Anonymous – 'this time with conviction' – in the hope that 'my pride might then help me beat the monster'. On 28 February, exactly a month after pouring out his heart to Thorne, Greaves found himself in a pub close to Warley Hospital. Having ordered himself a lunchtime Guinness, he heard the barman call last orders and watched his fellow-customers scramble to get themselves one more drink before heading back to work. 'Bugger this,' he thought, purchasing one final pint. It was the last alcohol that would ever touch his lips.

---

28 Star of ITV series *The Avengers,* in which over the course of two decades he played secret agent John Steed.

Giller quit drinking on the same day. 'I did it to encourage Jimmy,' he explains. 'I was a Fleet Street drinker and, while not having a problem, I was too fond of the hard stuff. It did us both the world of good.'

Thorne adds, 'That was the wonderful thing about it. It took Jimmy to be so rock bottom and ashamed that he never drank again. I didn't know that would be a spin-off and I regard it as an achievement that I helped to save his life.'

Of course, when you sum up the rejection of alcohol in a couple of paragraphs, it sounds easy. It was anything but.

'It was incredibly difficult for him,' says his son, Danny. 'Try telling some people to go without a drink for a week and, by the way, the week you have decided not to drink it is your son's 18th birthday or your daughter's 21st. That is tough. And after all the people he drank with throughout his life, he has never had a drink with the two people he would most love to have had a drink with – his two boys. That brings it home. He would have loved to have a pint of Guinness with us and he has never done it. Every year, we have gone on golf trips and family outings and we are sitting there with pints or a glass of wine and he is having a Coke with plenty of ice. Quite incredible.'

Friend and agent Terry Baker adds, 'His willpower was immense. The way he did it was to completely give up his former life; disassociate from all his drinking pals. He never went out socially with those people again. Other than his golfing weekends with the boys he retreated from his former life. He never went to restaurants, he kept away from people, and I think my 50th birthday was the first event he went to – outside of family gatherings – where there was alcohol. Occasionally, over the years, I would even have to taste a dessert for him in case it had something in it.'

Fully committed to his AA meetings, Greaves discovered that the opportunity to expand upon his newspaper confessional in a supportive, non-judgemental environment was 'a lifeline' for him. Used to the close bonds of a dressing room, and discovering that the loss of such an attachment had hastened his descent into alcoholism, he was relieved to find himself back within an environment of camaraderie, care and shared goals. 'I had never been a member of such a team as this,' he recalled.

By following the AA creed of going without a drink 'just for today' – or, in the beginning, an hour at a time – he was able to see a road ahead where previously there had been merely an abyss. 'When I managed that single hour, my goal was to get through another,' he would write. After enough hours, he discovered he had made it through an entire day without a drink. The following day he would find the resolve to go through the whole process again, his craving for alcohol failing to match his desperation to have his life back.

He welcomed the shared experiences of others at his meetings and he accepted the organisation's 12 steps to recovery, beginning with the admission that his life had become 'unmanageable'. Raised as a Catholic but not considering himself a religious man,[29] Greaves even found enough spirituality within him to connect with the various different steps that require acceptance of God and a willingness to be guided by Him along the path to recovery. And from that he mined the stronger will required to see him through that next hour, next day, next week.

Getting back on the football field for Barnet and facing up to the inevitable mocking from opposing fans was another important step; although such was the esteem in which he was held that it was only ever light-hearted, even bordering on affectionate. Having been absent for only a couple of Barnet games after his January announcement, he was back at Underhill and ready for a second season in 1978-79. 'I was once again a hungry footballer,' he said, describing Barnet as 'a marvellous little club'. He went as far as saying, 'The atmosphere was great, we had a terrific side, and

---

29 He once said, 'I grew up without much religion at all, so when they pick the All-Time Catholic XI I won't be in it.'

the whole scene was reminiscent of my early Tottenham days – at a lower level. When it was finally made public and I decided to crack it, the club were 100 per cent behind me and they gave me a tremendous amount of help.'

Inconsistent form meant that the FA Cup once again became Barnet's focus, with Bracknell Town, Feltham and Wokingham Town beaten in the first three qualifying rounds. Greaves, who had scored twice in the second of those games, was the match-winner when Barnet travelled to Edgware Town in a bid to secure a first-round place for the second year running. Ten minutes into their fourth qualifying round tie, he took a return pass from John Fairbrother, dummied to send the goalkeeper the wrong way and stroked in the only goal of the game. Manager Billy Meadows called it 'one of the best goals ever'.

This time, there was to be no Football League opposition for Barnet, who were given a home draw against Isthmian League side Woking. Greaves still managed to make headlines, however, by being sent off in the first half. Noticing the Woking defenders attempting to organise themselves, the swift-thinking Greaves quickly curled the ball into the corner of the net. As the Barnet players celebrated, referee Mike Taylor ordered the kick to be retaken, explaining that neither he nor the Woking players were ready. 'That's their look-out,' Greaves responded angrily, reminding Taylor, 'You awarded us the free-kick and now you're punishing us for taking it quickly.'

The official's answer was to send Greaves to the dressing room. 'I sent him off for foul and abusive language,' he said. 'I had little alternative. His attitude seemed to be that he was Jimmy Greaves and I could not do things like this to him. As far as I was concerned he was just another footballer in breach of the rules.' Astonished, Greaves at least left the field this time, while assorted debris, including cheese rolls and even a fragment of brick, was hurled into the penalty area by home fans behind the goal at the top end of the sloping ground.

Having earned a 3-3 draw via a last-minute penalty by George Cleary, Barnet were without Greaves for the replay, another 3-3 draw. Five days later, Greaves played his final game in the competition that had rewarded him with two winners' medals, a low-key 3-0 defeat in the second replay at Brentford's Griffin Park.

Barnet's next two League games were heavy defeats, 4-0 and 5-0 against Weymouth and Redditch United. Meadows resigned as manager and was replaced over Christmas by Barry Fry, the man who would eventually go on to lead Barnet into the Football League in his second spell at the club. Fry was quick to realise the continuing battle Greaves was waging. He might not have been drinking any more, but that did not mean he was no longer suffering. 'Jimmy was attempting to overcome his alcoholism and my heart went out to him many times. He would sit alone at the front of the team bus while the rest of the lads were in the bar having a beer and it must have been very difficult for him. A football club was hardly the place to be for a recovering alcoholic and I knew that we would not have Jimmy around for long.'

Fry's observations and his desire to build a younger team meant that, by the end of February 1979, it became easy for Greaves to decide that it was time to retire from football once more. His final start for the club was in a heavy defeat at Bath, although he did come on as substitute in one final game a few weeks later. Living in his flat, weekends had become his best opportunity of spending time with his children. This time he left the sport without regret, safe in the knowledge that his two years at Barnet had contributed enormously to the recovery of his life. 'They were two of my most memorable seasons,' he would recall years later. 'When people introduce me as Tottenham, Chelsea, AC Milan and West Ham, I always say "and Barnet".'

A footnote to Greaves's competitive football career was to be written the following season when he was persuaded by Joe Kinnear to play a handful of games for Athenian League team Woodford Town, where his former Spurs colleague was player-coach. In his autobiography, Kinnear recalled Greaves receiving around £250 – 'which was about 10 times what the rest were getting'. He added, 'He'd given up the drinking, but I think he was still having treatment. So our club, with its own nightclub [under the stand] was perhaps not the best place for him. He did get depressed a lot.'

As well as maintaining his relationship with his children, the opportunity to be around his family without the distractions of the fixture list gradually brought Greaves closer to Irene once more. Before long, they found themselves courting again, supported and encouraged by their sons and daughters. 'I had lived in despair; now I lived in hope,' was the way in which he would summarise this period. As plans were made for daughter Lynn's wedding in June 1979 and days passed without alcohol, Greaves could feel Irene's trust being rekindled and sensed the re-emergence of the love he'd hoped had been buried rather than destroyed. When Irene finally told him, three months after their divorce had been finalised, that he should leave his flat and return to the family home – by now a somewhat smaller property in Upminster – he fought back the tears and gave a prayer of thanks for his redemption.

The weeks after the exposé of his alcoholism had found Greaves locked away with Giller, working on an updated version of his autobiography. Entitled *This One's on Me*, the book's advance from publishers Arthur Baker would not only help to pay some important bills, but the process of further confessional was another stage of rehabilitation. 'The bottom line is that Jimmy needed money,' Giller admits. 'The taxman was chasing him and his businesses were being wound up. We started out writing the book to help clear some of the bills, but it finished up as Jimmy using our interview sessions as therapy. I was almost cast in the role of psychiatrist as I prompted him to remember the good and bad times.

'It was a relief for him to talk about things, as if he was at an AA meeting. He used to visit me at my home in Thorpe Bay and loved it so much he tried to buy it off me! At the time he was living in a rented one-roomed flat in Wanstead, selling ladies' sweaters from the back of his mustard yellow Jaguar sports car, the one luxury he clung to. Irene had kicked him out and told him he was not allowed to visit the kids unless he was sober. This was his greatest motivation to kick the bottle; winning back Irene and spending dad time with his children.'

Brutally honest in its admittance of how far Greaves had fallen, the book lacked the stomach-churning detail to which Tony Adams would expose himself in his autobiography two decades later. It was not until a future publication that Greaves referred to vomiting and admitted, 'I had humiliated myself on some of the best carpets money could buy, as well as in the gutter.' In that regard, however, the book was a product both of its time and its author's reticence in the area of self-analysis, which had also shown itself when he had discussed the relatively mundane matter of scoring goals. Besides, as he freely admitted, the most extreme excesses of his alcoholism had been obliterated from his memory. There was more than a thread of truth running through one of his standard after-dinner jokes in future years: 'George Best and I are going to collaborate on a book about our lives in the 1970s. So, if anyone can tell us where we were...'

Greaves did hope, though, that 'talking openly about my problems will be therapeutic for me and if what I have been through opens the eyes of just one potential alcoholic or brings comfort and hope to anybody already hooked on the habit, then all the misery and suffering I have undergone will at least not have been entirely pointless'.

The book would contain the belief that he had become closer than ever to his children, Lynn, who was now into her 20s, Mitzi, Danny and Andrew, who were at various stages of teenaged life. He described them as 'a little shaken but unscarred' by events in their father's life. He closed the book with the acknowledgement that he was far from being fully rehabilitated. 'The eyes of the world are on me and I must prove to everybody – particularly to myself – that I have the courage and the character to conquer my problem.'

To promote the book's publication on 22 March 1979, Greaves appeared five days earlier on the chat show *Russell Harty*. His first inclination had been to turn down the appearance with ITV's interviewing equivalent of Michael Parkinson, but he realised that he was better served by not 'running away' from addressing his problems on television. And, of course, he had a commitment to his publishers. It took every remnant of resolve, however, to force himself on to the set.

In the green room at the London Weekend Television studios, Greaves found himself in the grip of nerves – or more like outright fear. He threw up in the toilet, wiping his mouth with fiercely shaking hands. He wanted nothing more than to walk out. Only the greater dread of what it might trigger if he gave in prompted him to assure a concerned production assistant that he was fine. He was relieved when fellow-guest, the author Arthur Hailey, confided that he was glad Greaves was on first as it gave him more time to control his own nerves. 'If you had told me that less than six years later I would be back in that self-same studio co-hosting a national networked show with Ian St John I would have accused you of being more pissed than I'd ever been,' he would reflect.

Called to the stage and greeted by the looming figure of Harty, perspiring heavily under the studio lights, he sat down and awaited his interrogation. Stripped of the protective shield of faceless pages of print, he now had to deliver his confession to millions of viewers, able to study his every tic and twitch for signs of sincerity, remorse and even relapse. He described it as one of the hardest things he had ever undertaken.

'The important thing for me is that I must be a non-drinking alcoholic,' he stated after retelling the story of his addiction. To do that, he explained, he simply had to continue not having a drink on that particular day. After a 20-minute interruption while a boom microphone was fixed, Greaves described the methods he was learning from Alcoholics Anonymous, based around admission, adjustment and achievement, and urged anyone with drink problems to contact the organisation. Ironically, he would hear later that some AA members, far from believing he had given a great advertisement for the group and its work, were angry at what they saw as betraying confidentialities.

Harty would confess to Greaves some years later that, seeing the way he was shaking at the interview, he harboured doubts that he would overcome his addiction. But for now, Greaves's ordeal was done. He returned to the hospitality lounge and, with all eyes upon him, downed a mineral water. It was another step taken.

Having achieved another milestone in walking daughter Lynn down the aisle,[30] a giant leap occurred in the summer of 1979, when Greaves was contacted by Frank Nicklin, sports editor of *The Sun*. He was offering Greaves the opportunity to write a weekly football column in the country's best-selling newspaper. For a man who was attempting to make ends meet by flogging ladies' sweaters, working in insurance for Abbey Life and selling off anything he possessed of value – with the exception of that beloved Jaguar – it was like receiving a call-up for England. 'I am still grateful to Frank Nicklin, who had faith in me when others were closing doors to me,' he would write a quarter of a century later. The column not only offered him much-needed income, it gave him back a degree of self-esteem that had seemed lost for ever and, significantly, it gave him a reason to reconnect with professional football.

In February 1980, almost a year after his interview with Russell Harty, Greaves participated in what proved to be perhaps the most

---

30 Greaves was back on the news pages when Lynn's marriage to Frank Bishop, a former Chelmsford City footballer, broke up after three years. Greaves was reported to have gone at Bishop with a seven-iron golf club. 'Actually it was a five-iron,' he wrote in 1990. 'I took the golf club with me only to force entry into my daughter's house, where my gorgeous granddaughter, Victoria, was waiting to be reunited with her mother. I had a bit of a barney with her now ex-husband but it was all ironed out ... after a few words with the police, and everything has since been settled.'

significant television engagement of his life. Lifelong Tottenham fan Berny Stringle, the producer responsible for turning the PG Tips chimpanzees into national icons, was very familiar with his hero's story. As a recovering alcoholic himself, he believed that there was a lot more to be said by, and about, Greaves and his problems than the sound bites he had given to Russell Harty, especially with several more months of recovery behind him.

'I was working with [comedian and writer] Willie Rushton,' Stringle explains, 'when Donald Langdon, who managed Peter Cook and Dudley Moore in those days, said that Peter was a huge Spurs fans and asked if we would write something for them. I was talking about the fact I was lucky enough to dry out in about 1973 and it started out with this sort of conversation.'

The project that formulated in Stringle's mind was far from being a comedy vehicle, even though Cook would be involved. It would be the story of Greaves's alcoholism, told by the subject, his family and those in football. 'I put up an idea to the documentary department at ATV.[31] They had already booked the one documentary spot they had left, but they said they preferred this idea if I could get Jimmy to talk on screen about being an alcoholic. Everything moved very quickly. They gave me an office, a research assistant, whatever footage they would have allowed and 10,000 feet of film.'

Now he just had to get Greaves to participate, a process that began by Stringle convincing him to visit him at his home in Enfield. 'I said, "Do you realise what this is going to do; what I am asking you to do? There is no documentary here if you are going to hide anything." I think two things convinced him, because I didn't have much money to pay him. One, I am an alcoholic. Two, I had managed to shake it off. The fact I was so deep into Spurs helped, too. He started describing many of the things I had experienced: the missing days; turning up in places and not knowing how you

---

31 ITV's regional television network covering the Midlands, later to be relaunched as Central.

got there. We got on like a house on fire. I had been through the same experience and we were talking the same language. I was very honest with Jimmy, which is maybe what persuaded him to take part. And he realised it might open other people's eyes to alcoholism.'

What proves to be a powerful hour of television gets off to a stilted start. Without knowing that what they were about to see would be honest, poignant and thought-provoking, many viewers might have watched the sequence before the opening titles and assumed that *Just for Today* was merely a vehicle for Cook – and not a particularly funny one. His schtick is a somewhat laboured juxtaposition of Greaves's football career and his alcoholism. Sitting at a pub bar, smoking a cigarette, while a suited Greaves stands nervously drinking tea, Cook suggests, 'What I was thinking about – very tasteless – was discussing drinking as a sport. Greavsie is the greatest finisher in the game … a member of the great double side; used to come in here and started with the double, then on to the quadruple … the quickest man over 10 yards to the toilet I have ever seen.' Hilarious.

He continues, 'I understand that the football started off like it normally does, as a social footballer, with other people; then gradually over the years it built up and became this addictive compulsive process.' And so on. It is a set-piece that does little justice to what is to come and appears to have been included as a nod towards Cook's place in the genesis of the project.

The programme really begins three minutes in when, after a title montage showing drinks being poured and bottles and cans littering gutters, Greaves, framed against a black background, turns to the camera and announces, 'My name is Jimmy Greaves. I am a professional footballer and an alcoholic.'

In settings ranging from outside White Hart Lane and on the pitch at Barnet to jogging through the woods and sitting on a park bench with discarded beer cans around him, Greaves proceeds to tell the story of how alcohol seized control of his life. Through his candidness, and the involvement of Irene, Lynn and Danny, the documentary offers the most revealing and intimate portrait of Greaves as an alcoholic, attaining greater depth and insight than his tale achieved in newspaper and book form.

'In the early point of agreeing to take part he felt a little nervous about suddenly becoming an actor and holding this thing together,' says Stringle. 'But the minute he started work he picked up things very quickly and realised that he had got to talk to the lens like he was talking to one person. He was so easy to work with. He was apprehensive, but after the first couple of days things were moving along fine. We finished it very swiftly and ITV were very keen to get it on the air as soon as possible.'

Stringle could recognise that, once again, the unburdening had been cathartic for Greaves. 'Some of the things we talked about together privately he initially said he didn't want to talk about on screen, like how it affected his marriage. But eventually I got to interview Irene as well. I think it did help to get the whole thing off his chest.'

Throughout the programme an impressive footballing cast speak about Greaves's phenomenal talent and, later, offer their observations, reactions and theories relating to his drinking. Denis Law, Terry Venables, Malcolm Allison, Alan Gilzean, Alan Mullery, Geoff Hurst, Billy Wright and George Best all contribute. 'Best was the biggest problem,' Stringle laughs, 'because he was drinking very heavily and kept disappearing. Eventually he turned up after letting us down six times. I thought I was going to have to put the film to bed and forget him but then he showed up and he was perfect. Every single footballer I contacted was quite willing to be interviewed because they admired Jimmy so greatly. It was strange, though. No one I spoke to would own up to ever seeing Jimmy take a serious drink. No one had thought he was a drinker or that it had affected his play.'

Early in production, Greaves remembered the letter he had received from Nick Charles and managed to get his number via

Stringle, who had already spoken to him about appearing in the documentary. 'Nick had been to the depths,' Stringle explains, 'drinking boot polish and meths. He had become a guardian of alcoholics who had really fallen off the end of the world and who nobody would deal with. He had managed to get a hospital in Ealing to let him have some disused buildings.'

Charles recalls, 'I had a phone call from Jimmy and he said, "I don't know if I have done the right thing. I am scared shitless." I knew exactly how he felt. I said, "You are not on your own, you are a very brave man and the only person who can say that to you and not be patronising is another drunk who has been through what you have been through."'

Recognising the stage Greaves had reached in his rehabilitation, Charles was able to offer him comfort and advice. 'Twelve months into my sobriety I was still mentally unstable,' he explains. 'I would switch from a high to a terrible low in five minutes. When you are two years sober you realise how bad you were in the first year. You are not wise enough to evaluate it.' Greaves was just approaching that important two-year landmark. 'I told him that you can either learn from what I have done or you can go out there and make the same fucking mistakes all over again. I told him, "None of my mates have survived."'

Charles also recalls an incident during the filming of the players that Greaves found instructive. 'I didn't have a big wardrobe and someone told me there was a shop around the corner that had what looked like white cricket jumpers and I thought that would be just the job with a pair of jeans. I bought the pullover, but there was a rip in it, which was why it was cheap. It was stitched up for me.

'During filming I felt this rustle and it was constant, like an electric shock though your clothing. Jimmy leaned forward and said, "It's a good job they are not filming you right now." I looked down and this pullover had unravelled all the way round my body and all that was left was like this cream-coloured ruffle around my neck. I hadn't noticed. Jimmy said, "You said alcohol is an anaesthetic and there will never be a better bloody example than that.'"

Aired after ITV's *News at Ten* on Wednesday, 27 February and gaining an audience well into double-figure millions, the documentary includes one scene where a group of English football journalists who reported on his career – including Desmond Hackett (*Daily Express*), Laurie Pignon (*Daily Mail*), Bernard Joy (*Evening Standard*), Geoffrey Green (*The Times*) and Brian James (*Daily Mail*) – sit around a table with Greaves discussing various elements of his life, most notably Sir Alf Ramsey's selection decision in 1966. 'I still think he was wrong,' insists Hackett. 'I would never have taken this man out of my team.'

Every one of this group knew that Greaves was a heavy drinker – even if they were unaware of the severity of his addiction – and James wonders why he was unable to ask them for help. 'Drink doesn't suddenly come on you,' is Greaves's reply. 'You don't know what is happening to you.'

Greaves asserts at another point that 'the average person doesn't really know the difference between an alcoholic and a heavy drinker'. He enlightens his audience. 'An alcoholic is somebody who takes drink and then ceases to function as a normal human being. You basically become a walking vegetable in many ways. Although you appear to be functioning normally, you are not.' To a viewing audience used to hearing footballers in this Wednesday night broadcast slot declaring themselves to be 'over the moon' or 'sick as a parrot', it was something of a revelation to hear a sportsman discussing such a complex issue.

In one of her final comments, Irene discusses an unforeseen consequence of Greaves going public with his addiction. 'The strange thing to me, which I can't understand, is that we have been ostracised,' she explains, by 'people who would never have known the wide spectrum that we opened for them. Very close people I am talking about, who got business principally because they have known Jim, have not wished us well.' Making it clear that public support had been overwhelming, she concludes, 'I suppose the nicest thing is the people who did stick by us, and the new friends we have made because he is an alcoholic or in spite of being an alcoholic – as opposed to pretending to be friends because he is a famous footballer and what he can represent.'

Having been interviewed separately throughout the piece, Jimmy and Irene are seated together on their sofa for the final scene, the Christmas tree behind them not only illustrating when it was filmed but also adding an extra air of domestic cosiness that is in stark contrast to so much of Irene's earlier testimony. Greaves, his wedding ring visible on his right hand, admits:

> One has had to grow up and believe the sun doesn't shine every day for Jimmy Greaves. You walk outside and it is pissing down with rain and you have got to accept the fact. And it is no good running to the nearest pub like a spoilt child and saying, 'Someone up there doesn't like me, it's raining.' Sure it's raining, but it's raining on every other bugger. So you have got to accept the world for what it is. The real context is that the world doesn't revolve around you as an individual; it doesn't any more revolve around Jimmy Greaves. I have to take the world for what it is and fit myself into its moods, not the world fitting itself into my moods. Those days are over and, sure, it's a sign of immaturity in the first place, and if you want to say that accepting it on those terms is a sign of maturity then possibly I have grown up a lot over the past two years.

After closing shots of Greaves jogging along the sea front, the final credits roll alongside a still of Jimmy and Irene, underneath a Stringle-composed song in which a husband pledges to make up to his wife for the pain he has caused.

Greaves considered that he was done with talking about his problems for now. He had confessed all in a newspaper, expanded upon that in his new autobiography, faced up to the rigours of a television studio and now dug a little deeper in a documentary. It was time to move on. While alcoholism might be an ever-present companion, it was not going to be – outwardly at least – the aspect of his life that became its chief characteristic.

Which is not to say that it became a taboo subject. Not only was he happy to share his experiences with those close to him, such as Cliff Jones and Billy Wright, who found themselves similarly afflicted, he was able to take a joke at his expense. In the early '90s, he would appear on BBC's *Fantasy Football League* in a 'Phoenix from the Flames' section, in which hosts Frank Skinner and David Baddiel, with the help of their guests, staged comedic reconstructions of famous football incidents. With Greaves kitted out in all-white and Skinner in canine costume, they played out the incident in the 1962 World Cup when Greaves had captured a stray dog and been urinated on for his trouble. 'Hey, Jimmy,' laughs Skinner. 'I bet that wasn't the only time you went home smelling of piss.' Greaves was a good sport about it and duly followed his scripted role of wagging a scolding finger in response.[32]

Meanwhile, the *Just for Today* programme turned out to have unexpectedly welcome consequences. 'It opened so many doors for me,' says Charles. 'Have you ever seen 5,000 letters on the floor of your front room? Berny asked me in the documentary how I would define alcoholism. I replied, "Alcoholism is cancer of the soul. It gets right in there and eats away at everything that is good and leaves behind nothing but rubbish." Within a fortnight, that post came along, six of those big Navy kit bags in the hallway. That opened so many doors for my work. I have Jim to thank for that.'

As well as setting in motion a chain of events that Charles reckons has helped tens of thousands of people, the documentary proved pivotal for Greaves himself. Later that year, ATV executives

---

32 Greaves and his broadcasting partner, Ian St John, would be regularly lampooned in the show – to the point where St John, in particular, felt it went beyond good-natured humour and ended any hope of their *Saint & Greavsie* show returning to TV screens after ITV cancelled it in 1992.

found themselves looking for an analyst to work on *Star Soccer*, the Midlands region's football highlights show. The stakes could not have been higher. It was the first season in which ITV had wrested Saturday night football away from the BBC in what the newspapers had delighted in calling 'Snatch of the Day'. The 1980-81 season was the one in which *Star Soccer* – and regional counterparts such as *The Big Match* (London) and *Match Night* (Granada) – would begin alternating season-by-season with BBC in the Saturday evening and Sunday afternoon slots.

It was something of a gamble, then, for *ATV Today* producer Tony Flanagan to interrupt the conversation about Midlands football figures to suggest, 'How about Jimmy Greaves?' Sports editor and *Star Soccer* presenter Gary Newbon recalls, 'We looked at lots of people. They were quite keen on Derek Dougan, who was a big mate of mine, but he was very verbose. Although I loved the bloke and he was a great talker, he would not have been my choice. They were finding it difficult to get me comfortable with it, but then Tony Flanagan was reading *The Sun* and suggested Jimmy. I had just seen the documentary ATV had done and thought, "That will be great."'

Flanagan felt that Greaves's newspaper columns proved that he had strident, interesting opinions and agreed with Newbon that his performance in *Just for Today* was evidence of a gift in front of the camera. Nick Owen, who was the station's sports reporter, continues, 'They had decided that if we were doing a Saturday night programme then we needed a pundit. Derek Dougan was a Wolves legend and very much a Midlands man and when Jimmy was suggested people like myself said, "Well, he has got no connection to the region." But they decided to go with him. Then it was, "How do we get in touch with him?" I had first met him when he brought out his book, *This One's on Me*, and was doing a promotional tour. It was during my earliest days on television, so it was an absolute thrill for me. I don't know how it came about, but he gave me his phone number.'

Newbon and *Star Soccer* editor Trevor East were instructed to make initial contact with Giller, who was representing Greaves, as well as working on his column for *The Sun*. 'We were laying the foundation for his new career,' Giller explains. 'I used to accompany him around the country, introducing him as an after-dinner celebrity. In the early days I used to write his scripts for him, but he hated reading and started to ad-lib his own material and was much funnier than me. I was acting as his agent, while up to my ears in my new career as an author and TV scriptwriter, and we decided perhaps I was not right for the job when I booked him for a speaking engagement at what I thought was Bognor Regis – but it was Lyme Regis, many miles further away.'

The final decision lay with former England captain Billy Wright, who had been one of televised football's first analysts after his unsuccessful venture into management at Arsenal and was now head of sport at ATV. He shared with Giller his concerns that the pressure of the job 'could drive Jimmy back to the bottle' but was intrigued enough to pursue the idea.

Stringle explains, 'Billy Wright rang me and said he thought Jimmy had come out of it so well. He asked, "Do you think he could handle a sports programme on television?" The thing I had noticed was that he had that sense of timing that made him such a skilled goalscorer. His timing and personality made it work. I told Billy how easy he was to work with, an absolute dream. It is nice to think that the programme led to a new career for Jim. I think it made him realise what he could do. I am proud of that.'

Wright duly contacted Greaves. 'It was only a few days before the first programme,' says Newbon. 'Jim said, "No, thanks," so we were back to the drawing board and we still hadn't got anybody. Then, on the Thursday, Jimmy rang Trevor and said, "Is that job offer still open? Irene says I have got to go and do it."'

Greaves admitted that he had 'got the jitters just thinking about it' and had discussed the idea with Irene, hoping that she would discourage him from committing himself to a new career that would necessitate traipsing back and forth between Essex and Birmingham. Yet, like the scene in *Rocky II* where the hospitalised Adrian instructs Sylvester Stallone's character to 'win' when he offers to quit the ring, Irene had turned to her husband and ordered, 'Get your backside up that M1!'

17

SCREEN SHOTS

'With Saint & Greavsie *we had a lot of fun and that was what it was all about. I think some of the shows now are a bit too serious. I think there is too much talk about tactics … it's still a game, whatever anyone says.'*

THE Midlands has in recent times been the forgotten region of English football. The north-west has seen the big clubs situated at either of the East Lancs Road bring trophy after trophy back to Merseyside and Manchester, and when anything has evaded their voracious grasp it has usually ended up in the hands of one of London's glamour clubs. Even the north-east, for all its frustrations on Tyneside and Wearside, is revered for its passion and its people. It is easy for those teams and cities in the middle of the country to feel bypassed.

In the early years of the 1980s, however, it was a different story. Derby County, under Brian Clough and Dave Mackay, had won the League Championship twice in the previous decade; and now Clough, astonishingly, had brought two European Cups, a Division One title and a couple of League Cups to Nottingham Forest. Wolverhampton Wanderers had beaten Forest in the latest

League Cup final, while Aston Villa were about to follow Clough's path, winning the League in 1980-81 and conquering Europe the following season. Jimmy Greaves was going to work within a genuine hotbed of success in the sport.

'Everything was happening,' recalls Gary Newbon, who would succeed Billy Wright as head of ATV's sporting output. 'Things were fantastic up here. It was pre-Sky, so the ratings were huge. It was a golden period for the Midlands.'

It meant that Greaves's first foray into football broadcasting would be exposed to widespread scrutiny, especially given *Star Soccer*'s new home on Saturday evenings. This was no get-to-know-the-ropes assignment out in the sticks of regional television. Greaves's distrust of life beyond London had prevented him considering a transfer to Derby, a move that he came to recognise might have altered the perilous trajectory of his life. Now, with the blessing of Irene – with whom he was happily re-settled, although not remarried – he headed north to Birmingham with the kind of butterflies he'd rarely felt when turning out for new teams on the football field.

'He came up to *ATV Today* to promote the new season and he was understandably incredibly nervous,' says Newbon. Assigned to look ahead to the weekend's games on Friday evenings and then review the action on *Star Soccer*, Greaves described his first couple of performances as being 'worthy of a Monty Python sketch'. He stumbled over the basics; looking into wrong cameras, tripping over the script and struggling with his timing. It was not the kind of debut to which he was accustomed. 'It made me realise how naïve I was about television,' he said. Sitting and chatting amiably with Berny Stringle in a less pressurised atmosphere of a documentary was no preparation for this. He was relieved to have maintained his interest in the insurance business, feeling it offered him his own security against an early departure from the world of TV.

The dyslexia that had been with him throughout his life made the autocue an almost impossible barrier. Instead, he would prepare his own notes and use them as a prompt; a method far more suited to the relaxed style of presentation he hoped to master. Greaves recalled Newbon looking after him in his early shows 'like a mother hen' and would record, 'I learned a great deal from Gary and I will always be grateful to him.' Director Syd Kilby was another who offered sound advice, reminding Greaves that he had been invited into viewers' homes and that he should conduct himself as a guest. Even the station's fishing expert, Terry Thomas, chipped in with the advice to smile more on screen.

As had been his approach on the field, Greaves was not about to try anything for which he was not suited. Detailed tactical analysis, he decided, was better left to the likes of Jimmy Hill. By his third show, he was settling into a method that would serve him well for the next decade; chatting as though he was sitting among a group of friends. Fun, he recognised, was as valuable as formations.

Newbon remembers, 'I was teaching him the art of it, everything I could. At first, I took a lot of abuse; there were terrible letters in the local papers and phone calls saying, "Why do we want a bleeding Cockney on our screens?" Then, when he started making people laugh, suddenly he became a huge hit. We didn't know how funny it was going to be. We got lucky with his humour. He started to get used to television and he was as good as gold. Bev Bevan, the drummer of ELO[33], told me that when they were recording in Munich they would tape the show and take it with them, just to watch Jimmy.'

Nick Owen, who joined Greaves and Newbon to complete *Star Soccer's* presenting line-up, has little memory of any early struggles by the rookie of the team. 'He was just himself from the word go,' he says. 'My advice for anyone going on television is that you have got to be yourself. You cannot be an actor. If it works it works, if it doesn't, bad luck. You are reacting, ad-libbing, expressing views,

---

33 The Electric Light Orchestra, originating in Birmingham, were one of the UK's biggest music acts in the late 1970s and early 1980s.

so all the time you have got be yourself. That is what Jimmy did par excellence.'

According to Norman Giller, 'The secret of Jimmy's success was that he was one of the few totally natural people in front of the camera. Because of severe dyslexia he could never read the autocue, so he became conversational while most others were robotic. He came across exactly as he is; a cheeky chappie, with a quick wit and the background of having been a genius of a footballer.'

Greaves's new career was a talking point for the newspapers. Inevitably, in something so subjective, there was good and bad. 'Jimmy Greaves has brought something almost unheard of to football punditry – a sense of humour,' wrote *The Sunday Times*, while *The Sun* argued that he brought 'a rare and much-needed smile to the face of soccer' – which was what you might have expected from the publication that employed him. The *Daily Mail* said that 'he is irreverent, savagely honest, often hilarious and sometimes bordering on the irresponsible, which makes his act compulsive viewing'.

However, another reviewer asked, 'Why doesn't Greaves go the whole way and put on a clown's suit?' and accused him of poking fun at the 'game to which he owes so much'. Perhaps that was unfair. Commenting with humour was a long way from being disrespectful. Greaves viewed such remarks as pure snobbery. 'He was a joker,' Owen continues. 'Up until then it was still quite a stiff broadcasting world; people were quite tight-lipped and didn't expand much. He was suddenly a breath of fresh air. He was not just a pundit, he was an entertainer. He was great value.'

Greaves loved the atmosphere in the studio. 'Just like being back with a winning team,' was how he described it. Once more, he was experiencing the satisfaction he had got from the dressing room, or the collective drive of an AA meeting. It was Greaves who used to get the crew's Saturday night takeaway from the local Chinese restaurant – until that practice was banned because it was discovered that the leftovers were attracting mice into the studio. 'We developed a great relationship on air and off,' says Newbon. 'Billy Wright had let me get on with it and Jimmy felt really safe with everything.'

Owen, a Luton Town fan who would go on to serve as club chairman for a decade, continues, 'I loved Jimmy's company and he had a great sense of humour. We used to take the piss out of each other all the time; he was always being rude about Luton. It was a magical time. And we talked a lot about his alcoholism, especially the day he decided to finish after he'd been dredging around the dustbins looking for bottles Irene had thrown away. The fact that the date of his last drink, 28 February 1978, sticks in my mind shows how much he talked about it with me.'

Greaves made a big enough impression with his new employers to be given a wider remit, as *The Greaves Report* was added to the station's output. The segments required him to take a light-hearted look at sport and found him, over the ensuing years, playing tennis with John McEnroe; facing England fast bowler Bob Willis in the nets; getting on the back of a motorbike with world champion Barry Sheene; playing darts with Eric Bristow and squash against Jonah Barrington.

He even headed into the ring on occasions, most eye-catchingly in 1986 when he wrestled the masked Kendo Nagasaki at London's Hippodrome. Dressed in a cerise pink body suit with 'Griller Greaves' emblazoned on the back – 'I thought it was quite fetching, but the trouble was I couldn't have a pee in it because it had no flies' – he did what most scripts called for in Nagasaki fights; he headed straight for the headgear and tried to pull it off, even though the mysterious grappler had originally been de-masked nine years earlier. Unsuccessful, he suffered a few body slams and an aeroplane spin before being pinned with a cross press. All over in roughly a minute.

He donned the gloves to conduct an interview between punches in a staged sparring session with heavyweight Frank Bruno, before discovering he was too out of breath to get his questions out. He would also stand nervously as world heavyweight champion Mike Tyson showed him some of his moves during an interview at his US training camp. And he survived a crash landing after hitching a ride with a hang glider. Greaves was clearly never likely to win a BAFTA for highbrow journalism, but the public, already on his side after his football career and battle against alcoholism, quickly came to embrace him as a broadcaster. He said he was stopped in the street more often now than he had been during his playing days.

According to Nigel Spink, Aston Villa's goalkeeper throughout the 1980s, he was equally popular among the players. 'It was ironic that he ended up in the Midlands as I was breaking into the Villa team,' says his former Chelmsford City team-mate. 'Every week he was part of what I was going through. The kind of programmes Jimmy would be involved in were unique at the time. You see any number of those kind of shows these days, but it was unique then and he brought the humour of the dressing room to the TV screens.'

For a couple of years, Greaves would make appearances alongside presenters Tommy Boyd and Isla St Clair on ITV's *The Saturday Show*, the morning successor to cult favourite *Tiswas*. He was offered a rematch with Bruno and this time the interview was halted when Big Frank forgot how hard he was supposed to punch and felled Greaves with a blow to the head.

But it was football, specifically the 1982 World Cup, that gave him another breakthrough opportunity. It was the first time he had been seen nationally on the ITV network talking about his sport.

ITV had led the way in presentation of World Cups when head of sport John Bromley came up with the idea of a World Cup panel for the 1970 tournament in Mexico. While BBC carefully placed the likes of Brian Clough and Bob Wilson into its coverage, Bromley decided to throw Malcolm Allison, Derek Dougan, Pat Crerand and discarded England squad member Bob McNab on air at the same time and let Jimmy Hill and Brian Moore try to keep them under control. Dressed as though they were on their way to a nightclub, the panel brought a new, accessible style to football analysis, helping ITV to match the BBC viewing figures – a previously unthinkable development. Bromley explained, 'Crerand, the tough little Scot, and Allison, the hard-nosed Cockney, were the baddies, and the charming Dougan with the lovely McNab were the goodies. The whole mix was absolutely right and it took off and they became folk heroes in four weeks.'

For fans of a certain age, the first tournament to be televised in colour remains as memorable for Allison puffing on cigars, blowing smoke in Dougan's face and making politically incorrect remarks about all sorts of foreigners as it is for the magnificent vibrancy of Brazil's football and shimmering yellow shirts. Greaves, however, had hated it. He 'detested their pontificating and thought they made right wallies of themselves'.

For the 1982 finals in Spain, the first to feature England since 1970, ITV were again packing their line-up with big names in preparation for showing more live games than before. Greaves was prepared to join the 'wallies' as part of a squad of experts that included George Best, Jack Charlton, Denis Law, Ian St John, Brian Clough and John Bond. ITV's leading commentator, Brian Moore, would once again be kept at home to present.

Newbon recalls a battle, however, to make Greaves part of that line-up. 'Things were going really well with Jimmy, but when the 1982 World Cup came up there was a lot of politics and we went to war in the end. As a region, we paid our share towards the ITV network, but London Weekend Television wouldn't let anyone else in. We were all blocked. They didn't want Jimmy Greaves in London. One of their guys said, "We don't want him, he is a disaster." I said, "Have you seen him on television in the Midlands?" He hadn't. Trevor East was very helpful and the two of us went and argued with John Bromley that he should be one of the panellists. Of course, they then discovered that he was a huge hit.'

When England came up against the host nation in the second phase of the tournament, Greaves found himself sitting between Clough and Bond while they argued over the tactics of manager Ron Greenwood. When it began to get personal, with Bond complaining that viewers were bound to side with Clough because he had won two European Cups, Greaves, whose neck had been working back and forth like a tennis umpire, interjected, 'If this is a discussion and not a row, I don't want to be between the two of you when you have a row.'

Off air, he and Best discussed the ills of the modern game and thought that only Tottenham's Glenn Hoddle and Manchester United's Bryan Robson of the England squad were world-class. Greenwood disagreed, picking Arsenal's Graham Rix throughout the tournament ahead of Hoddle.

Having successfully tipped Italy at the outset as eventual champions, Greaves signed off his contribution to a gripping few weeks of football by telling Moore, 'These finals have all been about long balls, short balls, square balls, through balls, high balls, low balls, and to you, Brian, I would just like to say … it's been a pleasure being on the panel.'

His performance continued to appeal more to the fans than critics. In *The Times*, Dennis Hackett – not to be confused with namesake Desmond – opined that 'Greaves was far more eloquent on the field, all those years, than he is off it.' As an example, he noted his remark that 'I'm a bit choked for Bryan Robson' after an injury during the group game against Czechoslovakia. 'To a viewer, he appears somewhat choked most of the time. Mr Moore should realise the futility of asking him for a quick comment.' The power brokers in ITV Sport spent little time reading such reviews.

'The problem with TV critics,' says Newbon, 'is that they are writing for their own effect and they don't care who they pan. Panning a programme is much more interesting than writing nice things about it. At the end of the day, the viewers will watch what they want to watch. Some people might have battered him, but he was a huge success.'

While fate and circumstance combined to launch Greaves's television career, Ian St John had decided, even while a regular in Liverpool's first team in the late 1960s, that he fancied a future in broadcasting. When BBC Television staged a national competition to identify its fourth commentator for the 1970 World Cup, St John had finished as runner-up behind Welshman Idwal Robling. After venturing into management with Motherwell and Portsmouth, St John had realised his TV ambitions, eventually being asked to take over presentation of Saturday lunchtime's *On the Ball* slot during ITV's *World of Sport* from the overworked Moore.

'It was suggested Jimmy should have a regular spot on the programme,' says St John, 'but he was up in Birmingham doing his Saturday morning children's show and I was in the London studio. So each week we would link up from different places. It worked very well.' Well enough that potential for a more productive partnership between the two was quickly recognised, although in the meantime another television executive had taken note of Greaves's unique style. It was, he decided, worthy of waking up to.

Greg Dyke had a daunting task on his hands. Newly-appointed programme director at TV-am, holders of the ITV breakfast television franchise, he was looking at audience numbers that were barely high enough to register in the ratings as the BBC emerged as the clear leaders in the new early-morning television war. The idea of conversation over the cornflakes was a new one, BBC's *Breakfast Time* having hit the screens first in January 1983. Fronted by long-time master of sports presenting, the avuncular Frank Bough, and the likeable Selina Scott, the show's format and tone was in stark contrast to what was to follow a few weeks later from TV-am.

Featuring a powerhouse presenting line-up of David Frost, Michael Parkinson, Anna Ford, Angela Rippon and Robert Kee, the serious, news-heavy approach of the *TV-am* show in its early weeks failed to connect with viewers distracted by preparing for the working day ahead. Within two months, Dyke, who had made a success of London Weekend Television's *Six O'Clock Show*, was brought in to create a new identity for the station. The heavyweights were out – which represented a big break for Nick Owen.

'Greg Dyke had come in when the station was struggling and decided to inject some new faces,' Owen recalls. 'I was the sports presenter and suddenly I was asked to take over as main presenter. Only eight weeks into this new station I took over from the mighty David Frost. I was a comparative unknown. I had done quite a lot of network sport, but I was a regional sports presenter essentially. After Angela Rippon and Anna Ford left, Greg said to me, "Who, in a perfect world, would you like to present this programme with?" and I said, "Anne Diamond." He asked who she was and I explained that she and I had co-presented stuff in the Midlands.'

Dyke's open-minded, experimental approach was to create an influx of on-screen talent and personality. Disc jockey Paul Gambaccini would arrive as film reviewer, 'Mad' Lizzie Webb was offered a fitness slot, the likes of Gyles Brandreth and actress Diana Dors were given regular roles and a furry puppet called Roland Rat became a cult character who appealed to a far wider audience than children. Newsreader Gordon Honeycombe added a touch of gravitas. Horoscopes, celebrity gossip, fun and games became the staple of the station's content. And Dyke had a role in mind for Greaves.

'What do you know about television?' he asked him.

'Well, I know to look into the camera with the red light,' Greaves replied.

What Dyke intended to ascertain was how much television Greaves watched – which, since he had given up going out drinking, was a lot. Greaves was offered a five-minute segment on Fridays as a TV previewer.

'We're looking to go down-market,' Dyke explained.

'That's very flattering of you. You can't get much more down-market than me.'

Owen continues, 'It was wonderful to be reunited with Jimmy. Joe Steeples was his producer and he and Jimmy would talk about the programmes and work out gags and thoughts and lines. Jimmy couldn't just walk in and do it. If his slot was, say, 8.15 then he would be there by seven, in good time to get sorted and talk it all through and rehearse. He was very conscientious.'

Greaves would recall, 'I was only a part-time contributor, but there was such a strong team spirit that I felt a total commitment to what had become a fight for survival.' Dyke's dream team did more than just survive. A year later, the audience had grown to well over a million and was beginning to overtake the BBC. Now it just had to wipe out its massive debts.

Dyke, his job done, would move on after 12 months, but Greaves would stay for several more years, contributing his thoughts on various topics. Most famously, he ruffled some feathers in 1987 by describing the weather forecasters as 'useless ginks' after there had been little warning of the intensity of a hurricane in the south-east. 'The fact is the weather people this year have got nothing right,' he argued. 'You remember January and February – "a couple of inches of snow" – I couldn't get in one day because there was two feet the following morning. Most of them are more interested in going on *Blankety Blank* and bloody *Call My Bluff*. They are paying no attention to the weather. When Trish [Williamson] and the other gink was sat here there was no apologies. It was all excuses. "Oh well, it's not our fault. We didn't predict this." If I came on here and said, "Right, on Wednesday we have got *Minder* and *The Bill*" and we got totally different programmes, the wizard of Oz[34] upstairs would call me in and sack me.'

Criticising his fellow presenters might not always have gone down well in the studio – 'I do remember him getting into a bit

---

34 He was referring to TV-am chief executive Bruce Gyngell, an Australian.

of trouble for that,' says Owen – but it was, of course, the kind of no-nonsense honesty for which he had been employed.

In 1988, he would make the headlines for beginning a campaign protesting at the number of repeated shows appearing on British television. *The Sun* even ran a cartoon showing him kicking a football through his TV set, while other newspapers speculated about whether he would be fired for biting the hand that was feeding him. 'We're not really getting a fair deal,' he argued, citing a survey in which the public had named 'too many repeats' as its biggest complaint about television, well ahead of violence, bad language and other issues. 'Television cheats the public because at peak times when they should be showing new and entertaining and different programmes they are showing repeats.' He advocated new channels specialising in re-running old shows, leaving the main stations to concentrate on new output, and accused TV companies of being 'bone lazy'. At least his prescience about the kind of stations that would arrive with satellite TV compensated for a degree of naivety over the budgets available for original programming.

The following year, he proved himself happy to lay into ITV once more, although he ended up being called a 'small-minded bigot' by broadcaster Mike Smith after he'd criticised the antics of comedian Julian Clary on a show called *Trick or Treat*. Greaves had said that Clary, whom he called a 'prancing poof', was using suggestive material unsuitable for an early-evening family audience. His choice of phrase was thoughtless and insulting – although not an uncommon expression at that time – but again demonstrated that he was not afraid of taking shots at his own network.

He could talk himself into trouble when speaking about football, too. Commenting on the 1985 FA Cup final between Manchester United and Everton, he accused referee Peter Willis of 'trying to get his name in history before he retires' after he made United defender Kevin Moran the first player to be sent off in the sport's showpiece game. Willis sued Greaves and London

Weekend Television for libel and, almost a year later, accepted an out-of-court settlement and an apology from Greaves, who said his remark was 'an unintended slip in the heat of the moment'.

LWT's lawyers advised him that in future he should preface his most strident comments with the words 'in my opinion' in order to safeguard himself and his employers. There was never any possibility of the station deciding that Greaves was more trouble than he was worth. The ratings argued against that. Instead, by the time the Willis case was being resolved, Greaves was in the process of securing his broadcasting profile and his place in the cultural history of the decade thanks to the launch of a show born out of those weekly link-ups with St John during *On the Ball*. 'ITV sports chief John Bromley spotted the chemistry,' says Giller.

At the end of September 1985, the network's 20-year-old *World of Sport* aired for the final time, its demise hastened by the loss to Channel 4 of its rights to horse racing, which had been the backbone of the show. It was announced that wrestling, another staple, would be shown at lunchtime, with a new football preview show preceding it, *Saint & Greavsie*.

A mixture of action, analysis, previews, offbeat stories and characters, plus lots of general larking about, it was the programme that came to define Greaves's second career. 'We didn't want viewers to see football the way the so-called experts saw it, as a very serious game in which there was no place for humour,' he recalled.

The rapport that had been developing through their remote segments during *On the Ball* achieved a three-dimensional life of its own once Greaves and St John were together in the studio. St John's staccato chuckle became a feature of the show and is never far from reappearing even now when reminiscing about his old partner. 'I had great admiration for Jim as a player, but I think we hit it off on TV because we had the same sense of humour,' he suggests. 'We had lots of laughs at the same thing. What he was doing on TV was what he did on the pitch. He had his own individual style of doing it. Off the cuff, like he had been as a player. It would make me laugh because he was so funny. I was trying to learn to do the right things as a TV presenter, but you are talking about two old footballers doing a programme with absolutely no training. We just did it, helping each other along the way.'

St John's respect for what Greaves had been through a few years earlier grew quickly. 'He should be commended highly for being able to just come off the drink. I am quite a social person myself, but when I was with him I never had a drink. Jimmy would obviously say no when the drinks were getting handed out and I would say no as well because I would not want to be the person that was drinking around him. So both of us would abstain. It was an unspoken thing because he would say, "Go on, Saint, you have one." But I would have a Coke with him. I just felt it was the right thing to do; not to have his partner in crime drinking while he was not drinking.'

Living at opposite ends of the country, there was little socialising between the two away from work; no staged get-togethers to deepen affinity or to plan ahead for the following weekend's show. 'It's very much a close working relationship,' St John once said. 'The truth is we don't even phone each other.'

Instead, they would meet up for a 10.30am 'brekky meeting' in the LWT studio canteen on the day of the broadcast to go through the proposed running order and create a general outline of their talking points. According to St John, that planning consisted of little more than him suggesting a topic and Greaves chipping in with, 'Great, Saint. I'll have a go at that.' If any detailed tactical analysis was called for, Greaves would delegate the duty. 'He would not do that at all,' St John confirms. 'Jimmy would say to me, "You do that." He would give me a square pass and that was it.

'There was no coaching from the producers, or much rehearsal. Jimmy would turn up on set five minutes before the programme went on air. There was no character more laid-back than Jimmy when it came to that. Whether he had done any homework during the week I don't know, but I don't think he did. It was just always off the cuff and ad-libbed. We would reminisce about the game or talk about characters and it was just a lot of fun. One of the key members of the staff was [editor] Bob Patience, who was a Scot and great admirer of Jimmy. He let it ride like that. He could see that was the way the programme was going. "You know about that, Saint. You know about that, Jim. Let's get on with it." He was brilliant at keeping the show on the road like that.'

Greaves proved no more interested in the technicalities of television than those of football, declaring that he had no desire to wear an earpiece linking him to the production team. St John continues, 'Jimmy would not have talkback. For years, he didn't know what Bob was saying to me in my ear. The girls in the gallery would be counting down to you, letting you know when we were bringing in action or whatever, but Jimmy had no clue about that. He didn't want to have a clue; didn't want any information in his ear. Towards the end of our partnership, he suddenly wanted to have it. It amazed everyone. "What does Greavsie want to have talkback for?" they were all asking. He thought it was fantastic. It was like he was talking to somebody from the moon. I don't know if it helped him, but I always thought it confused him and he would be better without it.'

Frequently, things failed to run according to whatever plan there was, but, as St John points out, 'Because it wasn't like a BBC-type show, nobody knew when there had been a cock-up. You would never know because we would ad-lib anyway. There was never a case of "these two don't know what they are doing" and if there was a cock-up we would laugh about it. For me, that was the thing that covered up our lack of professionalism in presenting.'

Far from worrying about the appearance of broadcasting competence, the viewing public appeared to lap up the haphazard, good-natured humour of the show, with audiences exceeding five million. In April 1986, Greaves was named Sports Presenter of the Year in the Television and Radio Industries Club Awards; a year later viewers named him leading Sports Personality in the *TV Times* Awards.

Greaves's claim that *Saint & Greavsie* 'went some way to re-establishing in the minds of supporters that they were all part of the family of football' might be open to accusations of overstatement – especially given the way football hooliganism was continuing its escalation – but it was rightly considered a forerunner of the likes of *Fantasy Football League* and *Soccer AM* and is still fondly remembered and discussed more than a quarter of a century since it went off the air. 'To this day,' says St John, 'when I go to a match up at Liverpool it's always, "Hello, Saint," and the next thing is, "How is Greavsie?"'

Writing on the Football365 website in 2017, John Nicholson paid this tribute:

> The football bit of the show was the usual goals and interviews package over half an hour (45 minutes in the last series) but the reason we tuned in was to watch Saint cracking up after some off-hand comment from Jimmy. His laugh being that distinctive repeated single note. Even now, you know what it sounds like. To do an impression of Ian, all you need to do is that dry 'ha-ha-ha-ha'.
>
> They had a massive cultural resonance in the country. Prior to them, football was always treated with reverence. Cup final day aside, there was little or no room for jokes, for taking the pish, for being irreverent. Yet it all came from a place of love. There was no nastiness. The fact that the jokes came from possibly the greatest English footballer ever only made it better.

The impact of the Greaves and St John double act was such that the satirical comedy show *Spitting Image*, itself an iconic piece of 1980s broadcasting, created puppets of the duo and featured them in its

Sunday night shows. And that led, indirectly, to the catchphrase with which Greaves would be forever bound. Yet it was not his lips from which it first fell.

Central TV decided that it would be fun for Greaves to be interviewed on air by his puppet and he arrived at the studio to be greeted by his latex lookalike and Harry Enfield, the comedian and impressionist who supplied the voice of Greavsie. At the end of the scripted interview, the director failed to call 'cut' and there was silence. Having delivered the final line of dialogue, Greaves decided it was his puppet's responsibility to ad-lib something in response. The puppet turned to the camera and Enfield declared, 'It's a funny old game.'

In late 1990, it was St John who came face to face with the fake Greaves when his partner was ill in bed and unable to record *Saint & Greavsie*. Vocal duties for the Greaves puppet were taken by Peter Brackley, a renowned impressionist as well as being one of football's leading football commentators and a regular contributor to the show. Richard Worth, who had succeeded Patience as producer, called Brackley to inform him that he was needed to co-present the show. 'Not as yourself, though,' he added. 'The puppet will present the show sitting next to the Saint and you can impersonate Jimmy's voice.'

Brackley recalled, 'I actually had to crouch under the desk to do the voice, while the puppet was being worked on the top by an unseen technician. Not exactly the most comfortable position for me to operate in for the entire duration of a half-hour live show, but I managed to get through it, and although I couldn't see the Saint, I could certainly hear him and the studio crew as they fell about in response to this puppet answering his questions in typical cheeky Greavsie fashion.'

The clip that still exists on YouTube is a delight, defying anyone not to laugh along with the audible guffaws of the crew as 'Greavsie' sings a Christmas carol, cracks jokes at the expense of everyone from Dave Bassett to Ken Bates and even mocks 'himself' during a look at elaborate goal celebrations by stating that his own method of marking such a feat was 'a few lagers and a couple of vodkas'.

As the 1980s continued, Greaves had become an omnipresent force in the media. Following their collaboration on *This One's on Me*, Giller and Greaves began to pump out a series of varied publications. Among them were four knockabout football-themed novels featuring a playboy superstar named, ahem, Jackie Groves. Giller admits that the addition of Greaves's name as co-author was merely a way of heightening the profile of the books and generating income for his pal. 'It was totally me, I'm afraid. We were trying to turn him into the Dick Francis of football. Failed.' More successful were the myriad quiz books, histories and humorous looks at the sport that the duo produced.

Greaves had no more envisaged being an author than a chat-show host, but even that opportunity presented itself in 1987. Central offered him the chance to interview ordinary members of the public about unusual events and achievements, a role he took to with some comfort, describing the programme, which aired at 7.30pm on Tuesdays, as 'low-key and interesting'. His mistake, as he would admit, was allowing himself to be persuaded by ITV network executives that he had proved himself capable of hosting his own full-blown celebrity chat show.

For a programme that would be aired nationwide from July 1988, Central brought in a new production team, led by former *This Is Your Life* scriptwriter Roy Bottomley. He devised a format whereby the *Jimmy Greaves* studio would resemble a kitchen – Greavsie's Gaff – and guests would drop in for an informal conversation over a brew. Understanding network television's need for famous names and faces rather than homespun tales of everyday folk, Greaves was nervous about fronting a show that would become a revolving door for product plugs by people in whom he had no interest. Which is exactly what happened – within an environment of amateurish presenting and painful scripting.

Admitting that his ego had been responsible for his agreement to participate in the show, Greaves acknowledged that he made a 'right pig's ear' of the three locally-aired warm-ups and was struck with the realisation that he was out of his depth, forced to work from autocue rather than ad-libbing his way through the shows in the manner to which he was more accustomed. He felt that he was being crowded out by too many guests, unable to engage in any depth of conversation. Inevitably, the critics slated the show, and this time Greaves had no real defence. Coming at the same time as a short-lived move to Cornwall – which lasted only a few weeks – and the death of his 80-year-old father after a heart attack, it was hardly the happiest period of Greaves's life. Never, though, was he tempted to seek solace in having a drink.

Instead, he eventually blew his top at Bottomley, whom he believed was obsessed with glamorous, lightweight guests instead of finding those with something interesting to say. 'If you book me one more bloody bimbo, you can fucking interview her yourself,' he screamed at Bottomley in a hotel bar, while grabbing him by the tie. 'It was stupid of me to tackle Roy in a public place,' he would admit, as the confrontation was inevitably reported to the newspapers, along with the suggestion that he must have been drunk. It was one of many occasions over the years when friends of Greaves were approached to verify 'rumours' that he was back on the booze. Every time he missed a show because of a cold or made a decision to alter his work pattern – as he did in 1988 when taking a rest from live-game analysis on ITV in order to reduce a busy schedule – reporters would start ringing around. Greaves wished more such stories had appeared in print as he might have made a killing in libel damages.

Meanwhile, he did believe that the incident with Bottomley cleared the air, although he never enjoyed the closest of relationships with the producer and *Jimmy Greaves* – which he would look back on as 'an absolute die-on-your-arse show' –

disappeared from ITV's early-evening schedules after only a few weeks.

By this time, however, Greaves was a regular in yet another show, *Sporting Triangles*. Made by Central, the programme launched in 1987 as the ITV network's answer to BBC's long-running *A Question of Sport*, but would end up creating a serious rift in the Greaves-Gary Newbon relationship that took a long time to be fully healed. To be fair to both men, Greaves put the problems down to 'the conceited Greaves', while Newbon admits that he was wrong in the way he attempted to handle the biggest issue arising from the show's production.

Giving his version of events for the first time, Newbon prefaces his comments with, 'I love Jimmy. As a colleague I loved the bloke and I still do. He was a fantastic success. The Midlands loved him, the nation loved him and he was a great operator and a very nice man. I am sorry we had some incidents, but it doesn't affect my relationship with Jimmy.'

He explains, 'Jimmy wanted to front *Sporting Triangles* and I didn't think he was the right bloke. I got Nick Owen, who was later replaced by Andy Craig. I appointed the team captains, who were Andy Gray, Tessa Sanderson, the Olympic javelin champion, and Jimmy Greaves. Jimmy was then worried about what the other people were earning, although he actually earned more than the others and more than I did. I was quite happy about that because he was the star. But he is a footballer and they are always worried about what the bloke on the next peg is making. The programme didn't do very well at first so I made a change of host and I also signed Emlyn Hughes as a captain.'

Greaves, who felt that the show's reliance on computerised technology encumbered Owen's relaxed presenting style and slowed the pace of the show too much, also believed that the level of questions was initially pitched too high – in an attempt to differentiate from the BBC's relatively gentle testing of its sporting guests. By the time Newbon made his changes before the third series, he felt that the show was heading in the right direction. But he was not expecting whatever success the show had achieved to be enough to tempt former England captain Hughes to switch channels. And Greaves believed he should have been afforded the courtesy of being informed before the story appeared in the media.

Hughes had been fulfilling a similar captain's role on *A Question of Sport* and his acquisition by ITV was reported as something of a coup, with newspapers, according to Newbon, 'reporting a salary which was exaggerated by several times, which didn't help'. Hughes was, in fact, making less than Greaves, but an issue arose out of Hughes having a sponsorship deal with Pierre Sangan, whose sweaters he was contracted to wear on screen. As part of his deal, Hughes suggested that the whole presenting team wore the company's knitwear.

Greaves recalled telling show producer Jeff Farmer from the outset, 'There is no way in a million years that I will wear an Emlyn Hughes sweater' – even though he knew there would be no company logo on the clothing. Farmer then agreed he could wear his own red sweater. Yet Newbon counters, 'Jimmy agreed. The sweater just had *Sporting Triangles* on it, you weren't allowed to show a manufacturer's motif in those days. Jimmy was fine about it until he got home.'

Both men agree that there was a heated phone call about it. 'We had a real slanging match that made the telephone wires sizzle,' according to Greaves. Newbon continues, 'Jim went bananas about it, asking, "What is Emlyn getting out of it?" I said, "Either you do it or you don't [do the show]." I was wrong, but Jimmy had pushed me on one or two things and I lost my temper, which I am very sorry about and is not like me. I think all the negotiation to get Emlyn on the show just got to me.'

Greaves explained that the conversation ended with Newbon hanging up. 'It stretched close to breaking point a friendship that had been good for most of the eight and a bit years I had been with Central. We barely spoke to each other over the next six months.'

He followed up by having a dig at Hughes's football knowledge on a subsequent edition of *Saint and Greavsie*, at which point his agent at the time, Barry Brown, was told by Central to ask him to back off. And having, he felt, made his point that he could not be ordered to wear a particular sweater, he informed Newbon and Farmer that he would wear the Hughes-endorsed item.

The footnote to the episode comes from Newbon. 'He wore the jumper and then it was his birthday and my missus came up with the idea of getting him a big cake because we had an audience in.' Yet, not wanting the fuss and attention, Greaves warned, 'If you bring that cake out in front of the audience I am going to get in my car and go home.' The cake ended up at a local children's hospital. 'I took it on the chin,' says Newbon. 'His presence on my programmes was more important.'

Sporting Triangles continued on into a fourth series before ITV blew its final whistle. *A Question of Sport*, meanwhile, has marched on towards its half-century.

18

THE LAST
PICTURE SHOW

*'Our attitude to football was not in keeping
with the way football now saw itself going.
Neither was it complementary to the way
television wanted to project the game.'*

BY 1992, the FA Premier League was waiting to explode into life. English football had been dragged kicking and screaming out of its complacent attitude by the tragic events of Hillsborough in 1989 and Sky Sports was poised to change English football, both in its broadcasting and its funding.

ITV would initially be excluded from the party that the sport was about to throw, with BBC having secured exclusive rights to highlights of the new competition. It meant a bleak outlook for *Saint & Greavsie*. Gary Newbon's view is that Greg Dyke, who had by then become ITV's head of sport, 'threw his toys out of the window and cancelled it'. Yet Norman Giller adds, 'Jimmy thought they deserved another couple of years, but once ITV lost their football franchise they had nowhere to go with it.'

As part of what would be the show's final season, there had been a visit late in 1991 to the USA for a special programme looking at preparations for the 1994 World Cup. They visited Trump Tower, where – in a clip that was shared widely during the 2016 American presidential elections – Donald Trump assisted in the draw for the quarter-finals of the League Cup, then going under the guise of the Rumbelows Cup. 'Donald, you don't know what you've done,' laughed Jimmy Greaves after the future leader of the Western world pulled out Manchester United to visit arch-rivals Leeds United. Trump gave little impression of having the first clue what was going on throughout the entire piece.

The final *Saint & Greavsie* broadcasts took place during the 1992 European Championship finals in Sweden. The last show opens and closes with Greaves – never afraid to pander to national stereotypes for a cheap laugh – wearing a horned Viking helmet in honour of Denmark's unexpected triumph as he and Ian St John record their links. In the final few seconds, St John turns to his partner and asks, 'What about next season?'

'It's funny you should say that,' Greaves replies, pulling a piece of paper out of his pocket. 'I had a chat with the head of ITV Sport and he said...'

'Oh, no,' exclaims St John as the note is held in front of him.

'In the immortal words of Norman Tebbit...'[35]

'Let's do it.'

At which point the duo step back from the camera, take their seats side-by-side on a pedicab and cycle off into the distance singing from an old Rolling Stones hit: 'This could be the last time. This could be the last time. May be the last time, I don't know.'

It was the last time. There would be no return journey. The show was absent when the new football season kicked off, with Greaves claiming to have discovered his fate when he picked up

---

35 In 1981, Norman Tebbit, Employment Secretary under Margaret Thatcher, had told the Conservative Party Conference that his father had been unemployed in the 1930s. 'He didn't riot,' he said. 'He got on his bike and he looked for work.'

The Sun to see a headline announcing that he and his partner had been axed. 'You look at the figures and they were great,' says St John, 'especially for a lunchtime on Saturday. The people at the station responsible for advertising would think the ratings were wonderful. Why would you pull a programme that was doing so well?'

In 2009, when the show was revived for a segment on Setanta Sports' coverage of the Chelsea-Everton FA Cup final, St John revealed, 'To this day nobody at ITV ever lifted the phone or wrote a letter. Isn't that terrible? Never lifted the phone and said, "Sorry, boys, it's all over for you." Nothing. And we waited and waited. Jimmy was saying we should turn up next week in the studio.'

In the same interview session, Greaves added, 'ITV had a big sulk. They'd lost the football to Sky, everything got wiped off the screen and we got wiped off with it. We knew we were getting the bullet long before.'

Greaves said his overriding emotion was sadness, although Nick Owen suggests that the manner of the deed had prompted stronger feelings. 'Jimmy was very bitter about it in the early stages,' he says. 'When I saw him speaking at a dinner he wasn't very happy with the way he had been dumped. Of course, I would never say this to his face, but I suppose the powers that be thought the world had moved on. Someone like Billy Wright or Stanley Matthews wouldn't know enough to talk about today's game because it is such a different era. And television moved into a much, much more sophisticated operation. Everyone has their time in the sun and, bearing in mind he had his as a footballer as well, he had an outstanding career.'

During the 1990s, there were frequent reminders of *Saint & Greavsie* on BBC's *Fantasy Football League*, whose presenters, David Baddiel and Frank Skinner, described Greaves and St John as 'the godfathers of football television comedy'. Playing Greaves and St John respectively, the comedy duo performed a regular feature called 'Saint & Greavsie talk about the Endsleigh

League as though it's important', which was intended to poke fun at ITV's lack of top-flight football more than it was to lampoon their two predecessors – although it came pretty close at times, especially when they progressed in a later series to a 'Saint & Greavsie Investigate' skit.

When *Fantasy Football League* was revived by ITV during Euro 2004, Greaves and St John were invited on as guests. St John's later complaint about their treatment on that show was echoed by journalist and author Rob Bagchi, who described it as 'graceless and rude abuse, using them as props for savage put-downs for the benefit of a pissed-up and baying audience'.

Bagchi's comment formed part of a 2009 reassessment of *Saint & Greavsie* for *The Guardian*. He had begun:

> It is easy to forget that at the beginning of the 1985-86 season, when the programme rose from the ashes of *On the Ball* on the cancellation of *World of Sport*, people genuinely feared about the game's survival. In the 10 years from Leeds fans rioting at the 1975 European Cup final to Heysel, football had sleepwalked to pariah status as far as the media was concerned and that season began with a stand-off between broadcasters and the Football League that led to a blackout for the first 12 weeks of the campaign. It was hardly an auspicious start for the show but they improvised, shot lots of funny segments and compensated for the lack of clips by talking about the game with authority. Two wonderful footballers, loquacious and mischievous, doubling up as presenters and pundits, managed to hold the fort until a compromise came and highlights returned to the screen.

Bagchi argued that they 'pricked football managers' pomposity and brought some humour back to a po-faced game'. And he concluded:

If they were seen to trivialise the game with their approach, perhaps the game back then was in need of trivialisation, to give fans a proper perspective.

What they deserve credit for, though, was forcing the BBC to raise its game, introducing Terry Venables as a trenchant pundit to counterbalance Jimmy Hill and ushering in Alan Hansen's first few incisive years on the sofa ... Sky's *Soccer Saturday* is its only heir and what we cherish in that format, ex-professionals talking candidly and wittily, was pioneered by St John and Greaves. Football has never really been 'a funny old game', but when it most needed some light relief, *Saint & Greavsie* provided it.

The show might have been, as Ian King on his Two Hundred Percent website described it, 'the last, dying breath of old football on the television', but Greaves at least had a few more years on Central, where he continued to work for Newbon. Having done some broadcasting with Andy Gray, the former Aston Villa, Wolves and Everton centre-forward, Newbon was told by the future Sky Sports pundit's agent that he would be interested in a full-time role. 'I haven't got room for two. I want Jimmy,' was Newbon's reply. 'I was very loyal to him,' he adds. 'I passed on Gray, even though I knew that he would get to be a star. Jimmy had done a great job for me.'

But when the opportunity to employ the former Republic of Ireland captain Andy Townsend came along, Newbon decided that he could not pass up another player he felt had a bright broadcasting future. Greaves recalled being left at Birmingham City with no car to get him back to the studio as an indication that he was on the way out, although Newbon relates a somewhat different version. 'My secretary booked the cab and it didn't turn up. Jimmy interpreted that as us having snubbed him and he came back pretty furious. I told him it was just a cock-up. He felt he wasn't wanted any more. Well, I'd had enough of that and his contract wasn't renewed.'

Greaves would return, however, thanks to being teamed with Newbon in a charity cricket match. Newbon explains, 'While we were having lunch I said to him, "Do you want to come back?" He said he did and we shook hands. I said, "I will pay you programme by programme" because I thought that would cut out the nonsense. I asked Andy Townsend to do the co-commentaries instead of the studio.'

With the 1990s coming towards a close, the television career Greaves had never expected finally came to an end. 'Two or three years later I felt things weren't quite right,' Newbon continues. 'Jimmy had done 18 years with me on and off. I met him, I think it was at The Old Bridge in Huntingdon, and we sat outside and I said, "Jim, I am not renewing the contract."

'His actual words were, "You should have done it a year ago." It was the hardest thing I ever had to do and I felt really bad about it, but I had to do it in the interests of my company. If you look at pundits, they don't last forever. It was my professional judgement that I needed something else. I would be failing in my duty if I hadn't moved to a more modern footballer. Look at all the pundits on television; which of those haven't been recent footballers? It was the most difficult professional decision I have had to make and I didn't enjoy it. But we had a lovely lunch and we talked about our years together and I thought we'd parted on the best of terms.'

That impression was contradicted when he read Greaves's account in 2003, claiming that he had been allowed to leave Central without explanation. 'That was was grossly unfair,' according to Newbon. But even that has been unable to sully his memory of working with Greaves, nor his affection for his former colleague. 'Ninety-nine per cent of the time he was absolutely magic,' he states. 'He did a great job and I am really grateful for what he did for me at that part of my career. I loved working with him.'

And he and Greaves would finally make their peace. 'It was Bob Patience's funeral,' Newbon explains. 'Jimmy gave me a lift back and I had a beautiful journey. I will always remember it. It was fabulous, just like the old times.' Newbon was inspired to invite Greaves to be a guest on his Sky Sports show, *Sporting Heroes*. 'We will do an hour, just like the old days,' Newbon told him, but Greaves declined. 'It was a shame because I was going to use it to canvass inside the building to find a role for him, but that was the end of it.'

The containment of Greaves on regional television meant that his broadest platform throughout the 1990s continued to be his weekly column in *The Sun*, where Martin Samuel had become his ghostwriter. Later to move, via the *Daily Express* and *The Times*, to become chief sports writer for the *Daily Mail*, Samuel was Greaves's ghostwriter throughout most of the decade. 'Jimmy was an absolute gift as a columnist; he was so generous that when I left *The Sun* and began writing my own column I wasn't terrified by it,' says a man who has since won multiple Sports Journalist of the Year awards. 'Jimmy's column was the perfect training ground.'

Samuel offers a revealing portrait of someone with whom he is proud to have collaborated. 'We started off meeting face to face and it quickly became apparent that we had a rapport and we thought the same way on a lot of things and we made each other laugh,' he recalls. 'In the end we used to talk on the telephone, often for an hour and a half, of which 10 minutes got into the column. I think it helped that we came from the same area and he lived not far down the road from me. We liked the same things – he liked his cricket and rugby, so we didn't just talk about football – and we shared a lot of the same opinions about some of the bullshit of modern football.

'Once he trusted you he was very generous. Everyone who worked with him – like Neil Custis and Dave Kidd, who wrote the column after me – loved doing so. You never got the feeling that you were the hired hand. He always talked about "our column". If you had a better line or a better joke he would prefer you to put your joke in. Obviously it was under his name anyway, but he didn't have the kind of ego that meant you had no input. The first few times I wrote with Jim, I sent the copy through to him, but it quickly became apparent that he just trusted me.

'I might have had a conversation with the sports editor about what we could get him talking about, but then we might go off in another direction. In the end, I spent so long talking to him that there were occasions when I could have gone off memory because we had discussed the subject before and I knew what Jimmy thought about it.'

Offered the biggest daily newspaper audience in the country, Greaves found an easy, natural connection with his readers. 'He had this way of cutting through stuff,' Samuel continues. 'After the Alan Sugar-Terry Venables split at Spurs, Ossie Ardiles took over and their form wasn't very good and people said the players were affected by the split. I remember Jim saying that it doesn't matter to players what goes on with the board and it doesn't matter whether everyone is mates. How can that affect how you are going to play football? He said it doesn't even matter whether you get on with the manager. He said, "When I played for Tottenham, we hated Bill Nicholson and he hated us. The only thing we all agreed on was that none of us could stand the board of directors."

'He was not the guy who was going to sit there talking tactics and moving salt and pepper pots around the table, but he had great instinctive ideas about football. His view on strikers taking penalties stands up 30 years later. He said that if you are a centre-forward you work all week in training to create you-versus-the-goalkeeper from 12 yards. Everything the team is doing is to get you in that situation. So why, when it is you against the goalkeeper from 12 yards, is the left-back taking the penalty? It is absolutely flawless logic.'

Greaves was not immune to upsetting some of those in the game to whom he had been close. Harry Redknapp was furious when Greaves suggested that his former team-mate, as manager of their old club, West Ham, had only employed Frank Lampard as his coach because he was his brother-in-law. 'That wounded both Frank and I deeply,' Redknapp admitted. 'I enjoy watching him on TV and reading the stuff he writes in *The Sun*, but the comments he made in one of those articles really put the knife in.' Yet no one, it seems, could remain cross with Greaves for long.

Samuel is unashamedly effusive in his appreciation of his writing partner. 'One of the reasons we had a good relationship was that I really, really admire Jim. Not as a footballer, because that goes without saying, but I really admire him as a man. I admire the decisions he has made and how he has conducted his life since dealing with the problem with alcohol. I admire his modesty and the way he took control of his life.'

The popularity of their work created a situation that gave Samuel even greater insight into the discipline of Greaves's existence. 'I wasn't going to the 1994 World Cup in America, but then my sports editor, Paul Ridley, thought it would be great to take the Greavsie column there. I am thinking, "Fantastic, go to the World Cup, do a Jimmy column and a few other pieces, the States, brilliant." I phoned Jim and told him and he said, "No, Mart. I can't do it. It will be great, but I can't go."

'He was utterly honest about it; didn't make any silly excuses. He told me exactly what the situation was. He said, "We'll go to matches and it will be fantastic. But when the match is finished, we will go back to the hotel and all the lads will be in the bar and then I have got a choice. I go to my room and sit on my own when I know everyone is having a laugh downstairs. Or I sit there all night drinking Diet Coke while everyone gets pissed and the conversation gets more boisterous. Or I get involved. I can't afford to get involved and I don't really want to do the other two. It's better if I don't go."

'I said to him once, "Could you not have just one?" – which I know is a stupid thing to say to an alcoholic, but I was young. He said, "Yes, I could have one and go to bed. The following night I might have another one and think maybe two wouldn't hurt and then I would go off to bed having had two. The third night I might have two and then I might have three and then I wouldn't stop. You would stop and I wouldn't be able to. And that is why I don't have one." I thought that was fantastic self-awareness, discipline and self-control.'

The 1994 World Cup still prompted what Samuel considers one of Greaves's most powerful columns, after Argentina's superstar, Diego Maradona, failed a drugs test and was expelled from the tournament. 'Jim was brave,' he argues. 'It was just so easy to write Maradona up as this enemy of football because of his past history with England, but Jimmy wrote an absolutely brilliant column that was very sympathetic towards him. He talked about his brilliance as a footballer, but also how he had been kicked off the park throughout his career and if he'd ended up having to take a pick-me-up to get out of bed in the morning it was because he was never protected by football. It was a very brave thing to write. He might have ended up with drug issues, but Jim saw through it in a way that others didn't. It was very easy to caricature Maradona as a bad guy, but Jim didn't do that.'

Samuel continues, 'I don't think it came from a natural empathy with footballers because Jimmy was a footballer who didn't particularly like football. He liked playing it, but always preferred rugby and cricket to watch. But he had an empathy for people who had complex issues arising from football. He wrote brilliantly on Paul Gascoigne, George Best and Maradona. They were the columns that really stand out for me because he was never one to sit there and analyse the game. He made observations about those guys that stick with me now. Jim said that George seemed almost content with the life he had chosen for himself and when you met George you never got the feeling he was unhappy. But with Paul Gascoigne, nothing makes him happy. Even football, in the end, didn't make him happy. There was this deep sadness about him that he never found with George. I thought it was a very interesting observation.'

As much as Greaves was, according to Samuel, 'brilliant at in-my-day' and able to bring his era of football to life, 'he was never an in-my-day guy'. He says, 'I never heard in his voice any resentment of what they earn now. And he had no ego whatsoever. He had one photograph in his house back then that could have made you guess that he was a professional footballer. It was a photograph of him and Bobby Moore in Zurich, I think, in the town square, dressed in normal clothes. It was the only clue that he had been a footballer.'

If Samuel ever detected any regret or resentment residing within Greaves it was not in relation to modern players' financial good fortune or even his memories of 1966. It was the loss of some of his own memories of his career to his years of alcohol addiction. 'He was talking to me once about the psychiatric treatment he'd had and he said, "I don't know who got my memory, but it wasn't me."'

'He used to say that he couldn't remember what it felt like to be good at football. I don't know if regret was the right word, but if there was one thing he would change, the one bit of ego he might have had, he would have liked to have remembered what it was like to be good at football. He said, "I know I was good because people tell me I was and every now and then I see a bit of film of myself, but I can't remember what it felt like to play a match and think that I am the bee's knees."'

Even that was something to which he became conditioned. 'The last interview I did with Jimmy,' Samuel continues, 'he was in great form. He said that a welder retires and no one ever talks to him about welding again, but people came up to him and wanted to talk about a goal he'd scored in 1965, which he couldn't remember. They would say, "I was behind the goal and Charlie went off to get a pie and everyone jumped up when you scored." He said to me, "Actually, it is a story about Charlie dropping his pie and the story is not about me at all. And that is all good." Most of Jim's stories are self-deprecating.'

The fact that Greaves created so many landmarks in so many people's lives – and could relate with such skill the ups and downs of his own – ensured that a successful third career was ready to gather momentum as his television work wound down. Terry Baker, a DJ and lifelong Greaves fan, first worked with his hero in the mid-90s when he engaged him to be guest speaker at a fundraiser for the ailing AFC Bournemouth.

After securing him a couple of additional bookings, Baker was told by Greaves, 'You can be my agent. You are getting me more work than mine does.'

Over the next two decades, Baker reckons he must have presented around 500 theatre shows with Greaves in approximately 125 venues. 'In that latter career he worked with me for longer than he'd ever worked with anyone and made considerably more money than he did from his other careers,' Baker says proudly. 'Like most players of his generation, he needed to carry on earning.'

Having become an admirer of Greaves after seeing him score in the first FA Cup final he remembers watching in 1962, Baker enjoyed a rewarding relationship that extended beyond money. 'He became one of the best friends I have ever had and I hope vice versa. We got on so well and laughed so much. For those two or three hours backstage at the shows we used to sit there and laugh and laugh and laugh. He is so funny.'

Touring with George Best and observing his relationship with alcohol served to heighten Baker's respect for the lifestyle Greaves had observed for so many years. 'The two of them had the same problem, or disease, but dealt with it so differently,' he notes. 'Jim has had a steely determination never to touch a drop. Even since his debilitation in later life, it has been suggested to him that it wouldn't matter if he had the odd pint now. He has steadfastly refused to countenance the thought.'

As it had been on television, the sharpness of his humour was the key to the achievement of Greaves as a stage performer. Baker continues, 'It would be five minutes of me giving an introduction and then Jim would come on and do 50 minutes and, after a break, he would come back on and do a Q&A, which he would conduct on his own. Every night was something different. He was such a clever guy and so quick-witted. If he got a bit of polite heckling, someone taking the piss, he had an immediate answer – not the stock one a comic might use, but he would come up with something straight away. He was the best after-dinner speaker on the circuit and in another life he could have been a Tommy Cooper, a top-class stand-up comedian.'

The everyman appeal of Greaves meant there was rarely any problem in selling tickets for his shows. 'They all think they know him,' says Baker, 'probably through the telly more than the football. But Jim is actually a very private person and, although he did mix well with people at the shows, he always would rather just be with us backstage. He is quite shy underneath. He would always sign an autograph and smile but he wasn't great with eye contact. He came alive on stage, like he did on television or on a football field.'

Baker and Greaves became close enough that when the non-playing members of the 1966 World Cup final squad were finally presented with winners' medals, they went together to 10 Downing Street for the ceremony. 'Everyone else took their wives,' Baker laughs. 'They were all calling me Mrs Greaves.'

At the end of 2007, it had been announced that Greaves and his 10 fellow-reserves on that famous day in 1966 would finally be awarded medals, in keeping with the modern practice. While some, such as Norman Hunter, expressed their delight and said that the lack of a medal had 'rankled' over the years, Greaves accepted the news with a shrug. 'He was the last person to be interested in getting it,' says Samuel. 'When I used to ask him about it he said, "What would be the point of that?" He saw it as a reminder that he didn't play.'

The decision had been made by FIFA to award medals to all winning squad members and coaching staffs from 1930 to 1974, although it took until June 2009 for the England men to receive theirs from Prime Minister Gordon Brown. After the presentation, the team-mates were taken to Wembley Stadium, where they were paraded on the pitch at half-time of England's 6-0 World Cup qualifying victory against Andorra.

'He went along that night as much to see the old faces as to get his medal,' Samuel adds, recalling the reaction to the television interview in which Greaves asked of Andorra, 'Have you ever seen a team this bad?' and wondered how many goals he would have scored against them. He even suggested his 1966 team-mates could have given them a good game that very night. 'They couldn't wait to get him off,' says Samuel. 'It was so not what the modern package of football is about, where everything is wonderful and everything is about accentuating the positive. For someone to come on and say "this is rubbish", they weren't ready for that.'

Greaves ended up owning his World Cup medal for little more than five years. In 2014, the 18-carat gold reminder of the worst moment of his football career fetched £44,000 in auction at Sotheby's. 'He couldn't give a toss about the medal,' says Baker. 'He didn't know what to do with it because you can't split it between your children.'

Within a matter of months, the money raised by the sale would take on even greater importance.

19

A DAY AT A TIME

'Football should be a joy, not a chore.'

ON another blazing morning during 2018's uncommonly hot summer, Danny Greaves rests his elbows on a picnic table in the front garden of a Brentwood hotel. He has left his wheelchair-bound father finishing off breakfast with friends while we talk; not about England's dreamy progress in the World Cup, which seems to preoccupy the entire nation, but about the recent reality confronting one of the country's greatest footballers. 'It's been a tough three years,' Danny admits. 'Whoever you are, when your parents or a family member gets ill it is incredibly difficult.'

Life for the Greaves family was turned upside down on 3 May 2015, when Jimmy was rushed into intensive care after suffering a stroke. The severity of his condition quickly became apparent and news of his misfortune left the community of football, and beyond, saddened and concerned. Two years previously, he had suffered a transient ischemic attack (TIA), an episode of neurological dysfunction, but still his full-blown stroke was a shock to most people around him. 'We'd been doing a show in Exeter only a couple of days before,' remembers Tottenham team-mate Phil Beal.

'There was me, Jim, Keith Burkinshaw, Alan Gilzean and Steve Perryman. He was right as ninepence and we were going to catch up again soon. And then he had his stroke.'

Terry Baker explains, 'It was a massive stroke and he had no right to survive it. Me and Jimmy and my wife, Freda, used to go and have something to eat before the shows. She would have a salad, I would maybe have pasta and Jim would always have cake. After he had the TIA, he was off for about three months and when he got back we were in a little market town somewhere and he had a salad. I nearly fell off my chair because I had never seen him eat a vegetable. Just before the stroke he had forgotten all that and was back on the cake again and had put a bit of weight back on.'

Danny discusses the strain of having to follow his father's battle for life in the media. 'It happens to people day in and day out, but there is a slight difference when you are dealing with somebody in the public eye. The best way I can illustrate what that feels like is that when Dad had his stroke we spent two days in hospital and then, when you finally get home at ten o'clock at night and sit down, the first thing that comes up on the BBC is, "Jimmy Greaves has had a stroke and is in intensive care." You have tried to walk away from it for a moment and have a little bit of time, but you can't because of the nature of the person means it is the headline on the news.'

As days turned to weeks, Greaves's condition stabilised. Mortal danger was now behind him, but the effects were devastating and long-lasting. Released from hospital after a month, he has never recovered his ability to walk, while it is his left hand only with which he greets visitors and clears his plate. As he sits among family and friends while they reminisce about happier days, there are flashes of recognition, a sparkle in the eyes at good times remembered, but speech is mostly beyond him. 'It has been a nightmare,' Irene had said when he left hospital. 'He is not the guy I know.'

Baker was able to convert the wave of public sympathy towards Greaves into a fundraising campaign that brought in a six-figure sum to contribute towards his ongoing care. Donations arrived from die-hard fans sending what little they felt they could afford to high-profile celebrity admirers. 'Phil Collins phones me regularly to see how Jimmy is and made a substantial donation,' says Baker by way of example. 'Even though he is a Manchester United fan because of his boys, wherever he has lived he has a signed picture of Jim on his wall.'

Close to a year after his stroke, Greaves was quoted in the *Sunday People* – for whom he had written a column for several years and who generously continued to donate his fee – as saying, 'I will never stop trying to get better – and the main thing is that I'm still here fighting all the way. I'm not feeling sorry for myself, I'm just taking each day as it comes and trying to make small improvements all the time.'

'He is settled and he is at home,' says Danny, 'and, like you are seeing today, we get him out at least once or twice a week so he gets away from staring at the same four walls. We get him interacting with people, which is important. It has not been easy, but he is here.'

There have been sporadic public appearances since illness struck, although he was not well enough to join fellow inductee Steve Perryman when entered into the Tottenham Hotspur Hall of Fame in 2016.

He did make a final journey to White Hart Lane in April 2017, a month before its demolition began, when he was filmed visiting the dressing rooms and making one last appearance on the playing surface he had graced for almost a decade. He managed a brief interview for Spurs TV, telling them that he fancied a kickabout.

Later in the year he visited his former club's sparkling training ground in Enfield and met Harry Kane, his modern-day successor at club and international level. 'His achievements at Spurs and his goal record for club and country are certainly things that I aspire to,' said the England striker.

Awarded a place on the Walk of Fame at the National Football Museum in Manchester, where he was represented at the ceremony by son Andy, the most touching of his engagements came in September 2017, when he and Irene were finally remarried, four decades after separation, divorce and reconciliation. Greaves had always insisted that he and his ex-wife were so happy in their second life together that there was no need to change things. But 60 years on from their first ceremony, they attended St John the Baptist Church in Danbury, close to their Essex home, to tie the knot all over again. 'Honestly, we'd never thought about remarrying,' said Irene. 'As far as we were concerned we were always married.'

Danny adds, 'I think they just thought that because of Mum and Dad's situation it was time to do it again. It was something they had spoken about for years even before Dad fell ill. The original plan was that they wanted to go to Lake Como, which was one of their favourite places they have ever been, but they had to settle for Danbury instead.'

After a service in front of their family, Irene reported, 'Jimmy did brilliantly. He was able to say most of what he needed to say and the reverend [Clive Ashley] helped him when he couldn't. It was a lovely day, very poignant and very emotional for the children. When we turned around I said, "Come on then, husband," and everyone roared with laughter.'

Son Andy, whose own son Harry proposed the toast at the reception, said, 'It was a very special day and great for all the family to witness Mum and Dad tying the knot. It was a lovely day for the children and grandchildren.'

The ceremony was also a sign that Greaves had lived up to the promise he made at the end of the 1980 documentary, *Just for Today*, that had told the story of his fight against alcoholism. 'What Irene has gone through,' he'd said, 'I could give her a million pounds and it would not be compensation for one minute of the mental torture I have put her through. I can't do anything about it. There is nothing I can do. All I can do is hope that over the rest of my life I can make it up to her, to the children, to other people and show that people who are lost in the world from one problem or another – and it needn't necessarily be alcohol – that you can overcome it, and you can succeed. And you can succeed by simple rules, a day at a time.'

It is a sad irony that ill health should reduce Greaves's final years to a different kind of day-to-day challenge; one that required his family to rally round to make that life as comfortable and happy as possible in the most trying circumstances. At least strength and support has been easy to find in the groundswell of genuine love that Greaves has attracted from a public moved by his plight and eager to express affection and gratitude. Via a Facebook page and Twitter account, Baker has given a constituency of Greaves admirers updates on his health and mood. Whenever he has shared details of an upcoming meeting with his friend, Baker has been inundated with messages, ranging from those wanting to deliver simple 'get well' wishes to confessionals explaining the important role he played in people's lives. One typical post read:

> Ever since my dad took me to Chelsea and said, 'That's Jimmy Greaves over there warming up. Watch him,' I did. [Around] 1961 or '62, I abandoned Chelsea and went to watch the Double team and, lo and behold, Jimmy moved there too. I watched every home game and the London games until 1965, when I went to university. I spent my lowly football career 'doing a Jimmy Greaves'. I was left-footed and was quite good. Jimmy was a god to me. Not just the skills he had, but the way he carried himself on and off the pitch. You could line up all the greats from Pelé to Messi and set up games. You would find me at the game where Jimmy was playing. He was quite simply incomparable and has been a

massive part of my life. If you could, tell him Bill Stapleton loves him and thank him for enriching my life so much.

'When you are the son or daughter of a famous person, there are always swings and roundabouts,' Danny notes. 'The outpouring of affection for my dad is absolutely incredible and means a lot to all of us. He must probably be one of the most loved footballers of all time. The lovely thing is that he has touched different generations, and whatever generation he has touched has loved him for whatever he has done. There was the generation who watched him from a 17-year-old at Chelsea and Tottenham and England; the next generation who were told by their parents how good this guy was and what he was; and then the next generation who saw him on *Saint & Greavsie* and then all the dinners and the shows. Over a long period, people have had no negatives about him. Whatever he has done, there has always been a lovely positive reaction.'

For some people, online tributes and anecdotal endorsements of Greaves as a player and a man are not enough. While football has seen many worthy recipients of honours ranging from MBEs to knighthoods, many of those would admit themselves that their achievements, both on and off the field, fail to match the 366 senior league goals and extended media career on Greaves's résumé.

The Sun took up the cause in its main editorial column following the announcement of the 2018 New Year's Honours List, noting some of the dubious political recipients.

Meanwhile footie genius Jimmy Greaves, highest-ever scorer for Spurs and fourth on the all-time England list, has nothing, not even an MBE. When top honours are dished out like sweets to establishment cronies but not to genuine sporting heroes, the public is right to hold them in contempt. Give Greavsie his gong.

Son Danny argues, 'You look and think that if anyone deserves an honour for services to football it has to be Dad. Have a look at this guy and the generations he has touched, not just as a footballer, but over 50 years. He has not got a single cap or medal left because he has given them to charity and not made that public. Some people are getting honours for charity work, but the old players have all done that years ago. They didn't shout about it. Whether he was playing football, standing up in front of a theatre audience or sitting in a studio with Ian St John, Dad was entertaining people. It is a massive art to be able to do that and a real shame that it has not been recognised.'

As much as those close to Greaves would love to see him formally decorated, they also know that, even before his illness, he would have been the person least bothered about all the fuss. 'He couldn't give less of a shit,' states Baker, while Martin Samuel adds, 'I would love him to get the MBE; he thoroughly deserves the MBE for what they are worth and it would be lovely for his family. But even without his recent illness I get the feeling it would not be something he'd be fascinated by. It wouldn't make that much difference to him.'

Danny continues, 'He kind of disappears into the background because he is so modest and humble and he would be the last one that would worry about it. It will never happen now.'

Yet preservation of his father's memory remains an important motivation for Danny, even though his own career in football was made doubly difficult by the name he was forced to bear. A junior at Tottenham, player of 49 League games as a striker for Southend United and manager of non-League Witham Town, he states, 'I enjoyed my brief football career and I have made some wonderful friends through the game and wouldn't change it.

'With all four of us, Dad's view was if we wanted to play sport, fantastic. If we didn't, it didn't matter. And we chose what sports we wanted to play. But it is tough, of course it is tough, if you go into football. Everybody expects you to be the next Jimmy Greaves

– and we have been waiting 50 years for the next Jimmy Greaves. The fact that it has taken Cristiano Ronaldo this long to go past his European goals record and Messi is still not there tells you the kind of level he was at.

'I remember some of the comments. I remember playing Norwich, who were in Europe at the time, and we beat them 4-2 and I scored a couple of goals. As we came off, the assistant manager of my team at Southend said, "Yes, but his dad would have got four." You were constantly up against being compared rather than being you. It was enjoyable, but there were times when people would judge you when they hadn't even seen you play. Because of the name, that kind of thing comes with it.'

So now, with his father stricken, Danny has created the Jimmy Greaves Academy in his honour. Based at Beauchamps School in Wickford, Essex, the academy was in the planning stage before Greaves suffered his stroke, with its website stating that his desire was to help children to 'get the most out of the beautiful game without breaking the bank or bankrupting their parents'. The academy aims to place boys and girls who are good enough at one of the many professional clubs with whom Danny and his fellow coaches have contacts.

'There are two things behind it really,' Danny explains. 'From a personal point of view, I have tried to organise my working life to support Mum and Dad as much as I possibly can. It frees up time so we can do things like this morning, rather than doing a nine-to-five job where I can't get Dad out. The second part of it was: let's put a legacy out there for him.'

While Greaves might not have been, as many have said, the most avid fan or follower of professional football, the childhood he spent watching his local part-time clubs and the fond memories he retained of his own years in the non-League game speak of deep passion for the sport itself. 'Dad would love coming and watching Witham Town play when I was manager,' Danny continues. 'He could never work out why more people wouldn't want to just drive and park your car, pay a few quid, have a burger and a pint, watch a decent game of football and go home. Instead, they were travelling the length and breadth of the country to watch Tottenham play Liverpool.'

Greaves's great connection to football at a lower level had been highlighted a few years earlier when his grandson James Robinson, son of his second daughter, Mitzi, reached the first round of the FA Cup with Redbridge FC, who were drawn against Oxford City. Robinson, who had previously played under Danny at Witham, naturally became a focus for media previews. In one interview he explained, 'At Witham, my granddad would be at every game. He would wander into the dressing room at half-time with his cup of tea and take over the team talk. I'm sure if he wasn't a footballer he would have been a comedian. He loves non-League football, I think he can relate to the players. There are no egos. I don't think he relates easily to players at the top level anymore.'

Danny continues, 'Ultimately, he loved grassroots football. He would kick about with kids and would love watching kids kick about. So the thought was: can we tailor working life to support Dad and can we help kids by getting them running around kicking a ball about? That is what the academy is all about.'

There appears to be a deep irony in a developmental institution named after a player who famously eschewed coaching and railed against the multiple tactical layers imposed on the game throughout his own career. 'We don't do it that way,' Danny stresses. 'The emphasis is on letting the kids have fun; letting them run around and play football without all the tactics that can come later. We just want kids to turn up and enjoy themselves.' It is why the academy manifesto uses Greaves's own insistence about football being 'a joy, not a chore'.

Laps of the field, body-building press-ups and shuttle runs will be no more part of the academy bearing the Greaves name than they were an element of his own approach to training. A ball at the feet will do. 'Dad summed it up like this,' Danny continues. 'When he played, they were footballers who had to try to be athletes. Now they are athletes who are trying to be footballers. That is the way the game has gone. You have got to have this power and strength and now it is too much of a science. But the best players are still the most gifted, not the most athletic. Players like Ronaldo, Messi and Scholes were not man-made; they had their own gift that was nurtured. Just let them play football.'

If one professional footballer should emerge from Danny's realisation of his father's vision of how the game should be presented to youngsters, no one would be more delighted than Greaves himself, even if he were not around to witness it. And if those children find a lower ceiling to their ability, then that will be fine too. As long as they have experienced something of the pleasure that the young boy from Dagenham found kicking his prized leather football around the streets and fields outside his home.

Of course, the chances of another Jimmy Greaves emerging from the institution bearing his name may be close to non-existent. Geoff Hurst's comment to open this book, that 'I don't think we will ever see anyone like him again', is echoed by virtually everyone. Admittedly, greater all-round players have come before and since Greaves. Yet he would be considered remarkable even if one only considered his ability in front of goal. Factor in the way he overcame alcoholism, became a broadcasting icon and has continued to be the recipient of universal affection throughout his life, then you have a singular man – never mind just a footballer.

A goalscorer who thrived on instinct and nerve rather than training and tactics; a broadcaster who relied on wit and personality instead of scripts and autocues; an addict who refused to go under, making the decision one day that he'd had enough. And, above all, a man whose modesty, generosity and charm were genuine, not carefully crafted by an image maker.

Unique. Human. Natural.

APPENDIX

Jimmy Greaves: Career Record

PROFESSIONAL APPEARANCES AND GOALS

Domestic Competition

Team	Years	League	Goals	FA Cup	Goals	League Cup	Goals
Chelsea	1957-61	157	124	7	3	2	2
AC Milan	1961	10	9	1*			
Tottenham Hotspur	1961-70	321	220	36	32	8	5
West Ham United	1970-71	38	13	1		1	
Total		526	366	45	35	11	7

* Coppa Italia

European Competition

Team	Fairs Cup	Goals	European Cup	Goals	Cup Winners' Cup	Goals
London	3	3				
AC Milan	2	0				
Tottenham Hotspur			2		12	9
Total	5	3	2		12	9

International Competition

Team	Games	Goals
England Under-23	12	13
England	57	44

HONOURS

FA Cup: 1961, 1967

European Cup Winners' Cup: 1963

World Cup: 1966 (squad member, awarded medal in 2009)

First Division Leading Goalscorer: 1958-59, 1960-61, 1962-63, 1963-64, 1964-65, 1968-69

NOTES

- Greaves played in two FA Charity Shield games, scoring two goals
- Most goals in a club season: 43 in 1960-61 (41 League, 2 FA Cup)
- Greaves scored 28 hat-tricks in senior club football (13 for Chelsea, 15 for Tottenham), plus six hat-tricks for England

MOST SEASONS AS ENGLISH TOP-FLIGHT LEADING GOALSCORER

6	Jimmy Greaves	1958-59, 1960-61, 1962-63, 1963-64, 1964-65 (joint), 1968-69
5	Steve Bloomer	1895-96 (joint), 1896-97, 1898-99, 1900-01, 1903-04
4	Thierry Henry	2001-02, 2003-04, 2004-05, 2005-06

HIGHEST ENGLISH TOP-FLIGHT GOALS-PER-GAME RATIO
(200 goals to qualify)

0.86	Dixie Dean	310 goals in 362 games, 1924-38
0.82	Dave Halliday	211 goals in 257 games, 1925-33
0.69	Hughie Gallacher	246 goals in 355 games, 1925-38
0.69	Jimmy Greaves	357 goals in 516 games, 1957-71
0.69	George Camsell	233 goals in 337 games, 1921-35
0.68	Vic Watson	203 goals in 295 games, 1923-32

* Greaves's exact ratio was 0.6918 per game. In November 2018, Manchester City's Sergio Aguero reached 150 Premier League goals in 217 games (0.6912 per game).

FASTEST PLAYERS TO 200 GOALS IN ENGLISH TOP-FLIGHT FOOTBALL

194 games   Dixie Dean (Everton)

230 games   Dave Halliday (Sunderland, Arsenal, Manchester City)

240 games   Jimmy Greaves (Chelsea, Tottenham Hotspur)

* Alan Shearer is the fastest since the Greaves era, reaching 200 goals in 375 games.

FASTEST PLAYERS TO 300 GOALS IN ENGLISH TOP-FLIGHT FOOTBALL

304 games   Dixie Dean (Everton)

399 games   Jimmy Greaves (Chelsea, Tottenham Hotspur)

505 games   Steve Bloomer (Derby County, Middlesbrough)

* Greaves reached 100 top-flight goals in 133 games, tied for 15th fastest. Harry Kane's 141 games marks the quickest to the landmark since Greaves. According to the English National Football Archive (www.enfa.co.uk), Sunderland's Johnny Campbell was the fastest to achieve the feat, in his 102nd game.

ACKNOWLEDGEMENTS

JIMMY Greaves knew that no matter how many goals he scored, he could not do it alone. It was why he spoke so highly of so many team-mates over the years. Similarly, I could not have told the story of his life without the input of many people, including the following interviewees who have shared memories of Greaves's life and times with me for this book and other titles: Les Allen, Terry Baker, Phil Beal, Frank Blunstone, Terry Bradbury, Nick Charles, Charlie Cooke, George Cohen, Peter Coker, Tommy Docherty, Bryan Douglas, Terry Dyson, Les Eason, Mike England, Norman Giller, Danny Greaves, John Hollins, Norman Hunter, Sir Geoff Hurst, Cliff Jones, Roger Jones, Bob McNab, Billy Meadows, John Mortimore, Alan Mullery, Nick Owen, Steve Perryman, Keith Pike, Steve Ragan, Harry Redknapp, Jimmy Robertson, Martin Samuel, John Sillett, Nigel Spink, John Sprinzel, Ian St John, Berny Stringle, Frank Thorne, Stuart Turner, Tony Waiters and Bob Wilson, along with the late Jimmy Armfield, Ronnie Clayton and Alan Gilzean. Special thanks to Sir Geoff Hurst for contributing the foreword to the book.

The cooperation of Jimmy Greaves's family was at the top of my wish-list when I embarked on this project. For making that possible I am indebted to Jimmy's long-time friend and agent, Terry Baker, who was most helpful in setting up interviews and ensuring the support of the entire Greaves family: wife Irene; daughter Lynn and granddaughter Victoria; daughter Mitzi Robinson and grandchildren James, Tom, Louie, Gemma and Shane; son Danny and grandchildren Sam and Hannah; and son Andy and grandchildren Harry and Madeline.

Others who do not appear in the book, but helped in different ways include Clive Allen, Jeff Barnes, Simon Felstein, Richard Knott, James Lawton, Paul Mace, Mary Mortimore, Mark Ragan, David Selby, Tony Stevens and Richard Wilson. Thanks to Kathleen Dickson at the British Film Institute, while special mentions are due to Roberto Gotta, for his assistance in my research into Greaves's period in Milan, and to Tony Young, for shared memories and a lifelong friendship that includes many afternoons and evenings at Underhill watching Jimmy Greaves playing for Barnet.

My agent, David Luxton, worked diligently and offered his usual invaluable advice throughout this project, while it was a pleasure to have my old friend Richard Whitehead bringing his knowledge and sensitivity to the job of editing the manuscript once again. Pitch Publishing have been hugely supportive of my work over the years and I am once more indebted to Paul Camillin, Jane Camillin, designer Duncan Olner and their entire team. Thanks also to the English National Football Archive for helping with some of the statistics of Greaves's career. Their excellent work is online at www.enfa.co.uk.

Finally, my own family. I have been blessed by four wonderful daughters, Amy, Sarah, Laura and Karis, and now I am thrilled to be able to give my grandson, Jacob, a first mention. Oh, the stories of old footballers I am going to bore you with. My wife, Sara, is always a little embarrassed by the dedications she receives in my books, but while she continues to make my writing possible through the love, support and patience she shows me every day, she is stuck with it.

BIBLIOGRAPHY

Adams, Tony, with Ian Ridley, *Sober* (Simon & Schuster, 2017)

Armfield, Jimmy, *The Autobiography: Right Back to the Beginning* (Headline, 2004)

Baker, Terry and Michael Giller (edited by Norman Giller), *Jimmy Greaves at Seventy* (NMG, 2010)

Banks, Gordon, *Banksy: The Autobiography* (Michael Joseph, 2002)

Best, Clyde, with Andrew Warshaw, *The Acid Test: The Autobiography of Clyde Best* (deCoubertin Books, 2016)

Bonds, Billy, *Bonzo: An Autobiography* (Arthur Baker, 1988)

Brooking, Trevor with Michael Hart, *My Life in Football* (Simon & Schuster, 2014)

Charlton, Sir Bobby with James Lawton, *1966: My World Cup Story* (Yellow Jersey Press, 2016)

Charlton, Jack with Peter Byrne, *The Autobiography* (Partridge Press, 1996)

Chivers, Martin with Paolo Hewitt, *Big Chiv: My Goals in Life* (Vision Sports Publishing, 2009)

Clough, Brian with John Sadler, *Cloughie: Walking on Water* (Headline, 2002)

Cheshire, Scott, *Chelsea: A Complete Record 1905-1991* (Breedon Books, 1991)

Cohen, George, *My Autobiography* (Greenwater Publishing, 2003)

Dickinson, Matt, *Bobby Moore: The Man in Full* (Yellow Jersey Press, 2014)

Dyson, Terry with Mike Donovan, *Spurs' Unsung Hero of the Glory Glory Years* (Pitch Publishing, 2015)

Ferris, Ken, *The Double: The Inside Story of Spurs' Triumphant 1960-61 Season* (Mainstream, 1999)

Flowers, Ron, *For Wolves and England* (Stanley Paul, 1962)

Fry, Barry, *Big Fry: The Autobiography* (Willow, 2011)

Garanzini, Gigi, *Nereo Rocco: La leggenda del paròn continua* (Mondadori, 2012)

Giles, John with Declan Lynch, *The Great and The Good* (Hachette Books Ireland, 2012)

Glanville, Brian *The Story of the World Cup* (Faber & Faber, 2001)

Goodwin, Bob, *Spurs: A Complete Record 1882-1988* (Breedon Books, 1988)

Goodyear, Simon, *From Mine to Milan: The Gerry Hitchens Story* (Breedon Books, 2009)

Greaves, Jimmy, *A Funny Thing Happened on My Way to Spurs* (Nicholas Kaye, 1962)

Greaves, Jimmy, *Greavsie: The Autobiography* (Time Warner, 2003)

Greaves, Jimmy, *It's A Funny Old Life* (Arthur Baker, 1990)

Greaves, Jimmy, *My World of Soccer* (Stanley Paul, 1966)

Greaves, Jimmy, *Soccer Techniques and Tactics* (Pelham Books, 1966)

Greaves, Jimmy, *The Heart of the Game* (Time Warner, 2005)

Greaves, Jimmy, *This One's on Me* (Arthur Baker, 1979)

Greaves, Jimmy and Reg Gutteridge, *Let's Be Honest* (Pelham Books, 1972)

Greenwood, Ron with Bryon Butler, *Yours Sincerely* (Collins Willow, 1984)

Haynes, Johnny, *It's All in the Game* (Barker, 1962)

Hill, Jimmy, *The Jimmy Hill Story: My Autobiography* (Hodder & Stoughton, 1998)

Hunter, Norman with Don Warters, *Biting Talk: My Autobiography* (Hodder & Stoughton, 2004)

Hurst, Geoff, *1966 and All That: My Autobiography* (Headline, 2001)

Jones, Cliff, *It's a Wonderful Life: My Story* (Vision Sports Publishing, 2015)

Kinnear, Joe with Hunter Davies, *Still Crazy* (André Deutsch, 2000)

Law, Denis with Bob Harris, *The King: My Autobiography* (Bantam Press, 2003)

Lyall, John with Michael Hart, *Just Like My Dreams: My Life with West Ham* (Viking, 1989)

Mackay, Dave with Martin Knight, *The Real Mackay: The Dave Mackay Story* (Mainstream, 2004)

Marsh, Rodney, *Priceless: The Autobiography* (Headline, 2001)

McDonald, Tony (editor), *West Ham: In My Day* (Football World, 2007)

McIlroy, Jimmy, *Right Inside* Soccer (Nicholas Kaye, 1960)

McKinstry, Leo, *Sir Alf: A Major Reappraisal of the Life and Times of England's Greatest Football Manager* (HarperSport, 2006)

McLintock, Frank with Rob Bagchi, *True Grit: The Autobiography* (Headline, 2005)

Mears, Brian with Ian MacLeay, *Chelsea: Football Under the Blue Flag* (Mainstream, 2001)

Miller, David, *The Boys of '66: England's Last Glory* (Pavilion, 1986)

Morgan, James, *In Search of Alan Gilzean* (BackPage Press, 2010)

Morse, Graham, *Sir Walter Winterbottom: The Father of Modern English Football* (John Blake, 2013)

Mourant, Andrew and Jack Rollin, *The Essential History of England* (Headline, 2002)

Moynihan, John, *The Soccer Syndrome* (MacGibbon and Key, 1966)

Mullery, Alan, *An Autobiography* (Pelham Books, 1985)

Nicholson, Bill, *Glory Glory: My Life With Spurs* (MacMillan, 1984)

Peters, Martin with Michael Hart, *The Ghost of '66: The Autobiography* (Orion, 2006)

Powell, Jeff, *Bobby Moore: The Authorised Biography* (Everest Books, 1976)

Redknapp, Harry with Derek McGovern, *'Arry: The Autobiography of Harry Redknapp* (Collins Willow, 1998)

Robson, Bobby, *Time on the Grass: An Autobiography* (Arthur Baker, 1982)

Robson, Graham, *The Daily Mirror 1970 World Cup Rally 40* (Veloce Publishing, 2010)

Saffer, David (editor), *Match of My Life: FA Cup Finals 1953-1969* (Know the Score, 2007)

Sandbrook, Dominic, *Never Had It So Good: A History of Britain from Suez to The Beatles* (Little, Brown, 2005)

Saunders, Donald, *World Cup 1962* (William Heinemann, 1962)

Tossell, David, *Alan Ball: The Man in White Boots* (Hodder & Stoughton, 2017)

Tossell, David, *Big Mal: The High Life and Troubled Times of Malcolm Allison, Football Legend* (Mainstream, 2008)

Tossell, David, *In Sunshine or In Shadow: A Journey Through the Life of Derek Dougan* (Pitch Publishing, 2012)

Tossell, David, *Tommy Doc: The Controversial and Colourful Life of One of Football's Most Dominant Personalities* (Mainstream, 2013)

Venables, Terry and Neil Hanson, *Venables: The Autobiography* (Michael Joseph, 1994)

White, Rob and Julie Welsh, *The Ghost: In Search of My Father the Football Legend* (Yellow Jersey Press, 2011)

Wilson, Jonathan, *The Anatomy of England: A History in Ten Matches* (Orion, 2010)

Annuals (various years)

Charles Buchan's Soccer Gift Book, Goal Annual, Rothmans Football Yearbook, Shoot! Annual, Topical Times Football Book

Magazines and periodicals

Charles Buchan's Football Monthly, Goal, Jimmy Hill's Football Weekly, Shoot!, Soccer Star

Newspapers

Barnet Press, Daily Express, Daily Mail, Daily Mirror, Daily Sketch, Daily Telegraph, The Guardian, The Independent, The Sun, Sunday Express, Sunday Mirror, Sunday People, The Times, Tottenham Weekly Herald

INDEX